CULTURALLY SPEAKING

INTERSECTIONAL RHETORICS
Karma R. Chávez, Series Editor

CULTURALLY SPEAKING

THE RHETORIC OF VOICE AND IDENTITY IN A MEDIATED CULTURE

AMANDA NELL EDGAR

THE OHIO STATE UNIVERSITY PRESS
COLUMBUS

Copyright © 2019 by The Ohio State University.
All rights reserved.

Library of Congress Cataloging-in-Publication Data
Names: Edgar, Amanda Nell, 1981– author.
Title: Culturally speaking : the rhetoric of voice and identity in a mediated culture / Amanda Nell Edgar.
Other titles: Intersectional rhetorics.
Description: Columbus : The Ohio State University Press, [2019] | Series: Intersectional rhetorics | Includes bibliographical references and index.
Identifiers: LCCN 2019013969 | ISBN 9780814214060 (cloth ; alk. paper) | ISBN 0814214061 (cloth ; alk. paper)
Subjects: LCSH: Voice—Social aspects. | Sound—Social aspects. | Rhetoric—Social aspects. | Rhetoric—Political aspects. | Voice culture.
Classification: LCC PN4162 .E34 2019 | DDC 783/.043—dc23
LC record available at https://lccn.loc.gov/2019013969

Cover design by Andrew Brozyna
Text design by Juliet Williams
Type set in Adobe Minion Pro

CONTENTS

List of Illustrations		vii
Acknowledgments		ix
INTRODUCTION	Speaking Identities	1
CHAPTER 1	Singing in the Key of Identity: Adele and the Vocal Intimacy of the Blues	24
CHAPTER 2	Voicing Uncle Tom: The Resonance of the South in Morgan Freeman's Films	50
CHAPTER 3	Sounding Presidential: *Saturday Night Live* and the Politics of Impersonation	83
CHAPTER 4	Whitevoice 2.0: Online Speech and Comedians of Color	116
CONCLUSION	A Call to Listen	148
Appendix	Using Audacity and MuseScore for Critical Cultural Vocalic Analysis	161
Notes		169
Bibliography		189
Index		207

ILLUSTRATIONS

FIGURE 1.1	Vocal discontinuities in Adele's "Rolling in the Deep"	37
FIGURE 1.2	Vocal strain in Adele's "Rolling in the Deep"	37
FIGURE 2.1	Morgan Freeman's vocal rhetoric in *Million Dollar Baby*	64
FIGURE 2.2	Ostinato pattern in Morgan Freeman's vocal pitch in *Deep Impact*	65
FIGURE 2.3	Morgan Freeman's vocal pattern and pitch in *Evan Almighty*	65
FIGURE 2.4	Morgan Freeman's pattern of breath in *Evan Almighty*	75
FIGURE 3.1	Sarah Palin in Charlie Gibson interview	94
FIGURE 3.2	Tina Fey impersonating Sarah Palin on *Late Night*	95
FIGURE 3.3	Sarah Palin in Katie Couric interview	96
FIGURE 3.4	Tina Fey on *SNL*, impersonating Sarah Palin from her Katie Couric interview	96
FIGURE 3.5	Tina Fey on *SNL*, the oft-quoted Russia line	97

FIGURE 3.6	Barack Obama's rhetorical style in "More Perfect Union" address	105
FIGURE 3.7	Barack Obama's campaign disclosure	106
FIGURE 3.8	Barack Obama in "State of the Union Address"	107
FIGURE 3.9	Fred Armisen's impersonation on *SNL*	107
FIGURE 3.10	Barack Obama's campaign disclosure	108
FIGURE 3.11	Jay Pharoah impersonating Barack Obama on *SNL*	108
FIGURE 4.1	Jay Walker's bit	128
FIGURE 4.2	Dave Chappelle's white character	129
FIGURE 4.3	Richard Pryor's white character	130
FIGURE 4.4	Russell Peters's whitevoice	134
FIGURE 4.5	Dave Chappelle's whitevoice	135
FIGURE 4.6	Aries Spears's white character	139
FIGURES A.1–6	Steps in Audacity's "Plot Spectrum" Analysis	162–67

ACKNOWLEDGMENTS

WRITING IS a communal process, and I am grateful for the community who supported this project throughout the process of writing, revising, and publishing. I am indebted to the bold feminist women who mentored me through writing my first book. Melissa Click's support and feedback made this book much more than it ever could have been without her. She is a constant role model, friend, confidant, and the strongest woman I know. Those who know Lisa Corrigan's scholarship will recognize her influence in this text. I am forever grateful for her promotion of me and my work and for her fierce mentorship in professional matters and elsewhere. I am fortunate to have gathered quite a community of feminists who challenge and inspire me. Jamie Kern, Holly Holladay, Sara Trask, and Mallory Raugewitz provided the emotional labor of supporting me through the grind—truly no small feat.

I am so appreciative to have had institutional support in this writing process. "The Juniors" writing group deserves much credit, and I am especially thankful for the perspectives of Andre Johnson, Christi Moss, Michael Steudeman, and Lori Stallings. I could not have asked for better support from my department chairs, Craig Stewart and Sandy Sarkela, and I am grateful that they along with Tony de Velasco and the Center for Research on Women at the University of Memphis found my project deserving of research support. Speaking of which, my research assistants, Kelly Ford, JoAnna Boudreaux, Cameron Brown, and Dakota Yates were world-class and truly made the revision process much more manageable. Ben Warner and Rebecca Dingo offered enthusiastic support and solid suggestions for shaping the project early on, and their contributions continued to influence this project even after revisions were well underway.

So many in my professional communities have supported this project. Thank you to those who read, responded to, published, and encouraged my scholarship along the way, and to those who offered feedback at the various places I presented pieces of this book as colloquia and job talks. My editors, Tara Cyphers and Karma Chávez, as well as the manuscript reviewers were incredibly generous and helpful, and I am so grateful.

Finally, challenging projects at work are always dependent upon support at home. Aaron Dechant has unwaveringly offered his support and praise, never once questioning that I could finish this project and finish it strong. Not only has he been enthusiastic about the project; he has also taken on more than his fair share of labor at home so that I could rest and focus on completing this book. His love and support, along with that of Mom, Dad, Andi, Milo, Raptor, Anekin, Kate, and Roxie, have been so important to me. Thank you.

An earlier version of chapter 1 was published in *Critical Studies in Media Communication*: "Blackvoice and Adele's Racialized Musical Performance: Blackness, Whiteness, and Discursive Authenticity," Amanda Nell Edgar, *Critical Studies in Media Communication,* May 27, 2014, Taylor & Francis Ltd, reprinted by permission of the publisher (Taylor & Francis Ltd, http://www.tandfonline.com).

The appendix of this book is based on an article that appeared in *The Velvet Light Trap,* Number 74, Fall 2014. The work was published by The University of Texas Press, copyright 2014.

INTRODUCTION

Speaking Identities

EACH FRIDAY, my colleagues and I gather to discuss the week's wins and losses. As we share ideas and experiences, we focus on the messages we are constructing and hearing. Sometimes, when topics are delicate, we are careful with phrasing and vocal tone, and when the space fills with people, we adjust our volume or move our bodies into closer proximity. The televisions in the space add voices to the mix: Tony Kornheiser, Van Jones, and Greta Van Susteren have all joined us occasionally from speaker and screen. Bobby McFerrin, Eric Clapton, and 4 Non Blondes, too, are among our regular visitors via jukebox. All are voices sharing space and being heard or ignored. All are voices communicating more than their intended messages, speaking or singing as much through tone and timbre as through language. All are voices coded with unique identities, inviting listeners into relationships and sharing, through vocal sound, the intimate inner workings of bodies and their ways of being.

Voices both unite listeners with speakers and highlight difference, aurally communicating shared cultural space as well as the uniqueness of individual bodies. Speech and song bring people together, organizing cultures, institutions, organizations, conflicts, and other relationships. The experience of hearing those who sound like us, Dolores Inés Casillas points out, is a powerful experience of communal comfort, particularly in settings of marginalization.[1]

Since learning to speak and sing is based originally in listening to surrounding voices, vocal sound can be understood as developing from and continually constituting community.[2] Yet, as important as familiar voices are to a sense of aural environmental comfort, the "manyness" of sonic communication means that we are most often surrounded by a diversity of voices.[3] Expressions of vocalized language, emotion, and identity are continually encouraged or disciplined by those around us, and in so doing, particular sounds are integrated and recirculated or excluded altogether, forming those combinations that we find individually or culturally familiar. Eric King Watts argues that "voice announces the felt experience of one's immediate relation to and inseparability from the world and others," but voice can also indicate difference and isolation.[4] The communal nature of speaking and listening relies on the functions of the human voice to circulate culture in particular ways. As natural as this experience often feels, it takes place within the social pressures of oppression and privilege. In this way, culture is constantly shaped and reshaped through the invisible and often overlooked sonic channel. As such, the voice is central to cultural rhetoric.

Aided by technology, media listeners/viewers experience a greater range of voices than are accessible in the local community alone. Yet the mediated voices we hear are constructed, edited, and filtered in ways that invisibly impact our understanding of how racial and gendered identities sound. Racialized mediated voices, for example, have historically been marked by the exaggerated sonic rhetorics of minstrel archetypes and immigrant ridicule. Mary Bucholtz calls this type of speech "linguistic minstrelsy,"[5] noting that media's sonic presentation of Black voices as a "stereotyped and highly simplified fiction"[6] carries historically oppressive representations into contemporary media. It is not only Blackness that is vocally caricaturized in popular culture; as Kent A. Ono and Vincent N. Pham write, Asian and Asian American characters have been mockingly portrayed by white actors "using an accent imagined to 'sound Asian,'" exaggerated dialects and pitch patterns are frequently attached to Latinx characters, and "brown voice" is often used to disparage Indian and Indian American characters.[7] Examined in this light, media has extended both the types of voices available to the average media listener and the sonic elements of taboo racist logics. Racialized sonic representations further intersect with cultural understandings of gender to compound and complicate issues of vocal marginalization and privilege. Along the intersecting axis of gender, differences in spoken pitch patterns are commonly understood to be biologically sex-linked, despite the considerable overlap between adult men and women's vocal pitch.[8] Thus, listeners may now experience the voices of a broader variety of racial and gendered identities than they would have previously encountered, but diversity is not necessarily liberating. Rather than advancing social justice, this vocal diversity may just as easily build and reinforce the assumptions of some listeners about how particular voices should be produced by particular gendered, racialized bodies.[9]

While mediated examples of sonically gendered and racialized speakers abound, some voices are more quintessentially identifiable than others. We are much more likely to recognize the voice of our favorite television star, for example, than that of a walk-on actor. Likewise, voices that are culturally understood as either aesthetically pleasing or jarringly repulsive often pique our interest more readily than those that seem ordinary. These culturally privileged voices communicate a great deal about the vocal sounds idealized by media and public sphere gatekeepers. Not only do authoritative or sexy voices tell us what kinds of sounds are desirable; as Jacob Smith argues, voices that incite laughter or derision discipline culturally unacceptable expression, a mechanism often linked to particular raced and gendered bodies.[10] Media's most celebrated or criticized voices, then, can index culturally idealized vocal sound, marking the sonic dimension of racism and sexism.

Culturally privileged voices, which I conceptualize as widely mediated and popularly recognizable celebrity voices, therefore represent individual bodies shaped through processes of social discipline and possibilities for resistance. While some strong work exists documenting practices of vocal discipline, examining the resultant sounds poses a number of unique challenges. To argue that women's voices have been restricted from or incorporated into radio play, for example, is to make a fairly straightforward claim.[11] More complex is the examination of how such restriction results in particular, socially constructed vocal identities, and how other axes of identity complicate and reinforce racial, sexual, class-based, and other intersections of oppression and privilege. Moreover, broad-strokes discussions of racialized and gendered vocal identities offer a limited explanation of how certain voices grow to feel intimate, familiar, and widely recognizable in mainstream media culture. Race and gender are an important aspect of the disciplinary and resistant forces at work in shaping culturally privileged vocal sound, but more nuanced individual differences must be involved in determining which voices are normalized in the US mainstream media landscape, which achieve positions through moments of struggle, which remain marginalized, and how. This is the challenge I take up in this book.

CRITICAL CULTURAL VOCALICS

In this book, I propose a perspective I call *critical cultural vocalics*, a theoretical and methodological orientation that resists the idea that voices are biologically sexed or naturally racialized and that instead embraces vocal sound as a socially shaped material text. This approach centralizes identity as articulated through a web of intersecting oppressions and privileges. All voices, in this perspective, develop through a cyclical process of speaking and listening situated within a context of cultural politics such that white supremacy, misogyny, homophobia, and other oppressive systems imprint themselves onto the voice. Critical cultural vocalics can be understood through the interrelated concepts of vocal intimacy and vocal identity. *Vocal intimacy* points to the voice's ability to create physiological and affective relationships between speaker and listener. I define vocal intimacy as the familiar and comforting connection between voice and ear. This concept is rooted in the physical exchange that links the corporeal processes of speaking and hearing regardless of whether the communicative exchange occurs in person or across mediated space.

The concept of vocal intimacy structures and is structured by the character of the voice and centralizes relationships of familiarity ranging from feelings of warmth to disgust, authority to disparagement, and awe to apathy. These connections shape the ways that identities are received and understood. I refer to the character of the voice as *vocal identity*, a lens for understanding vocal sound through established critical identity theories. On its surface, vocal identity describes traits of the voice including pitch, pitch movement, rate, tone, enunciation, dialect, volume, and other characteristics. In this book, I am particularly interested in how racial and gendered disciplinary mechanisms shape the voice, but vocal identity might also be used to explore other identities, including region, profession, generation, or group affiliation, to name a few. In any vocal exchange, listeners hear both a speaker's body and the meaning of that vocal body as defined by the listener's experiences, expectations, contexts, social power relationships. The body and the contextual reading of that body are both aspects of vocal identity. Vocal identity, in short, points to what vocal sound tells us about who the speaker is. The development of a speaking voice and the understandings of that voice are dependent upon relationships of intimacy, and relationships of intimacy are shaped by the voice's identity characteristics. The processes of vocal intimacy and vocal identity, then, are inseparable. In this book I explore critical cultural vocalics by applying the interlocking concepts of vocal identity and intimacy to a series of mediated voices, thereby grounding my theoretical analysis in concrete examples. I argue that mediated voices represent the complex interaction of bodies, the social forces that mold those bodies, and the media formats that circulate them. Repetition of particular vocal components creates the sense that voices naturally emanate from particular physiological structures, but voices are always ideological, formed through a cyclical process of listening and speaking.

Understanding the impacts of vocal intimacy and vocal identity on real lived experiences requires a concept that synthesizes the two components. This concept is the culturally privileged voice. Culturally privileged voices are those voices that are widely familiar in mainstream media circulation. They are voices that contribute to the publicity and career stability of the people who speak or sing, and the voices that, even when mediated separately from their visual bodies, prompt audience recognition. The concept of the culturally privileged voice is not meant to indicate a vocal identity that is predictable or stagnant in its ideological commitments, particularly given that the contours of vocal intimacy are dependent upon historical, cultural, regional, and political contexts. Therefore, at times a culturally privileged voice emerges that seems to violate traditional understandings of "privilege." This is because the concept of the culturally privileged voice does not indicate that the speaker will move through the world unmarred by systemic oppression; rather, the "privilege" in the concept of the culturally privileged voice indicates only the ease with which vocal identity and vocal intimacy combine to facilitate media circulation. Often, as this book elaborates, culturally privileged voices are extensions of culturally oppressed bodies whose vocal identities allow audiences to maintain unchecked assumptions of how race, gender, sexuality, region, ability, and other axes of oppression translate to vocal sound. Vocal intimacy, in these cases, is particularly accessible because we are comfortable listening to voices that do not challenge the ways we have heard and understood vocal sound across history. Some culturally privileged voices emanate from culturally privileged bodies. Many others enjoy privilege precisely because the bodies that speak them do not.

Culturally privileged voices benefit from and set the standards for vocal popularity, which often results in economic success in specific industrial and political contexts including music, television and film, journalism, government, and other arenas. As such, they are produced through an ongoing system of discipline and reward, and they consequently shape and reshape that same system. This system situates the voice not only as a conveyor of language but as a conduit for emotional and corporeal meaning, extending the body's vocal organs as they move in tandem to express ideas and feelings. To borrow Mladen Dolar's phrasing, "it is *precisely the voice that holds bodies and languages together . . . like their missing link, what they have in common.*"[12] From this perspective, neither language nor body fully encapsulates the meanings encoded in and through vocalization. Instead, the messy corporeality of vocal production is fused to any utterance's symbolic value.[13] The culturally privileged voice, then, must be understood not only for the linguistic messages it facilitates but also for the residue of spit and sinew present in the bodily processes of vocal production.

This explanation alone smooths over the effects of social context not only on the various ways we move our bodies to make particular socially acceptable sounds, but also on the ways the body itself is shaped by cultural norms and expectations. Like all voices, culturally privileged voices are marked by socially constructed signs of gender and race. Judith Butler argues that the physical body is shaped by gendered cultural expectations that dictate proper size, shape, movement, and other performative elements.[14] Although gender is a copy of a copy with no origin, she asserts, the myth of ideal gender's attainability has powerful effects on shaping the ways that bodies perform and, consequently, the ways that bodies are structured.[15] Bodies that resist these normative standards are disciplined by mainstream culture through marginalization. Since vocal sound is influenced by the body's composition and movement, mechanisms of social discipline must impact not only the body's appearance, as Butler theorizes, but also the body's vocal sound. Scholars like Greg Goodale note that "we believe . . . we can hear race when we cannot."[16] Conversely, I suggest that historical mechanisms of discipline and oppression actually do shape the sounds that emanate from racialized, gendered bodies from the outside in. By molding bodies into alignment with mainstream cultural understandings of gender and race, society's disciplinary processes encourage subtle but important sonic differences that can be traced through the text of the voice. These differences are not biologically determined but a result of how power shapes bodies. Thus, the physiological and the socially constructed work together in the production of voices.

The unique sound of an individual's voice often communicates politically coded information about the speaker, a process aided by cultural assumptions that characterize the voice as unconstructed and natural. Through a combination of physically and discursively constructed aural characteristics, voices become associated with the visually mediated bodies from which they emanate. Listeners then build intimate sonic relationships with these vocal bodies through their audiovisual presence. This book aims to dissect the physical and culturally constructed interactions between a speaker's voice and body and to extend that interaction through the media that makes culturally privileged vocal bodies available to listening ears. For critical rhetorical scholars to study the relationship of voice and identity, we need methods and theories of analysis that highlight oppression and privilege in the material conditions of communication. We need guides that allow us to translate, to borrow Laura U. Marks's germinal terminology, "the relatively more sensuous audiovisual media to the relatively more symbolic medium of words . . . to make the dry words retain a trace of the wetness of the encounter."[17] In this way, we can resist the assumption that voices are biologically or technologically determined and instead highlight the ways that material practices of speaking and singing influence and are influenced by bodies in relationships of power. Goodale, Watts, Joshua Gunn, and others have considered the rhetoric of vocal sound, and much of this work takes up issues of political power.[18] Beyond rhetoric, sound studies scholars including Jennifer Lynn Stoever, Dolores Inés Casillas, and Adriana Cavarero offer excellent analyses of the voice and sound generally.[19] This book builds from these to offer a programmatic approach to the rhetorical practices of vocalizing and listening that considers how these everyday practices perform hegemony and resistance in the realm of identity.

VOCAL INTIMACY AND VOCAL IDENTITY

The intimacy of the physical act of communication is complicated by mediated rhetorical forms. Through media, voices can produce a heightened sense of connection between listeners and mediated speakers, as listeners bring media into the soundscape of the home, workplace, public sphere, or, via earbuds, the interior physical canals of the body. Mediated voices, like all voices, are marked by particular vocal identities that imprint cultural assumptions about racialized and gendered bodies onto speech sounds. As intimacy connects bodies to one another, it shapes practices of listening. Listening, in turn, shapes the ways we speak, solidifying or challenging racialized and gendered expectations for vocal sound through our reproduction of speech. Particular ways of speaking, or vocal identities, influence the production of intimacy, and the cycle continues. Since all of this takes place within the ideological and material contexts of culture, each stage of the process is shaped and reshaped by elements of domination and resistance.

Since the physiological elements of lungs, lips, teeth, tongue, and the body as a whole work together to create the sound of the vocal instrument, the voice can be understood as an aural map of the physical body. Roland Barthes called this effect "the grain of the voice."[20] Writing specifically of singers, Barthes argued that some performers allowed the sounds of the vocal instrument to be heard in their performance. When the sounds of "the cavities, the muscles, the membranes, [and] the cartilages" were present, listeners could effectively "hear a body . . . as though a single skin lined the inner flesh of the performer and the music he [sic] sings."[21] This presence of the raw body in the voice was, for Barthes, a source of increased pleasure and aesthetic enjoyment as well as a mechanism of intensifying the connection between singer and listener. This effect of "hear[ing] a body" is also a key factor in encouraging vocal intimacy.²² By allowing the body to manifest in the vocal instrument, listeners gain intimate aural access to the performing body.

Although Barthes's concept of vocal grain is based primarily on the singer's production of voice, his essay serves as an autoethnographic account of his listening experience. For Barthes, listening to vocal grain is "erotic," positioning speaker and listener in a physically intimate relationship.²³ The space of listening is always intimately constructed since the voice moves from the body of a speaker to enter and envelop the listener's body.²⁴ As David Suisman explains, "Sound is a means by which the world enters the body . . . through the ear, you hear the world in your head; it enters *inside you*; you perceive the world from the inside out."²⁵ By entering the body through the ear's cavities, sound becomes a part of the listener, uniting speaker and listener at the level of corporeal interiors. The experience is further intensified by the relative inability of the listener to resist the hearing of sounds. Viewers may close their eyes to escape overly intimate images, but closing the ears is simultaneously more difficult and less effective at blocking unwanted stimuli.²⁶

The process of vocal intimacy is important because of its power to influence through connection but also because of what it reveals about the nature of the voice itself: in the text of a spoken voice is both the body's production of sound and the meaning of that sound within a particular political context. Like all instruments, the physical body produces a voice through a variety of components moving and working in concert with one another. Therefore, the voice registers the "interior structures" of the body's vocal organs, pointing to a physical, live person: "it communicates the presence of an existent in flesh and bone; it signals a throat, a particular body."²⁷ Like the voice it produces, this body exists within particular material circumstances which shape not only the body but the voice as well. The voice, then, is a direct extension of a politically shaped physical body. This body is the voice's instrument in production as, simultaneously, cultural experiences with various vocal instruments influence listeners' understanding of the relationship between speaking voice and speaking body. Culture shapes both voices and how voices are perceived.

The relationship between speaking and listening can be conceptualized both as an intensely intimate experience and as one of the most common ways of experiencing another person's body. Even when speaking and listening bodies are geographically separated or invisible to one another, listeners often conjure fabricated images of the speaker's physical appearance. Gunn calls these bodies, present only through vocal sound, *vocalic bodies*.²⁸ These imagined bodies are usually based on listeners' learned associations between a certain type of speech and a certain type of body. In other words, listeners learn which types of voices match which types of bodies through cultural experience and use these experiences to imagine "appropriate" bodies for disembodied voices. In making audible the physiological movements of the vocal organs, the voice is layered not only with the cultural cycles of speaking and listening but also with "the interior state of the body and its pathology."[29] In fashioning vocalic bodies, listeners imbue voices with bodies, marking physical characteristics, personality traits, and intelligence levels.[30] Thus, as we use the voice to form "an index of the body," we apply our cultural experiences of wanted and unwanted aural intimacy to our understanding of others through their voices.[31]

The precise cultural connections drawn between particular vocal and visual bodies owe much to the conventions of synchronization, or the practice of splicing together separately recorded sounds and images into a single audiovisual text. Despite the necessarily constructed nature of piecing two separate recordings together, Michel Chion argues, "we are often given to believe, implicitly or explicitly, that the body and voice cohere in some self-evident, natural way."[32] However, early film technologies could not encode both sound and image simultaneously, necessitating the practice of splicing together the soundtrack with the picture after both had been recorded. Since the purpose of this practice was to enhance verisimilitude, synchronization practices were designed to hide the seams between sounds and bodies, meaning that the relationship between the visual and vocal performer on screen was constructed and manipulated to match audience expectations.[33] These expectations are formed within cultural and media contexts. In fact, they are often based on audience experiences with other mediated voices and bodies, as the attachment of particular bodies to particular voices is repeated across media forms and throughout history, forming racialized and gendered conventions. For those who have no direct experience with Indian accents, for example, recorded representations are the only access to these sounds. The limited variety in Indian characters' speech across media formats naturalizes for these audiences the connection between the sounds of characters like Apu, from the popular series *The Simpsons,* and Indian people in general.[34] However, as characters like Apu illustrate, media's Indian accents are often exaggerated to appeal to anti-immigrant sentiment. As Shilpa Davé argues, these "brown voice" performances essentialize the actual sounds of Indians and Indian Americans, vocalizing Otherness rather than uniqueness and, through the suturing of image to sound, naturalizing the connection between particularly marked voices and particularly marked bodies.[35]

Vocal intimacy connects bodies to one another, but as with all relationships, this process is political. Contextualizing the corporeal intimacy of speaker and listener are complex social relations that affix assumptions about race, gender, class, sexuality, and other systems of power and domination onto vocal identities. The complexity of vocal identity is further complicated by the interaction of voices and bodies with mediated representations. Historical processes of media creation, particularly synchronization, as well as the market incentives of industry circulation impact the ways that vocal identities are matched with visual bodies. Through repetition, the components of voice, body, and media become inextricably linked, creating audience expectations of how particular identities should sound. These vocal identities, enhanced by their creation of increasingly expected vocal intimacies, are circulated and recirculated into naturalized, commonsense practices of speaking and listening. Within this process of normalized expectations, the culturally privileged voice emerges.

THE CULTURALLY PRIVILEGED VOICE AND THE CYCLE OF DISCIPLINE

The cycle of vocal identity and vocal intimacy at the heart of critical cultural vocalics has powerful implications for reifying or challenging social hierarchies. In a structure of systemic cultural oppression, particular bodies are labeled unfit or inappropriate for public discourse: they are racialized, gendered feminine or deviant, marked as poor, working-class, uneducated, or otherwise socially undesirable through the voice. This process is solidified through the cycle of vocal identity and vocal intimacy. The attachment of particular voices to particular bodies is a technology of maintaining status quo oppressions that takes place through the attachment and consequent naturalization of vocal types with mediated identities.[36] In a cycle of repetition without a clear moment of origin, the sonic extension of what Butler calls *citationality*, vocal identities are connected to particular mediated bodies.[37] Listeners/viewers who encounter these identities are drawn into a relationship of vocal intimacy with the speaking body, and this relationship shapes future listening and vocal performances. As this cycle repeats, new mediated vocal performances enter the mix, shaping perceptions and performances of others in the sonic environment, and these listeners and speakers contribute to the dynamics of discipline and reward. Through this cycle of speaking and listening, ideologies of racialized and gendered meaning seep into the aural environment and shape the ways that new voices are formed and understood.

Mass media are often imagined to be a less intimate form of communication than live interactions, but cultural understandings of vocal intimacy are shaped by media-circulated ideas. The spoken voice, mediated or not, continues to provoke a sense of intimate connection in the listener. This connection, I suggest here, is shaped through conventions, a primary mechanism of communicating vocal norms. Conventions, or "signs that signify efficiently," both are drawn from and contribute to existing cultural norms.[38] Sonic and vocal conventions are drawn from culture, as media aims to produce programming familiar to its audience's experience. For example, Ono and Pham argue that the exaggeratedly ridiculous yellowface portrayals of Asians and Asian Americans by white actors were so prevalent in twentieth-century media that Asian and Asian American actors faced a choice between replicating oppressive stereotypes in their performances or not working at all.[39] The power of racist cultural logics to dictate media performance conventions began at least as early as the transition from silent film to talkies, when casting practices were explicitly based on whether actors' voices fit stereotypes about gender, class, race, and ethnicity.[40] Such production techniques, which today are generally implemented implicitly rather than overtly, function as a reading and replication of current power dynamics, as producers attempt to tap into audience expectations for the sound of a particular performer's voice in order to please the listener and, ultimately, sell the media product. The conventions of vocal sound in media thus communicate information about which voices are normative and which are not.[41]

Furthermore, through massively scaled distribution mechanisms, media cements and circulates the sonic norms reflected by vocal conventions. Since the codes of sound that are reproduced and distributed are chosen by a powerful minority, Jacques Attali argues, the circulation of mediated sounds can never be understood as neutral.[42] Instead, the source of the message represents a great deal of power, and we should seek out these origins to understand the nexuses of ideologically based sounds.[43] Sound technologies in contemporary culture, from THX-equipped movie theaters to tiny earbud speakers, influence which vocal conventions are welcome in our cultural soundscape. As David Suisman notes, "If sound contributes to the shaping of the self, then control of the acoustic environment—the 'soundscape'—becomes an issue with real social and political consequences."[44] In other words, media's power to select which sounds are appropriate for distribution is also the power to define the sounds of our worlds, both public and domestic.

Naturalizing the link between marked voice and marked body is a primary mechanism of the disciplinary process. By solidifying the idea that particular voices (should) always emanate from particular bodies, links between bodies, voices, and public arenas grow consistent and therefore more difficult to challenge. These links form in a variety of ways. First, the legal sanctioning of noise has historically focused on society's unwanted voices; though immensely powerful sounds like airplanes and church bells are rarely disciplined legally, most noise violation codes focus on "the rougher voices of the lower classes."[45] Attali likens such legal selectivity to surveillance, noting that control of cultural sounds often reflects the disciplining of certain racialized and gendered bodies.[46] The association of women's voices with emotional irrationality, for example, has guided the rules sanctioning contexts appropriate for women's speech. Michele Hilmes points out that the voices of women across races have been "literally contained and controlled,"[47] regarded as appropriate in service of emotional displays like public mourning, but harshly sanctioned through accusations of excess in political or social advocacy.[48] In this way, laws that distinguish appropriate sound from inappropriate sound authoritatively discipline voices that do not align with cultural understandings of which voices belong and which do not.

A second form of vocal discipline uses vocal sound to restrict access to various forms of social privilege. Dolar argues that undesirable accents are determined by the "ruling norm" represented by "an accent that has been declared a non-accent."[49] The undesirability of a vocal identity Othered through dialect is solidified through practices of vocal training. Nineteenth-century education included speech training that targeted racially associated accents and ensured that upper-class white children learned to speak without these accents.[50] This training was exclusive and thereby exacerbated the differences between bodies based on how those bodies learned to sound. At the same time that white upper-class children were learning to speak "properly," Black radio actors were being trained to speak in exaggerated patterns of dialect and inflection in order to secure performance contracts.[51] Together these practices created a "vocalic hierarchy" that not only linked particular voices to particular bodies but that additionally promised educational, cultural, and subsequent economic access.[52] Similar practices cemented rules for mediated speech. Unlike Black actors, whose voices had been accepted by the industry as "pos[ing] no difficulties for sound recording,"[53] white women's voices were marked as incompatible with recording technologies. The reasoning behind this recording standard, the supposed variable pitch of white women's voices, follows the limiting stereotype that aligns femininity with emotional instability.[54] In other words, the assumption that white women's voices were too emotionally uncontrollable to be allowed in public discourse was both taken up and reified by media industry standards. As these industry standards were normalized in the proliferation of media represented by radio, film, television, and other formats, so too was the hierarchical divide between the voices that were suitable for public discourses and those that were not.

Speech training and education are powerful disciplinarians. They also illustrate potential for navigational agency. Voices are shaped by the environmental conditions of speech acquisition, but as speakers continue to move through various cultural spaces encountering, as listeners, more and varied voices, we also continually adapt our vocal sound depending on contexts of discipline and reward. At times this adaptation is conscious. Practices of code switching, for example, often include shifts in vocal identity such that, as bell hooks writes, speakers within oppressed groups "develop various styles of relating, talking one way to one another, [and] talking another way to those who have power to oppress and dominate."[55] Throughout history, performers of color across gender and women and queer performers of all races have found ways of vocalizing that allowed them to navigate unwelcoming environments. This type of navigation is commonly passed down generationally through consistent and repeated modeling, so that children of marginalized groups learn to incorporate situational vocal shifts from a very young age.

A final disciplinary mechanism that limits voices beyond the "ruling norm" is the sanctioning of voices marked as "mismatched" with the bodies from which they emanate.[56] Laughter and repulsion both set mediated examples of the social penalties for speakers whose voices do not match their bodies or contexts. Midcentury radio dramas, for example, crafted immigrant characters whose voices were exaggerated to ridiculous effect. As Susan Douglas writes, these characters were written to break the "ruling norm" to demonstrate

> that the speaker isn't going to play by the rules, either because he or she doesn't know better or because he or she refuses. Not knowing better makes you pathetic and even contemptible. Refusing, however, sets you apart from the herd, and can make you scary. It can also make you funny.[57]

In this reading, laughter is a seemingly innocuous form of vocal sanctioning.[58] By following particular vocal sounds with laughter, early radio programming imbued certain presumably nonwhite immigrant voices with an air of ridiculousness. This ideological work was continued by early sound films that attached silly, exaggerated voices to immigrant bodies, belittling the ethnically marked body by constructing an ethnically marked voice and then laughing at it.[59] White-supremacist media conventions vary depending on the particular racializations of time, space, and genre, as well as the influence of other intersections of oppression and privilege, but the pressure to choose between adopting subordinate vocal identities or not performing at all has been broadly experienced by Black, Latinx, Jewish, Asian, and other racialized and immigrant entertainers.[60] For instance, Claire Jean Kim points out that even though Asian Americans are often held up in "'relative valorization'" to other US Americans of color, mediated vocal identities very often mark Asian Americans (played by white actors) as "immutably foreign and unassimilable with Whites on cultural and/or racial grounds."[61] Even when characters of color are present in the media landscape, then, portrayals like these can do as much to essentialize as they do to include, flattening differences between the individuals onto whom these voices are projected.

The intersecting axis of vocal queerness, too, is often flattened by media conventions to entrench the binaristic performance of gender. Across racial and other axes of identity, pitch range and movement are the strongest predictors of whether listeners perceive a man's voice as gay; specifically, many audiences read typically feminized vocalizations including a wider range, higher overall pitch, and precise consonant pronunciation as "gay voice."[62] While queer actors like Vincent Price built careers on the basis of narrative voice-over, Harry M. Benshoff argues, his "oily, slightly effeminate presence and mellifluous voice" demonstrate the slippage in war-era films between "homi*cidal* maniacs and homo*sexual* ones."[63] Positioned, then, as the voice that narrates fear, Price's became a voice of both queerness and deviance, driven both by his association with horror and by his performance of feminized speech in a visually masculinized body. Likewise, women of all races who perform the narrower and lower pitch range associated with masculinity often become the butt of jokes, as when NPR's women journalists are mocked in terms of their sexuality on shows like *Saturday Night Live*.[64] Gendered conceptions of sexuality like these are bolstered by intersectional factors like race and region, leaving little room for voicing nonbinary gender. Media logics of vocal identity prioritize the match between voice and body, which requires discrete categories. When the socially constructed alignment of body and sound is experienced as mismatched, the disciplinary processes of laughter and derision mark these identities as undesirable and unnatural, reinforcing the idea that a "natural" voice is one that matches mediated conventions for how the speaking body is "supposed" to sound.

Together, these strategies of discipline and privilege, including differential sanctioning, education, and representation, cement cultural expectations of how particular bodies should sound. Given that these readings are all contextual and dependent upon the relationship between the speaker and listener, my point in this section has not been to offer concrete criteria for how particular vocal sounds are expected by various groups to communicate each possible axis of identity. Such a project would not only take more space than is available in this book but, more importantly, would risk essentializing and stereotyping particular groups' voices and listeners' contextually shifting patterns of reception. Rather, the project of this book is to highlight how pre-existing, culturally constructed marginalizations mark themselves onto bodies through the voice. As voices circulate through culture, they are taken up by listeners in processes that discipline, reward, and replicate, depending upon context. In this way, repetition structures the rhetoric of vocal sound, taking up the tools of media circulation and cultural structures of oppression. This process marks voices both as evidence of difference and as a naturalized extension of the body, thereby demonstrating a mechanism of marginalization that is literally invisible, and therefore difficult to discuss and dismantle.

WHY THE VOICE?

I offer this exploration of the culturally privileged voice through a lens of critical cultural vocalics as a contribution to the project of critical sound studies, particularly as a body of literature that can and should be incorporated into traditional practices of rhetorical and media criticism. Bemoaning the cultural tendency to privilege the visual over the sonic has become somewhat cliché because the logistics of incorporating sound into visual and textual analyses can be daunting. This book, then, provides a thorough discussion of the voice through a feminist, critical race, and cultural studies lens, offering a concrete method for considering the role of voice in music, speech, television, and film.[65] Why, though, is an understanding of mediated voices an important next step? The reasons are both scholarly and cultural.

First, this book aims to solidify a defined perspective on vocal ideologies, accessible to a variety of disciplines who have been, and should be more, interested in the ways that vocal sound shapes messages. In the rhetorical tradition, Gunn reminds us that the nineteenth-century elocutionists were deeply interested in how vocal sound influenced the emotional content of public address, and excellent work has been done in this area by scholars like Watts, Goodale, and others.[66] In media studies, the charge to understand vocal meaning has emerged primarily through radio scholars including Hilmes, Douglas, and Casillas, as well as in pioneering scholarship on sonic technology by Jonathan Sterne.[67] Still, though many disciplines have contributed interesting and important research to our understanding of the voice, the theoretical and methodological incongruity of the scholarship across fields creates challenges for interdisciplinary applications of vocal sound studies. This is not to say that projects in rhetorical analysis are unrelated to those in sociophonetics or psychoanalytic film theory. Rather, these disparate findings must be translated into a more standardized theoretical language to create a strong, unified subfield involved in understanding vocal ideology. By drawing from a variety of disciplinary perspectives, this book offers one interdisciplinary approach to studying the voice in hopes of solidifying a practical theoretical and methodological framework for vocal artifacts in rhetorical and media studies.

A second and related goal of this book focuses on promoting the importance of vocal sound as an accessible addition to other critical literacy projects, including and beyond rhetorical and media studies. To illustrate the potential connections between vocal sound and culture, broadly defined, I have chosen case studies that draw together cultural media studies and politically focused rhetorical theory to demonstrate the similarities between these two perspectives. Because the voices of governmental politics are often accessed through mediated forms like television, radio, and online sources like YouTube, techniques for studying mediated voices in entertainment forms are also applicable to political theorists. To a lesser degree, this book's focus on the affective ties formed between speakers and listeners offers a framework for studies of the voice in interpersonal relationships, organizations, and ethnographic contexts. This book therefore maintains a broadly communicative theoretical perspective as an entry point for additional applications of critical cultural vocalics.

Third, guided by the principles of feminist studies, critical race theory, and cultural studies, I ground the theory of critical cultural vocalics in social issues and identity performances articulated through an intersectional framework. Originally developed for legal applications by Kimberlé Crenshaw, intersectionality is defined more recently by Patricia Hill Collins and Sirma Bilge as

> a way of understanding and analyzing the complexity in the world, in people, and in human experiences. The events and conditions of social and political life and the self . . . are generally shaped by many factors in diverse and mutually influencing ways. When it comes to social inequality, people's lives and the organization of power in a given society are better understood as being shaped not by a single axis of social division, be it race or gender or class, but by many axes that work together and influence each other.[68]

A primary goal of this book is to articulate how race, gender, and other axes of oppression and privilege intersect to shape the voice as it is spoken, sung, and heard, and how those processes contribute to the continuation of and resistance to social marginalization. As Bernadette Calafell notes, in a "post-feminist" and "post-racial" society, sexist and racist attacks often occur on subtler dimensions, making them more difficult to refute.[69] Given the (sub)disciplinary variations among theoretical and methodological perspectives on the voice, cultural processes of vocal gender and race remain critically challenging. By combining various vocal theories into a lens for the study of gender, race, and other axes of oppression and privilege, I offer this book's analyses as templates for future feminist, antiracist interventions.[70] Throughout the book, I combine vocal theory from various perspectives and apply this critical cultural vocalic lens to racialized and gendered examples of vocal privilege and discipline in popular culture. As concrete examples of vocal ideological analysis, the cases in this book demonstrate the importance of understanding racism and sexism along a sonic dimension.

Finally, this book concretizes a perspective on intersectional vocal patterns as a call to further research in sound studies in general and critical cultural vocalics in particular. These analytic tools are meant to be as accessible as possible across and beyond our discipline in part to encourage further developments of sonic theory and method, particularly as they relate to axes of oppression and privilege. As a study in voices and the intersections of race and gender, this book clarifies the goals and potentials of vocal ideological analysis. However, race and gender are only two dimensions implicated in vocal sound. By outlining a clear approach to vocal ideological studies, I hope to encourage more research in this area by demonstrating an open-ended technique for projects centralizing aspects of identity including class, sexuality, and regionalism, which play a secondary role in this project. Such emphases are beyond the scope of this book, but they represent important dimensions of sonic oppression and privilege. This book therefore encourages and provides a framework for further research on the voice, especially in regard to the vocal elevation and disciplining of particular mediated bodies.

CONSIDERING METHOD

The core argument of this book is that understandings of vocal identity, or how the body presents itself through the voice, and vocal intimacy, or the connection forged between speaker and listener, are co-constitutive. The link between vocal identity and vocal intimacy is their shared development within particular political contexts, such that the social construction of these two elements happens in relationship to intersectional oppression and privilege. Therefore, this book approaches the concepts of vocal identity and vocal intimacy separately but analyzes them through a shared framework of feminist and critical race theory. My analysis of vocal identity follows Goodale's assertion that "sound can be read" similarly to public address transcripts or narratives.[71] First, utilizing Stuart Hall's *long preliminary soak* concept,[72] I listened to and watched each artifact several times to familiarize myself with its meanings and techniques. During this preliminary phase, I listened for the traits that made the artifact's voices identifiable, including repeated patterns of pitch movement, variety of speech rate, and vowel and consonant articulation. Once I had a general understanding of the patterns that made each speaker's voice identifiable, I used the particular contours of these patterns to find smaller excerpts that exemplified those identifiable patterns. Then, extending the acoustic and sociophonetic transcription methods I adapted in my previous work on Hillary Clinton's and Beyoncé's voices,[73] I translated these "tunes to which we set the text of our talk"[74] into a visual representation of their pitch, rate, and timbre.

The first component, *pitch,* describes the way that a voice is perceived as "high" or "low" to the human ear, whereas *rate* describes the speed at which speakers move from one syllable to the next. Pitch and rate can be transcribed simply by listening to a speaker's pitch and matching it to any musical instrument. However, this method, known as *impressionistic coding* in sociophonetics, is difficult to verify and occasionally somewhat ambiguous.[75] Therefore, I used Audacity, a freeware sound-editing program, to corroborate my pitch readings.[76] Once a sound file is loaded into the program, the researcher can run a variety of analyses, which, as I describe in detail in the appendix, provide verification for the impressionistic coding of pitch and rate of speech. This step simply provides a transcription of the sonic elements of the voice, which, as I explain at the end of this section, can also be analyzed through traditional textual analysis methods. In addition to pitch and rate, the concept of intonation includes timbre, or the tonal qualities of the voice. The International Phonetic Alphabet is useful for analysis, although since some readers will not be familiar with this type of transcription, I have taken care to explain the phonetic values of the speech samples I analyze in the most accessible way possible. This more technical approach to intonation, then, supplemented the elements I earlier noted as unique and distinguishable traits associated with the particular speaker. Given vocal identity's focus on the ways that bodies are apparently heard through the voice, the information collected in this step regarding intonation can then be interpreted through a lens of critical race theory, feminist theory, and other critical perspectives.

To approach the connection between speaker and listener/viewer at the heart of vocal intimacy, I examine this component through a textual analysis of that sound's linguistic, affective, and cultural context, offering a basic rhetorical analysis of discursive fragments surrounding my artifacts (such as online discussion boards and professional and fan-created critical reviews). Therefore, following Gunn's charge to perform "adjectival description followed by an analysis of how others similarly affix adjectives," I analyze vocal intimacy by placing voices in conversation with fragments of audience response and mediated positioning.[77] In considering audience response, I searched for contextual and intertextual fragments including any references to audience readings of particular voices in online forums, critics' reviews, and other internet commentary spaces (e.g., Twitter, Yahoo! Answers, personal blogs). Although online postings do not capture an audience as a whole, nor do they necessarily speak to the levels of intimacy that emerge from in-depth interviews, the public nature of these posts does mean that they contribute to the re-cycling of speaking, reading, and listening. From these audience fragments, I gathered references to the speakers' voices as well as evidence of the audience member's relationship with the speaker persona. As in my analysis of vocal identity, I analyze this information through a lens of critical theory.

As Smith and Goodale have pointed out, audio-recording technology can encourage a sense of immediacy through the amplification of intimate sounds like whispers and through techniques like voice-over that mimic the feeling of being directly addressed by media's voices.[78] In this way, "media establish a space between the origin of a sound and its listener,"[79] positioning audiences according to the actions in the narrative through the placement of recording devices. Therefore, my consideration of audience positioning centers the ways that voices solicit feelings of immediacy through recording technologies. For example, whispered voices may be amplified to allow the audience to hear, thereby positioning the audience closer to the speaker than to other background noises and speakers, or shouted voices may be paired with direct address, creating the illusion that the speaker is yelling at the audience.[80] My analyses therefore combine the connotations of tone (e.g., whisper, shout, mumble, cheer) with the connotations of linguistic content (e.g., secret, disagreement, announcement).

Central to my argument is the idea that vocal identity and vocal intimacy always coexist. Therefore, I consider these two components separately with the goal of better understanding how they interact. Grounding the analysis is a critical perspective that centralizes intersectional oppressions and privileges and considers how these frame readings of bodies and their relations to one another.

LISTENING IN

At the heart of critical cultural vocalics lies the exhilaratingly intense relationship that voices elicit as they travel from a speaker's mouth to a listener's ear.

This relationship comforts or repulses depending upon a complex interaction between the bodies, contexts, and ideological identifications of speaker and listener. Because the sinewy connection between speaker and listener is my core focus in this book, I have chosen a series of voices that carry cultural relevance *as voices*. This book includes the voices of a variety of perhaps seemingly disparate performers: blues singers, a film and voice actor, politicians, impressionists, and stand-up comedians, among others. The diversity of performance approaches and goals is by design. Since my purpose in this book is to illustrate the utility of critical cultural vocalics as an approach to studying the interaction of identity and mediated voices, I have chosen voices from an array of contexts. Additionally, these voices occur in a range of mediated settings including popular music, movies, television, and YouTube. Of course, in choosing voices to include, I also chose voices to exclude by default. The case studies I have chosen here are meant to illustrate my points about the voice and our scholarly approach to analyzing speech and song, so they are not exhaustive.

My choices were guided by the goal of making critical cultural vocalics useful and accessible to others interested in understanding and further studying how vocal sound shapes identity through the intimacy of speaking or singing and listening. The primary reason for choosing these particular speakers is that these voices represent moments in which the voice, a performance component that is not often discussed as such, came to the fore of public discourse. This provides access to publicly available traces of listener/viewer decoding in the form of popular press and social media discourses about the voices themselves, in addition to the performers who speak and sing them. Each of these voices also allows for a discussion of how sound interacts with intersectional oppressions and privileges in terms of both identity and context, as each of these performers either speaks directly to or works within a context that facilitates analysis of marginalization. In other words, the voices represented in this book have discussed racial and gendered identities and/or have been discussed in those terms. Finally, by choosing these cases, I demonstrate the ubiquity of cultural politics across everyday entertainment genres. An entire book could be written on the voices of satirical political impressionists, for example, but such a book might limit the scope of theory and method proposed here. I hope the diversity of vocal performances included in this book helps facilitate the use of critical cultural vocalics in a variety of contexts by a variety of performers for a variety of audiences. To this end, I chose case studies that follow in the tradition of cultural studies and feminist theory by allowing us to locate the ordinary and literally invisible politics of voices we hear in everyday life.

My remaining chapters are structured as a series of case studies that move through the features of vocal intimacy, vocal identity, and their combined potential for hegemonic reinscription and resistance. The methodological approach at the core of this book is based on the interpretation of sonic rhetoric through concepts of music. Therefore, I begin with a case study that emphasizes the ways that voice carries rhetorics of race and gender in the realm of popular music. In doing so, I demonstrate the value of musical analysis in a more traditional context, a move designed to concretize my musical approach to spoken voice in later chapters. This first case study, chapter 1, analyzes Adele's 2012 Grammy performance and surrounding discourses to explore the cyclical nature of vocal identity and vocal intimacy in a musical context. I first discuss the concept of Blackvoice as an example of the ways that vocal appropriation highlights the socially constructed nature of vocal identity. I then place this idea in the context of the popular music industry, before turning to Adele's voice, persona, and appearance to argue that the singer vocally adopts the identities of Black women blues singers. Since this vocal identity foregrounds the body as an audible feature of the voice, Adele's performance consequently heightens potential for vocal intimacy. Paradoxically, then, Adele's vocal racial passing, which might typically be considered inauthentic, instead contributes to a sense that her music reflects an authentic interior self. This move has been profitable for white men in the past, but for white women like Adele, the centrality of visual race to productions like the Grammy Awards limits her movement within the industry, keeping her performance grounded in the highly feminized pop genre.

Further exploring the ways that vocal identity and intimacy are socially constructed and mutually reinforcing, chapter 2 offers a case study of perhaps the most iconic voice in contemporary US American entertainment media culture: Morgan Freeman's. Other actors have found success in voice-over and on-camera stardom, but Freeman's voice is among the most iconic in contemporary, everyday media. The ubiquity of his voice therefore makes it a clear candidate to introduce critical cultural vocalics as an approach to the spoken voice in popular media. Therefore, in chapter 2, I examine the way Freeman's voice is marked by traces of his Jim Crow Mississippi upbringing. I first trace the ways that Freeman's career has often placed him in a position of subordination narratively, before exploring the obsequious characteristics present in his vocal identity itself. Vocal traits like breathiness, silence, and repetitive vocal patterns reminiscent of orchestral accompaniment frame Freeman as subservient to the white characters in his films. I put this contextual analysis in conversation with public responses to Freeman's voice to argue that the subservience of Freeman's roles is mirrored by relationships with some audiences that position him as servile. Just as Freeman's characters serve their white counterparts, these fans describe ways of imagining the actor's voice performing degrading or fan-centered dialogue. While certainly these fans do not represent the entirety of Freeman's listeners, these audiences' public responses position the actor as subservient, just as he is positioned as secondary in most of his roles.

The same type of vocal intimacy at the heart of Freeman's various media appearances works as an accessory to vocal identity to develop a sense of political ethos. Beyond cultural politics, critical cultural vocalics also offers a way of understanding electoral politics and presidential address through the lens of spoken voice, connecting this rhetorical approach to traditional public address. The voices of successful and unsuccessful politicians tell us much about a society's understandings of authority and credibility, and when these voices are satirized through imitation, such understandings are made even plainer. Therefore, chapter 3 foregrounds the role of vocal identity for political speakers by examining *Saturday Night Live*'s impressions of politicians Sarah Palin and Barack Obama. My analysis in this chapter foregrounds racial and gendered aural stereotypes. Tina Fey's vocal impression of vice presidential candidate Sarah Palin draws from stereotypical white femininity as infantile and emotionally unstable, whereas various impressions of President Obama by Fred Armisen, Dwayne "The Rock" Johnson, and Jay Pharoah caricaturize the masculine attributes that align Obama with a traditionally presidential sound. To ground this analysis, I argue that vocal impressions should be understood through three vocally intimate relationships: the connection between impressionist and audience, the connection between impersonated and audience, and the connection between impressionist and impersonated politician. Together these relationships reveal the cyclical ways in which voices are heard, disciplined, and reperformed based on racialized and gendered cultural lenses.

Saturday Night Live's demonstration of the role of imitation in defining racialized, gendered vocal qualities leads this book into the counterhegemonic and transformative potential of vocal performance. Individual voices, and imitations of those voices, influence and are influenced by structures of social (in)justice. In the final case study, I use critical cultural vocalics to explore how a multitude of voices work together within a tradition of sonic resistance. By examining imitations of white speakers, or *whitevoice* as I call it, by comedians of color like Dave Chappelle, George Lopez, Richard Pryor, and Carlos Mencia, I highlight the way that intimate vocal connections between audience and comedian push back against a dominating vocal identity that Dolar calls "an accent that has been declared a non-accent."[81] In these stand-up comedy performances on YouTube, comedians of color use techniques like hyperfeminizing their vocal rhetorics to weaken the threat of violence posed by their white speakers. As I explored in chapter 3, impressions demonstrate the citational performance of an audience interpretation, which becomes a vocal identity itself. Audiences who comment on videos depicting the comedians' reperformances of whitevoice demonstrate the shared cultural experiences of fear and oppression within white supremacy, so that vocal intimacy aligns comedians and particular audiences in opposition to systemic racism. Weakening this important project of antiracist community-building is the problematic tendency for these comic rhetorics to reify hypermasculinity for men of color and disparage women and femme nonbinary people of all races through the comedians' association of femininity with weakness.

Developed in each chapter is a concrete demonstration of the value of critical cultural vocalics in any exploration of cultural performance. By foregrounding vocal intimacy and vocal identity in analyses of everyday media, this book illustrates the complex politics hiding at the intersection of vocal sound and cultural histories. Racialized and gendered identities are not simply spoken, sung, or heard in the voice; myriad historical influences embed themselves into the physiological voice and the affective act of hearing in the intimate and revealing dance of voice and listener. Ultimately, *Culturally Speaking* articulates both theoretical and methodological approaches to exploring the ways in which the voice functions as a tool of hegemonic and resistant cultural politics.

CHAPTER 1

Singing in the Key of Identity

Adele and the Vocal Intimacy of the Blues

ON THE EVENING of her 2012 Grammy sweep, images of Adele's performance traversed the internet at a furious tempo. In the now iconic photographs, Adele wears a tailored black gown, emphasizing the glow of the singer's pale face against the dark background of the stage. Remarkably, these images of Adele's exaggerated visual whiteness spread in concert with an oppositional racial discourse, as fans and music writers began to question Adele's "Black" sound. Not only did online music communities ask "Do you think Adele sounds black?"[1] and "Is Adele part black because she sounds like it?"[2]; even the NAACP nodded to Adele's Black vocal sound, nominating her single "Someone Like You" for their Outstanding Song Image Award.[3] Discourses about the Black sounds of white artists like Adele are in conversation with those surrounding artists like Dusty Springfield and Amy Winehouse. In fact, singer Stephin Merritt referenced an ongoing debate about racialized sounds when he argued that Adele exemplified "British people who sound like American Black people."[4] The longevity of this conversation points to the historical and contemporary salience of the racialized voice, calling into question the ways that vocal sounds are understood through intersectional discourses of race and gender.

Singers like Adele, whose vocal identity can be read as racially oppositional to her visual performance, illustrate how voices structure and are structured by media industry practices. Music, film, television, and other industries operate through categorization, marketing products by grouping them into genres. Within this process, the practice of sorting musical performers and performances often depends as much on highlighting difference as it does on considering similarity. As Jennifer Lynn Stoever notes, cultural understandings of racialized differences stem from historical periods including Reconstruction and Jim Crow, and as such reflect the fierce struggle to maintain explicit material and economic domination of white, male, wealthy owners over African Americans, white women, immigrants, and workers.[5] In the entertainment industries, as in society at large, this project depended upon the exaggeration of difference. In this spirit, Adele's numerous 2012 Grammy awards were exclusively in traditionally white feminized categories like pop. Through these awards, Adele was distanced from Black performers with similar vocal identities, demonstrating and reinforcing mechanisms of sonic racial difference within the structure of popular music.

The racialized borders that structure popular music's genres are rhetorically defined and maintained. As such, these borders can be fluid and permeable, but only for those in positions of power; for the culturally oppressed, they restrict and discipline. Robert DeChaine argued that borders often travel discursively.[6] The immigrant "carries the border on her back," since her symbolic ties mark her as an outsider within her new national location.[7] Although the border burdens the immigrant, border flexibility can also enhance privilege; when the colonizer "carries the border on her back," the border signifies the dominance, power, and entitlement attached to the colonizing land. Musical borders work in much the same way, stretching to accommodate movement and exploitative colonization by those in power, but snapping punitively back into place for those framed as interlopers. Black musical forms like jazz and blues have historically been colonized by white performers, with the white music industry mining Black culture for profitable sounds. The vocal sounds developed by Black musicians have long circulated as culturally privileged voices. However, a culturally privileged voice does not necessarily allow a culturally marginalized body to travel, and performers of color have consistently been locked into racialized, and less profitable regions of the musical landscape.[8] Following Homi Bhabha, Ono and Pham argue that if racialized performances were not desired, they would not exist in the first place; at the same time, for white audiences, actual engagement with a performer of color is "undesirable and, hence, is excluded."[9] In the case of Adele's racially conflicting performance, R&B artist The-Dream lamented that "Blacks can't do *soul* records any more. [Audiences] love Adele singing it, but [not] Beyoncé."[10]

While comments like The-Dream's illustrate the racial tension between Adele's visual appearance and vocal identity, a third, and perhaps unlikely, discourse worked in tandem with narratives of Blackness and whiteness. Namely, post-Grammy articles and social media commentary drew attention to "the 'authentic' sounds of Adele,"[11] "the Scary Power of an Honest, Gorgeous Song,"[12] and her performance of "genuine music by a real person."[13] While the racial conflict between Adele's vocal identity and her visual appearance seems antithetical to authenticity, popular discourse surrounding her Grammy performance consistently marked Adele's legacy as a triangulation of Black voice, white body, and authentic performance. Clearly many listeners/viewers experienced a powerful connection in her performance, highlighting the ways that vocal identity and vocal intimacy work together, sometimes with unpredictable results. A rich singing voice like Adele's allows us, in Barthes's terms, to "hear a body," a concept at the heart of vocal intimacy. Yet which body, or vocal identity, we hear is less stable or predictable. Vocal racial passing, in which a singer identified with one race performs a vocal sound identified with another race, represents a racially conflicted vocal-identity performance, but that performance can still be intensely intimate. In fact, as I demonstrate in this chapter, performing a racially conflicted vocal identity can actually strengthen and enhance vocal intimacy.

Underscoring this book's focus on spoken voices is the musical approach from which critical cultural vocalics is drawn. Therefore, this first case study outlines the ways that vocal identity and vocal intimacy privilege particular voices in popular music. Specifically, I use Adele's 2012 Grammy performance as a case study to examine the interplay between the singer's apparently Blackvoice vocal identity and encouragement of authentic vocal intimacy. By *Blackvoice*, I refer to the performance of sounds historically associated with Blackness, especially by white performers.[14] Often, this type of performance reflects Blackness in the white imagination, at least in part, since even forms that originated with Black performers have been profoundly shaped by white distribution structures. I use *Blackvoice* here to refer to white singers, but in all cases these racialized sounds are socially constructed. Even when performed by Black women singers, these sounds cite previous performers and rhetorical conventions that mark them as "authentically" Black. In this case, I focus on Black women blues singers, but the concept of Blackvoice, and its corollaries in yellowvoice and brown voice, more generally highlights how particular racialized and gendered bodies become associated with particular vocal sounds which are, through this process, either culturally privileged or excluded from economic and cultural markets.[15] Adele's performance style incorporates vocal-identity components appropriated from Black women blues singers, particularly those elements that have corresponded to performances of pain. Supplementing the sonic attributes of vocal struggle are the lyrical and intertextual descriptions of suffering. This links Adele's vocal identity to early twentieth-century blues, but it does so only at the level of individual romantic struggles, displacing the Black feminist cause of historical Black women blues singers. This lyrical and contextual struggle in Adele's performance persona enhances her pained vocal identity, and both of these features highlight the sense of an interior body in the vocal sound, resulting in an apparently authentic sense of vocal intimacy. White men have often capitalized on this technique, but for white women like Adele, visuality renegotiates her apparent sonic authenticity, restricting her performance to the white feminine Grammy category of pop.

As in all critical perspectives, context and structure play important roles in critical cultural vocalics. Therefore, I begin this case study with a discussion of race in the entertainment industries followed by historical grounding in the role of Black women in the early blues genre. The chapter then outlines Adele's vocal identity in terms of Blackvoice and vocal racial passing and considers how lyrics and intertexts both shape Blackvoice vocal identity and encourage a vocal intimacy that is often read as authenticity. I then analyze the ways that visual whiteness interacts with these sonic components and conclude with a consideration of how the case of Adele's 2012 Grammy performance informs the concepts of vocal identity and vocal intimacy.

THE TWIN INDUSTRIES OF RACE AND VOICE

Media industries shaped racial bordering at many historical moments, but of particular concern to this chapter are the development of the music industry and the incorporation of sound into film. Initially, the development of a formal music industry marked the creation of genres that paralleled racial categories. It was the marketing demands of a new music industry, producing and selling sound in the Jim Crow South, that divided poor and working-class musical traditions according to performer race, resulting in categories of "hillbilly music" and "race records."[16] In the initial stages of industry development, the blues genre privileged Black women over men. Angela Davis characterizes this move as an extension of the "reductive marketing strategies" that assumed that since the first blues singers were Black women, only Black women could be successful blues singers.[17] Recording practices worked, and continue to work, alongside practices of circulation. In this case, radio played an important though complex role in delineating racial borders. Michele Hilmes characterizes the project of early radio as "constructing a national norm of 'whiteness.'"[18] This is not to say that radio play was limited to voices associated with white performers. Rather, radio caricatured differences between Black (primarily women's) blues music and white (mostly men's) country sounds. Thus, radio allowed Black artists to enjoy broader circulation and subsequent financial compensation, but only because the industry was built on the construction and incentivization of bifurcated racial and gendered sounds.[19]

Developing alongside these racialized music and radio industries was Hollywood's sound-film format.[20] As in music and radio formats, film producers actively created difference between the voices of white actors and actors of color. Often this meant actively training Black and immigrant actors to speak with exaggerated dialects, with spoken lines spelled out phonetically or coached to sound more stereotypically "ethnic" to white ears.[21] By this point in history, of course, Blackvoice sounds had been circulated through minstrelsy for decades, so the link between visually Black and brown bodies and "coarse," "loud," "strong," or otherwise racially marked voices was not originated through media technology but rather was "cited," to borrow Butler's term.[22] As standards differentiating Blackvoice from immigrant voice from whitevoice became repeatedly and consistently marked, explicit and intentional vocal training became less and less necessary; performers eventually learned which voices were more likely to become culturally privileged according to the genre in which they fit. The early sound-film industry capitalized on fetishized, but increasingly naturalized, Blackvoice in part by circulating the idea that Black voices "could be reproduced more faithfully than others," a discourse that had the effect of even more firmly reifying the constructed connection of vocal sound to visual body based on the performer's race.[23] The promotional strategies surrounding Black performance in sound film focused on "the fetishistic rhetorical strategy" of praising African American performance through a cartoonish lens of difference.[24] This meant, as Alice Maurice writes, that white audiences often brought simplified expectations of Blackvoice into theaters. It also contributed to the solidifying of stereotyped ideas of what race meant holistically. The sleight of hand involved in film sound and image synchronization naturalized Blackvoice as both markedly different and fundamentally sutured to Black bodies. Black bodies were, and are, far from privileged in US American culture. Still, a "Black voice" sutured to a Black body could easily become a culturally privileged voice, as long as it fit the exaggerated and, particularly in the case of historical spoken performance, degrading norms of the genre.

Furthermore, since the "talkie" format required sound and image to be recorded separately then synchronized, the race and gender of speakers and singers could be manipulated, increasing industry value when Black performance skill came in apparently white packages. Julie Dash illustrates this point in her award-winning film, *Illusions*. The film depicts the racial and gendered complications of the film musical industry through the story of a Black woman singer whose voice is synchronized to match the visual movements of a successful white starlet. Through the ease at which the singer's voice is edited onto the actor's body, Dash illustrates both the constructedness of racial voice in film synchronization and the ways that Black creative contributions are often appreciated more when attached to apparently white bodies. The film also works as a metacommentary, as the actor who portrays the Black woman singer in the film does not provide the musical vocals. Instead, Ella Fitzgerald's recorded voice is synced onto her, and by extension the white woman starlet's, body.[25] Thus, as was often the case in early Hollywood, the contributions of Black women are systematically erased, citing audience preference. As *Illusions* illustrates, synchronization so naturalizes the visual body as the producer of sound that a white woman with a dubbed Black woman's voice is understood not as sounding Black but rather as simply talented; in the same context, the Black woman singing is denied access to the financial and cultural benefits of screen visualization. The border dictating the necessity to "match" visual and sonic race, then, can be crossed, but only through the systemic power of whiteness.

As Dash's film makes clear, despite the dismissal and invisibility of Black women's bodies, Black women's music was highly profitable. Blues, in particular, highlighted Black women's ability to navigate the constraints of genre. Angela Davis argues that Black women blues singers offer an early and concrete example of how everyday Black feminist ideas can be circulated through power structures dominated by white men.[26] Even in the constricting social context of the 1920s and 1930s, she writes, Black women blues singers voiced messages that pushed back against both the domestic expectations of servitude that limited poor women and women of color and the expectations of maternity placed on middle- and upper-class white women. The transgressive rhetoric of Black women blues singers also highlights how the constructed nature of racialized vocal sound can be a foil for liberatory discourses. Since there is nothing biologically linking Blackvoice to Black bodies, the form can be co-opted or rhetorically marked in disparaging ways. For example, Black music critics often praised Lena Horne's success specifically as a Black woman, whereas white critics more often wondered at her ability to shift between established Black and white sounds.[27] This example illustrates that the difficulties of leveraging racially limiting genres for transgressive purposes are rooted in the social construction of those genres. The early construction of musical genre as racialized is thus double-edged in its potential to shift depending on context.

During the civil rights era, racial discourses grew even more deeply intertwined with popular music as the recording and circulation industries gained momentum. The continuing legacy of the racialized development of musical and film content in the 1920s is the classification of musical genres according to the perceived race, gender, and sometimes sexuality of the performer. While the blues genre had been somewhat complex in the era between its founding and the mid-twentieth century, allowing for racial crossover and experimentation, the 1960s saw a whitening and a masculinizing of the genre, particularly among British performers like Eric Clapton. The 1960s whitewashed blues culture continued to value performances of white-conceptualized "Blackness" largely through appropriation of the particular racially marked sound developed earlier in the century by Black women and men facing a great deal of structural oppression and violence.[28] The Blackvoice identities adopted by many white male performers "posited masculinized blues realism against feminized 'sappy teeny pop,'" ironically leveraging practices of appropriation for increased perceptions of authenticity.[29] In other words, white men blues performers defined others out of the mainstream, allowing themselves space to cross racialized genre boundaries but locking performers of color, white women, and gender nonbinary performers into genre-specific boxes. The new white blues sound was consequently reclassified for Grammy awards and *Billboard* chart categories, generic distinctions that not only influence cultural understanding of popular music but also contribute to the frequency of radio play and the subsequent financial benefits of musical ubiquity, demonstrating the cultural and economic capital attached to culturally privileged voices. These charts, David Brackett argues, elevate white performers to "Hot 100" lists and performers of color to separate categories like "R&B/Hip Hop" and "Latin."[30] The constructedness of these genres is highlighted by the similarity of sounds that cross over, so that divisions are most often marked by the visually apparent race and gender of the performer rather than distinct differences in vocal or instrumental sound.

VOCAL RACIAL PASSING, AUTHENTICITY, AND DIFFERENCE

Vocal racial passing is indecipherable without a concept of racial authenticity, which is in turn held firmly in place by widely held social understandings of difference. Debates over the meaning of authenticity have persisted over time, and the term has been used in discussions of performances, audiences, musical texts, and the contexts surrounding musical culture in general.[31] In contemporary conversations, authenticity is often situated opposite commerciality.³² Understood this way, *discursive authenticity* is a social construction that surrounds certain performers and performances, marking them as somehow more affectively real and less influenced by the music industry and economic incentives. This dualism, between the interior affective self and the exterior industry self, mirrors John L. Jackson Jr.'s discussions of racial authenticity, in which race is judged to be the exterior expression of interior racial identification.³³ Both authenticity and race are social constructions rooted in discourse, a fact that does not soften the intense and persistent material consequences of racism for people of color. When race is repeatedly performed as difference, that difference becomes ingrained in cultural expectations of how people of that race should sound, look, and behave. Consequently, these repeated performances frame an expectation for racial authenticity, creating a vicious cycle of performances and expectations.³⁴ With this in mind, this chapter explores the ways that, for musical artists, discourses of authenticity are tied to a vocal identity understood to match the visual race and gender of the performer. This performance generally runs alongside a sense of vocal intimacy enhanced by intertextual narratives about an artist's private life.

The salience of passing depends not only on authenticity but on authenticity to particular categories of being.³⁵ In other words, passing only makes sense in relationship to difference. Since hierarchical racial categories are a pseudoscientific fiction on which the structure of Western culture has been built, social practices must continually reinforce race as real and natural. This task has been taken up, in part, by entertainment industries who, as Stoever points out, engineered vocal difference explicitly and intentionally.³⁶ This manufactured difference, which she calls the *sonic color line*, naturalizes the idea that particular bodies produce particular sounds based on their racial membership.³⁷ Each time these racial categories are apparently confirmed through a matched vocal performance, racial difference is reified through sound. By crossing between categories of Black and white, on the other hand, speakers and singers simultaneously highlight the stubbornness of imagined racial boundaries and demonstrate their permeability. As Eric Lott argues, this is a primary reason for the success of Blackface minstrelsy, as the "small but significant crimes against settled ideas of racial demarcation" made the performance of apparent racial crossing both fascinating and compellingly unsettling for audiences.³⁸ Without stubbornly delineated racial categories and their translation to vocal sound, vocal racial passing and authenticity would be meaningless.

One extension of vocal racial passing is vocal appropriation. Vocal appropriation is most clearly problematic in its reallocation of ownership and capital from a marginalized group to a dominant group. Whether or not a particular act of appropriation in the media industry is intended as "love or theft," the point at which mediated, industrialized appropriation becomes representational violence is when it leverages racialized sounds to displace racialized bodies. As Greg Tate argues, the appropriation and subsequent marketing of Black cultural production is firmly tied to the rhetorical justification of slavery, a discussion that bears quoting at length:

> Capitalism's original commodity fetish was the Africans auctioned here as slaves, whose reduction from subjects to abstracted objects has made them seem larger than life and less than human at the same time . . . Something to be possessed and something to be erased—an operation that explains . . . the American music industry's never-ending quest for a white artist who can competently perform a Black musical impersonation.[39]

In other words, cultural profitability depends not only on co-optation but on rendering the original performer invisible. This process is complex, in that it appears to have originated from both entitlement and appreciative fascination, but the eventual financial result is clear.[40] For white women singers of the early twentieth century, including Sophie Tucker and May Irwin, performing in Blackvoice not only increased their individual incomes, it also meant they out-earned a majority of other women in the industry to an unparalleled degree.

Beyond profitability, vocal racial passing also offered political leverage for white women bolstered by race but struggling against gendered constraints. White women who performed on the vaudeville stage were propelled by audience interest in feminine spectacle but simultaneously limited by the strict racialized gender norms of the period.[41] By taking up the Blackvoice form of "coon shouting," white women could leverage Otherness to expand their own political possibilities. As Eden Elizabeth Kainer writes, performing in Blackvoice drew from the cultural capital of "black charisma," allowing white women to make the radical claims that they "could be sexy, they could earn money, and they could exist independently outside of the traditional roles of wife and mother."[42] Of course, the financial and political capital gained by white women "coon shouters" was less available to the Black women they emulated. Still, Angela Davis points out that Black women blues singers took notice of, and spoke back to, the differential standards of gender imposed on Black women and white women.[43] In "Sam Jones Blues," for example, Bessie Smith shifts between a bluesy, conversational voice when offering the perspective of a Black woman abandoned by her lover and a "teasing intonation to evoke white cultural conceptions" when voicing the expectations of white femininity.⁴⁴ Thus, intersecting the racialized performance styles of the early twentieth century was the key role of gender in complicating the content of blues and vaudeville performances. White performers continued to leverage their cultural power to appropriate and colonize the blues, even as Black women seized opportunities to critique this practice.

The colonization of Black music shaped discursive authenticity in three ways. First, as Debra Walker King notes, rock and roll grew around an unharnessed vocal emotion born from the culture of diasporic pain in Black blues culture.⁴⁵ Black musical performance demanded what Roland Barthes describes as "the grain of the voice."⁴⁶ The messy presence of spit and sinew in the voice was not a feature of white musical tradition since, as Barthes argues, a goal of classical vocal training is to remove the body from the song.⁴⁷ In contrast, the growl of vocal strain that propelled Elvis to fame did so by audibly foregrounding his sound-producing body within the music. Introducing a physical presence into the voice did not serve white women and Black singers in the same way, since their bodies were particularly constrained and stereotyped by law and culture. For white men, however, the throaty feel of rock and roll emphasized the music's genesis while pulling an imagined Black body into the voices of visually white performers. The body's indisputable presence in the music solidified the link between music and musician, giving rock and roll the feeling of being "true" to the performer, an element that Mark Butler notes is key to discursive authenticity.⁴⁸

Second, by injecting the body into the voice, Black music allowed white singers to claim authenticity as self-evident. The injection of the singer's physical body into the voice allowed the music's story to become intimately connected to the performer and the performer's community, a second trait of musical authenticity for Butler.⁴⁹ Jazz and other Black musical traditions grew and thrived on culturally and historically transmitted narratives of pain, giving them an air of truth not only for the performer but for the performer's link to past generations.⁵⁰ This appearance of history could be reproduced by white colonizers, Mike Daley argues, allowing white performers to associate with narrative tradition both through the content of jazz and blues lyrics and through the vocal identity associated with these genres.⁵¹ This application of discursive authenticity used the performance of an imagined Black body to colonize the experience of Black pain, further cementing the practice of white musical authenticity within traditions of Black musical expression.

Finally, Black musical performance was built on traditions of physical movement and dance, giving the music a feeling of radiation from the performer's body through movements. For white women and Black and Latinx performers across genders, whose sexuality was heavily policed in various ways, public performance of body movements in line with the strong beats of African musical tradition was socially dangerous. For white men, on the other hand, the visual focus on the body facilitated a performance of authenticity. Not only did a visual focus on white masculinity replicate conservative notions of performance for white US audiences, it also reinforced musical discursive authenticity by representing the white male performer as the source of a Blackvoice vocal identity. For white men, this type of performance was both new, in that white men had not previously embodied this specific type of performance, and a US tradition, in that the US entertainment industry, and the country in general, had always been built on theft from people of color. Reinforcement of the white body tapped into assumptions that, as Jackson explains, authenticity of the inner self could be read on the surface of the outer self;[52] sounds that originated in Black cultural forms were thus captured by the expanding borders of white authenticity as white men assumed control over musical production and the music industry as a whole.[53]

The space of musical authenticity represents a colonization that permeates the musical sphere, claiming white masculine music as the ultimate in "true" performance in a way that commodifies Black cultural heritage and delegitimizes women artists of all races. In crafting these racialized borders along generic lines, the white-male-dominated music industry constructed and naturalized musical binaries between white and Black music and masculine and feminine performers' bodies. The outward appearance of the performer thus becomes a symbolic demarcation, since, as Kent A. Ono has argued, "the body performs bordered identities, revealing aspects of identity that can be regulated as on this or that side of a given border."[54] Since, in DeChaine's phrasing, the performer "carries the border on her back," her body must be disciplined into hegemonic servitude to bordering.[55] The structure of the music industry depends upon performers remaining within the racial generic territories dictated by identity categories. Discourses of authenticity are one mechanism of reinforcing this structure, since they determine not only which singers belong to the privilege of white men's performance but also, in many cases, which singers' voices are culturally privileged and which are not.

VOICING STRUGGLE

As a white woman performer, Adele has a complicated presence within the musical space of authenticity. Although generally white women are not able to access the same level of privilege within the music industry, appropriation of a Black blues vocal identity is not new for white women, particularly those of British descent. Adele navigates her border crossing through a vocal identity that carries the same graininess used by Black women blues singers at the dawn of the recording industry. This vocal identity works alongside intertextual readings of her personal history and visual performance of whiteness to press her across the normatively white masculine border into a racially contested space. Authenticity is often framed as an affective intangible in rhetorical and cultural studies music literature, but the singer's success offers a framework through which authenticity can be examined for what it is: a racialized justification for vocal appropriation by the white-male-dominated music industry.[56] Adele's 2012 Grammy performance and the surrounding discourses demonstrate how vocal identity and vocal intimacy work together to facilitate this type of vocal racial passing through vocal, intertextual, and visual performances.

The border between whiteness and Otherness is policed by distinguishing individuals' interior racial identity based on exterior visual appearance.[57] This border can therefore be blurred by destabilizing racial binaries. John Louis Lucaites writes that most borders "tend to be seen but go unnoticed, observed only in the breach as we become habituated to—and truth be told, rely upon—their presence."[58] The "breach," then, represents observable performances of vocal racial passing, enacted through the voice, persona, and body, that make structural power and privilege visible. As Jackson argues, racial passing is dependent upon bordering practices; without discursively stabilized boundaries separating whiteness and Blackness, movement between these territories loses its meaning and value.[59] Passing is an attempt to perform another group's authenticity, or to capitalize on the culturally privileged vocal sounds created by consistent histories of reifying the match between racialized voice and racialized body. Such a transgression need not be intentional, and indeed often is not. Instead, as I discuss here, vocal appropriation may simply be a recognition of and desire for the cultural privilege that a particular group has negotiated within the racialized and gendered boundaries of the industry. When examined through this lens, Adele's performance of vocal racial passing demonstrates a renegotiation of white musical bordering, challenging the stability of white masculine privilege for musical artists, scholars, fans, and industry professionals.

Adele's racially conflicted performance is perceived largely through her voice. For Adele, this takes the form of a white singer performing Black vocal sounds, or simply "Blackvoice."[60] Kainer notes that many nineteenth-century publications advised white singers to adopt Black vocal identities by practicing "vocal breaks or discontinuities of the voice; large gaps in the melodic line

... nonverbal vocal interjections, such as 'peculiar humming sounds;' [and] a straining vocal quality ('exceedingly nasal and undulating,' and sustaining one's breath to the point of injury)."[61] These descriptions should not be read as the physical essence of a Black voice; in fact, a primary argument of this book is that the voice is *not* biologically or physiologically natural. Rather, the voice is constructed both through pressures that shape and reshape the body, often through forces of oppressive stress or privileged ease, and through citationality of vocal sound that is culturally made to seem "normal" based on exterior physical characteristics.[62] Stated bluntly, the racialization and gendering of voices is socially constructed, such that Blackvoice is no more natural or biological for Black singers than for non-Black singers. It is only through the frequent association of particular sounds with particular bodies that the characteristics identified in Kainer's historical research point to a culturally salient understanding of Black vocal identity. The perception of Adele's "Black sound" can therefore be understood along two overlapping criteria for a Black blues vocal identity: vocal discontinuities, including breaks in sound, melodic gaps, and emotional interjections; and vocal strain, including sounds that point to lack of breath, less intense engagement of the vocal cords, and forced distortion of the vocal tone. These two criteria, which I analyze below, push Adele's vocal style into a racially conflicted space.

A signature of Adele's musical vocal identity is her use of extended notes, particularly at the end of phrases; however, this technique is set apart by the singer's subtle use of vocal discontinuities that space and differentiate held notes within the melodic line. This is particularly clear during the singer's performance of "Rolling in the Deep" at the 2012 Grammy awards. During the first chorus, Adele sings, "The scars of your love, they leave me breathless; I can't help feeling that we could have had it all." While the focus of this phrase lies in the extended pitch of the word "all," the climax is framed by gaps in the previous pitch pattern; by breaking the line on the upbeats between "love" and "they," "leave" and "me," and "can't" and "help" (figure 1.1), Adele synthesizes the effect of gasping. Adele's vocal tone cracks slightly, leaving a space for the rhythmic high-hat taps behind her. In so doing, Adele conjures historical jazz and blues singers through both an increased focus on upbeat and downbeat alternation and a heightened emotional sound that radiates from inside the body. As Kainer's scholarship points out, these are the qualities embedded in the history of Black blues performance.[63] Through decades of repetition, these technically specific uses of vocal identity have come to represent a tone associated with Blackness, even as it has been colonized by white singers generations before.

Adele's performance of Blackvoice vocal discontinuities is enhanced by her alternation between a rich, pure vocal sound and a breathy, strained tone.

[Musical notation: yo-o-our luh they lee(f) me brea - (th)ul (ss) I can't help fee-lin]

FIGURE 1.1. "[The scars of] your love, they leave me breathless. I can't help feeling . . . ,""Rolling in the Deep."

"Rolling in the Deep" exemplifies this performance style, as the song's relatively wide pitch range paints a starker contrast between breathy and pure. At the climax of the previously examined prechorus, Adele's voice opens to a pure, round belt, as she holds the song's highest pitch on "all." Her tone at this point is much different from that of the song's opening verse; as the first verse begins, Adele's vocal cords seem to be only partially engaged, allowing some air to seep through the throat without vibrating the cords. This tone is often described colloquially as a fuzzy vocal tone, whereas nonlinear dynamic analysis of the human singing voice refers to the quality as "shimmer." This trait is found more often in genres like blues and soul than in genres like country.[64] This breathy sound gives the impression of vocal fatigue, which is often accentuated in Adele's performance of the blues growl. After several verses of airy timbre in the singer's 2012 Grammy performance, Adele's voice reveals distinctive signs of wear through a growling tone as she sings "you played it with a beat," followed by a yelping sound in her upper register (figure 1.2). This climactic performance moment not only includes hints of vocal strain; it actually features vocal strain as an integral element in Adele's vocal identity.

Adele's vocal strain links her performance to generations of Blackvoice singers through the tonal representation of pain, incorporating the authentic-

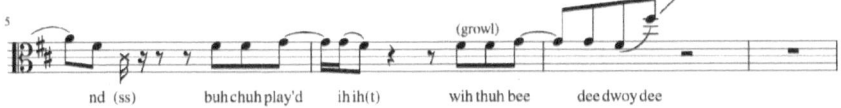

FIGURE 1.2. "[in your hands,] but you played it with a beat," "Rolling in the Deep."

ity of suffering as a decorative musical embellishment. For many Black women blues singers before Adele, the performance of pain has contributed to musical success. As King notes, "For the blues singer and those who benefit from her or his song, pain equals money, pleasure, and power."[65] In other words, for Black women throughout history, the price of a culturally privileged voice has been suffering. The performance of suffering that Adele adopts resonated with audiences as well. One Twitter user remarked, "I love that you can hear the pain in Adele's voice,"[66] and another commented that Adele had "so much pain in [her] voice."⁶⁷ However, blues performance is often conceptualized not simply as a performance of pain, but more specifically as a performance of Black pain. The link between Black pain and vocal strain is clear in Kainer's discussion of "coon shouting."⁶⁸ Popularized by Josephine Baker and Ethel Waters, coon shouting was a nineteenth-century practice that involved pitching a song above the singer's comfortable range to encourage audible vocal fatigue. The practice was associated with vocal health concerns, linking vocal strain to the apparently pained interior of Black women's bodies.⁶⁹ Indeed, the pained sound of vocal strain is so prevalent in Adele's performances that her fall 2011 vocal hemorrhage and consequent laser surgery seemed only to heighten audience enthusiasm for her Grammy performance a few short months later.⁷⁰ This "coarse" sound or "grain," Stoever writes, was often attributed to Black singers by white critics, not only creating a link between Blackness, physicality, and pain but also drawing a hierarchical division between white performers and those of color.⁷¹

Not only does the coding of physical pain in Adele's vocal performance frame her as a white woman deploying a Blackvoice vocal identity, but the presence of the body in her voice intensifies the experience of connection between singer and listener. In other words, the prominent "grain" of Adele's vocal identity also heightens vocal intimacy in a way that is necessary for a voice to become truly culturally privileged. Commenting on the grainy discontinuities in Adele's live performances, many social media users observed the singer's conflation of physical and emotional pain and the way this connected them to her. For example, YouTube commenter Alejandro Reyes⁷² wrote, "This is my favorite performance of Adele. I just love how much emotion she puts into it and how her voice starts to crack at the end like she wants to cry. This performance make[s] me cry every time."⁷³ In Reyes's post, the vocal crack in Adele's voice translates into his own listening body, encouraging affective simultaneity.⁷⁴ Key to the power of vocal intimacy is not only that Reyes feels moved to cry when listening to Adele. It is that the commenter feels moved to cry because Adele seems to be on the verge of tears. Similarly, Miss Cinabon roll's language explicitly demonstrates the connection between Adele's voice and her own physical listening experience: "She was getting really emotional towards the end that's why her voice was shaking and it left me shaking.Beautiful."⁷⁵ In both of these examples, which are representative of those found on YouTube videos and live tweets surrounding Adele's live televised performances, users express the experience of vocal intimacy as a shared physical experience of being. The singer's voice enters through the listeners' ear canals, connecting bodies through sound and allowing Adele's body to be intimately heard and experienced. As Adele sings to them through the television or internet, the movements of her vocal body connect with listeners'/viewers' ears to create an intimate sense of shared physicality.

Adele's performance of a Blackvoice vocal identity, then, extends beyond simple vocal appropriation. Through a critical cultural vocalic analysis, the singer's access to authenticity reveals itself as the interaction between identity and intimacy. Not only does the appropriation of Black women blues singers' ability to make audiences "hear a body"[76] allow Adele to borrow from a racialized genre; her skill at this appropriation similarly expands the connection of vocal intimacy.

THE SOUNDS OF AUTHENTICITY

White musical bordering exists not only through vocal identity but also in the way that the voice frames lyrical and intertextual identity narratives. In the case of Adele, the perception of her music as deeply personal is a function of her synergistic deployment of vocal identity and intimacy. Musical performance, according to Barthes, constructs meaning through the interaction of language and voice.[77] What Barthes calls "the grain of the voice" is the body's impact on the voice, through the sounds of breath, throatiness, and diaphragmatic movement, combined with, in Barthes's estimation, the soul's impact on the voice, perceived as messy passion in vocal identity.[78] Missing from Barthes's account is the intertextual relationship between the singer's body and soul and the communication of that body and soul to the listener,[79] a relationship that mimics Jackson's discussion of racial authenticity as the exterior judgment of a racial interior.[80] For consumers, this relationship forms the basis for what Richard Dyer calls *star images*, which consist of musical or film performances along with narratives of stars' images personal lives.[81] In Adele's case, the intertextual discussion of her experiences, primarily as the inspiration for both *19* and *21*, has been nearly as prominent as the textual discussion of her lyrical and musical expression of that personal life. The intersection of the textual and the intertextual, simultaneously displayed in her live performances, is the intersection of Adele's racialized and gendered vocal identity and intimacy, which run alongside claims to authenticity.

Adele's textual performance of Blackvoice presents not only through the physical sound of her white body in her vocal identity but also through her voice's projection onto lyrical expressions of pain and loss. Both of Adele's pre-2012 hit albums, *19* and *21*, focus entirely upon the narrative of lost love, leaving much of their lyrical content to reflect the pained sound of her physical vocal performance. In "Someone Like You," for example, Adele's raspy voice mournfully addresses a former lover as she sings "I heard that you . . . found a girl and you're married now." The conclusion of the melodic phrase extends through several beats as the word "now" is stretched into three distinctly separate syllables. Kainer identifies this technique as *linguistic deformation,* arguing that by splitting the line into several syllables, Blackvoice singers reference this Black blues technique.[82] However, this line does more than simply race the voice; it also makes apparent the interior body's physical presence in the singing, since by dividing a single syllable into several individual notes, the singer injects pulsing waves of breath into the song's meaning. This phrasing not only foregrounds the "grain" of the voice, then, but also places a certain type of interior body into the musical space, reifying vocal identity and enhancing vocal intimacy. In this case, Adele's performance of Blackvoice is present as a physical interjection of an imagined Black body.

Adele's strained Blackvoice characteristic combined with the lyrical text of pain prompts listeners to accept her performance as musically authentic. As Barthes argues, the "grain" of the voice incites a certain attentiveness to the physical existence of the performer: "If I perceive the 'grain' in a piece of music and accord this 'grain' a theoretical value (the emergence of the text in the work), I inevitably set up a new scheme of evaluation which will certainly be individual—I am determined to listen to my relation with the body of the man or woman singing or playing and that relation is erotic."[83] In other words, the constant presence of body in Adele's vocal identity promotes a deeper relationship between listener and singer than if her physical presence were more obscured. Still, the perception of this body is racially deceptive. This intersection comprises Adele's rhetoric of vocal passing, which challenges the listener to linger over the singer's white body; even these visuals are framed by Blackvoice vocal identity. The "erotic" relationship thus becomes not only one of voice, singer, and offstage performer but also one of the racialized borders of authenticity as Adele's fans confront conceptions about her interior and exterior identities.

Adele's racially conflicting identity seeps into her musical performance through her albums' intertextual focus on lived experience, complicating her Blackvoice vocal identity. King notes that the blues has long represented a connection to the culture of Black pain, and, as such, it draws its authenticity from the link between history and vocal-lyrical performance.[84] While her exterior white body denies her entrance into this particular location of racial authenticity, Adele's troubled romances infiltrate her music, linking her performance of interior pain to Blackvoice. For film stars, Dyer argues, the "overlap of performance and life . . . authenticates the former (she . . . 'really feels' the emotion she sings because it is an emotion from her life), but also fits into the film's treatment of the theatricality of experience."[85] In this case, Adele's history of lost love foregrounds her "authentic" performance. This personal pain interacts with her Blackvoice vocal identity, so that the individualized struggle of lost love is driven by, but does not engage with, the pain at the heart of Black women's blues history. She draws from communal intimacy without the work of community struggle. The connection of Adele's vocal intimacy is clear from the discourses surrounding her performances. YouTube posters, for example, commented, "She means every word. That's powerful you can see it comes from deep inside her heart,"[86] and "You are the real that makes fakeness shrivel in despair,"[87] and these comments were voted "Top Comments" by peers who apparently shared these posters' sentiments.[88] These comments demonstrate the ways that the intense vocal intimacy elicited by the graininess of her voice interacts with lyrical content to create a sensation of authentic vocal intimacy for particular audiences.

Working to make sense of the apparently contradictory nature of Adele's Blackvoice vocal identity and her white feminine visual identity, social media commentary drew explicit connections between race, gender, and pain in their conversations about Adele's music. Clearly posting in jest, one social media user shared, "Adele is a black girl. The pain in her voice, her itching her skalp on her album cover & she used to gettin her heart broken. I'm convinced."[89] That this poster identifies pain as communicating through Adele's voice foregrounds the centrality of vocal identity to the sense of intimacy elicited between the singer and her listeners/viewers. As this poster notes, it is not simply the lyrics of her music or knowledge of her previous romantic relationships, but rather the sonic components of her musical performance that mark hers as a culturally privileged voice. This type of joke was not uncommon in the Twittersphere. Another user quipped, "All that pain in adele's voice I swore she was black,"[90] again pointing to the connection not only of Adele, Blackness, and pain, but also to the explicitly pained vocal identity that the singer borrows from Black women blues singers. The pained voice, then, is a crucial aspect of Adele's vocal identity. Drawing from Black blues singers, Adele's music conjures the struggle at the heart of performances by the Black women who forged the early music industry before her. As Twitter user jbirdfly stated simply, "Adele got that pain & soul in her voice, that's why she sounds 'black.'"[91] *Black* is in quotation marks in this comment, labeling the Blackvoice sound as socially constructed. More typically, though, the quotation marks are omitted in online commentary, emphasizing the fact that vocal identity is frequently taken for granted as biological and therefore necessarily authentic.

The juxtaposition of Adele's interior Black sound and her exterior white identity complicates the political dimensions of her performance of racial passing. Adele's ability to pass between white feminine pop performance and Blackvoice blues foregrounds both whiteness and authenticity. Dyer argues that star images tend to paint celebrities as either wholly authentic or wholly constructed; in other words, "a star's image can work either way, and in part we make it work according to how much it speaks to us in terms we can understand about things that are important to us."[92] Put another way, celebrity authenticity is dictated more by how the performer makes listeners feel, or the success of vocal intimacy, than by any cognitive analysis of who they are and what they represent. While discourses about Adele's Black sound are prominent, many of the singer's fans come to her defense on this issue, refuting the idea of a racialized voice and often accusing the original poster of racism. This was the case following Stephin Merritt's comment about Adele's Blackvoice; a lengthy comment thread saw most posters reject Merritt's characterization of Adele's voice as an imitation of Blackness by insisting that her sound was an authentic expression of her inner self.[93] To stabilize the narrative of Adele's authentic voice, much of the internet community turned to postracial discourses, rejecting the presence of a Black sound in Adele's music. Indeed, a favorite quote attributed to Adele circulated the Twitterverse as a fan favorite in which the singer is cited as saying "I don't care if you're black, white, short, tall, skinny, rich or poor. If you respect me, I'll respect you."[94] Not only does this phrase follow the syntax of the popular claim to colorblindness, "I don't care if you are black, white, green, or purple,"[95] in announcing indifference to race, this quote does more to dismiss the complex differences in culture that produced genres like the blues than it does to reject racism. This type of postracialism, of course, is often used to justify ongoing racial aggression, violence, and exploitation, regardless of how well intentioned the discourse.

This conflict raises the question of cultural or vocal appropriation. As I discussed in the above sections, US American music and film industries were built on a foundation of exploitation that often took from people and cultures while concealing its sources. Still instances of appropriation are frequently more complex than they seem. Running alongside the postracial discourses surrounding Adele were those highlighting appropriation in as many words, including Rasheed Copeland's tweet in which he titled the singer's Grammy performance "The Gentrification of Black Music starring Adele."[96] If gentrification describes a system of entering a space of struggle, suffering, exploitation, and oppression and making it aesthetically pleasing to white middle- and upper-class visitors, then gentrification is perhaps a better reflection of Adele's effect on blues. Her topics of suffering are entirely romantic, rather than reflecting the complex structures of marginalization at the heart of Black women blues singers in the early twentieth century. Whereas Davis argues that women blues singers of the era offered a rich body of "quotidian expressions of feminist consciousness,"[97] the content of Adele's music disregards feminist themes in favor of the singer's own struggles to find love as a heterosexual white woman. Vocal appropriation, or Black musical gentrification, can also be understood through the lens of vocal identity and vocal intimacy. Adele learned to sing, and was subsequently trained as a singer, in a global culture that values the sound of Black women blues singers more than it values the singers themselves.

The concept of vocal identity maintains that voices carry sound from the depths of a body outward not as an inevitable result of biology, but through the shaping forces of the sonic environments in which we learn to speak and sing. Adele's vocal sound, then, is not, as one tweeter put it, "the most real voice,"[98] but rather a reflection of how her body learned to sound within a particular cultural moment. Her voice is not fully appropriated, in that she is not (as far as we know) lip-syncing to a Black woman blues singers' voice as in Dash's *Illusions*. Neither is her voice fully authentic, in that all vocal sound is shaped by social conditions. Similarly, the vocal intimacy forged with listeners is neither inevitable, in that it does not have the same impact on all listeners, nor devoid of raw material connection. The material experience exists within a particular cultural context, and that context shapes and reshapes material experience in a constant cyclical process of sound. The voice, its traits, and its connections always reflect both material and cultural influence, and these factors combine to elevate Adele's as a culturally privileged voice.

BLACK SOUND, WHITE FACE

The processes of colonization, appropriation, and gentrification require the constant visual presence of the clearly white, nonambiguous colonizer. Even as discourses about the race of Adele's vocal identity resonated throughout online communities, the singer's visual publicity rhetoric was recouping Adele's vocal racial passing by circulating messages about how Adele *should* be read: as a white female pop performer. As Dyer argues, the visual saturation of white bodies centers and reproduces whiteness as a dominant and naturalized power by constantly reinforcing its ubiquitous display.[99] The more constant the visual presence of the colonizers, Satya P. Mohanty contends, the more accepted their power becomes.[100] As the colonization is naturalized, it becomes common sense. The media's constant visual display of whiteness obfuscates its colonization of Black music, normalizing the music industry's white musical bordering. In Adele's case, these elements collide to reinforce her exterior racial identity, enhancing the colonizing power of her white feminine body.

If Adele's vocal performance prompts questions about the illusory "color" of her voice, the visual rhetoric of Adele's performances and album paraphernalia recoups the singer as a colonizer—and *not* a racial transgressor—by centralizing her white femininity. Most of Adele's publicity photography involves either close-up or extreme close-up frames of the singer's face, with the album cover for *21* obscuring all but the singer's face, arm, and hand. Notable in this shot is the high-contrast lighting: such bold light spills across the singer's face that only the foremost areas of the facial mask are illuminated, leaving the background behind Adele's chin and cheeks completely black. This technique, in which light is projected directly onto the face so as to produce a "darkening of the edge of the image where the light falls off, having the effect of softening the frame," is a way of emphasizing the glow of the white feminine form.[101] Indeed, what this black-and-white album cover most forcefully communicates is Adele's exterior whiteness. The contrast between the dark background of the frame's lower half and her literally white skin emphasizes her whiteness to the point of nearly matching the white text that bears her name. Adele thus becomes both clearly white and clearly feminine, as her face takes on the glow of an angelic figure.

Supplementing overt imagery of the singer's white skin in photographic depictions is the use of lighting in the singer's 2012 Grammy performance. By pouring cool, white light onto Adele as she sings, lighting effects push her skin's whiteness into the symbolic realm. Dyer explains that whitenesses of skin, hue, and symbol exist in constant representational slippage, with all three supporting the idea that white symbolizes purity and goodness.[102] For Dyer, this is the motivation for the standard technique of lighting performers from above, casting a visual heavenly glow onto the (white) performer.[103] This is highly pronounced in Adele's 2012 Grammy performance. White light spills from above the singer, isolating her whiteness through the stark contrast between her white body and the black stage. She appears to glow against the background as she begins to sing. The visual image of her white body, then, is juxtaposed with the breathy Blackvoice sound that is highly pronounced in her opening bars. Just as Dyer describes, the backlighting shimmers through her blonde hair, emphasizing the ethereal sparkle of whiteness as a divine and divinely endowed power.[104] Her command of the stage appears to come from her Blackvoice vocal identity, but this power is overwhelmed by the racial authority of her glowing white body.

As "Rolling in the Deep" moves into its up-tempo section, a floor light behind the singer spills an intensely cool white light upwards, giving the appearance that light is radiating upward from her blonde bouffant. In contrast to the upward facing light that seems to spill from Adele's crown, an extreme-upstage backlight is cast down upon her backup singers, all of whom are Black. In contrast to the glow created by backlighting Adele's blonde hair, the backlighting of the Black women's bodies is not balanced by facial lighting. Instead, this stark backlight paints their bodies as black silhouettes as they move slightly to the rhythm of Adele's voice. Later in the number, the stage is more fully lit, revealing the identities of the backup singers, but by this point authority has been established; lighting frames Adele as a divine figure, contrasted by the faceless followers who support her vocal prowess. While Adele and her backup singers perform similar vocal sounds, Adele's performance of these sounds is visually emphasized as masterful, whereas the backup singers' Blackvoice is expected and overlooked. The visual enhancement of Adele's vocal performance thereby justifies her colonization of Black blues performance style. Her presence in Blackvoice performance is legitimated as she becomes the face for Black music, lending her whiteness to a musical legacy of colonization in a way that confirms, rather than complicates, racial vocal appropriation.

Besides overwhelming her Blackvoice performance, Adele's visual whiteness also feminizes her, placing the singer in the role of colonizer but emptying her performance of colonizing power. Feminist popular music theorists have long bemoaned the dismissal of pop music, a genre inhabited primarily by white women and feminized white men, in the cultural sphere.[105] As Susan Fast notes, the dismissal of women's musical performances functions less as a reflection of performance talent and more as a mechanism for maintaining the "boy's club" of musical authenticity.[106] Indeed, although Adele's 2012 Grammy wins were nearly unprecedented, they were notably relegated to the white feminized category of pop music. Even her widely noted "soul" voice was not enough to move Adele into the competitive sphere of rhythm and blues, despite the similarities between her musical sound and that of R&B performance winners Cee Lo Green and Melanie Fiona. By relegating Adele's music to the "pop" category, the Recording Academy both feminizes and whitens Adele. As a result, the singer successfully crosses racialized and gendered musical boundaries through Blackvoice vocal identity, but she is held by restrictions on white femininity. Her culturally privileged voice can cross racial boundaries, but only so long as it matches gendered expectations for white women's performance.

The generic implications of white femininity are not absent from the vocally intimate relationship that Adele encourages with her listeners/viewers. Commenting on Adele's live performance of "Someone Like You," YouTube user LotusFlowerPower called the singer's work "Music for white,twentysomething females to cry into their cabernet sauvignon too!"[107] Here, whiteness and femininity together frame vocal intimacy as available only to a particular portion of listeners/viewers who match Adele's racial and gendered demographics. This observation is also supported by another user who follows a critique of the singer's weight with the comment "BAHAHAHAHAHAHAH HOW MAD ARE YOU EMO WHITE GIRLS NOW??"[108] On Twitter, too, users remarked, "I can admit I like white girl music"[109] and "It's a good thing Adele had her heart broken and wrote some songs, otherwise white girls wouldn't have any material for their [Facebook] statuses."[110] Pop music has historically been dismissed as a genre limited in its appeal; one Twitter user asks, "do gay dudes or white girls like [A]dele more?"[111] illustrating the ways that pop is imagined to speak to feminized domains that implicitly privilege whiteness and limit gay men across racial identifications in their socially acceptable range of gender expression. Situating Adele in the pop category, then, might be expected to result in her being dismissed as silly and shallow, and this was not uncommon among listeners/viewers on social media.

However, the attribution of whiteness to Adele's listeners is not so simple. Just as visual whiteness pushes Adele out of the blues genre, it creates dissonance for listeners who connect with her music but who were led to understand their relationship of vocal intimacy through a lens of race. In other words, listeners moved by Adele's vocal identity but who were under the impression that vocal identity came from experiences of Blackness in America often demonstrated surprise or disappointment with Adele's mismatched visual identity. In the days surrounding her 2012 Grammy sweep and performance, tweets pointing to a dissonance between the vocal and visual are common. Watching the Grammys that year, Twitter user Brett's father asked, "Who's this white chick who keeps accepting awards for Adele?"[112] and Zac Jackson shared, "Things I honestly didn't know 45 minutes ago: That Adele was white (or British)."[113] As Adele was presented visually for the first time for many listeners, and with her whiteness emphasized, the 2012 Grammy Awards offered a moment of realization. The sonic and visual dissonance that listeners/viewers perceived also prompted them to highlight, explicitly, the role of the music industry in maintaining racialized and gendered borders. Live-tweeting the awards, darkelem3nts asked, "I won't deny I like Adele, but why does she actually win awards having to do with pop? I thought she was a soul singer . . ."[114] This reading was often shared that evening, as reflected in sentiments like "Lol wtf adele is put under best pop vocal? Her album isnt POP is it?" and "Calling Adele 'pop' is like [calling] a funeral gathering 'a party.'"[115] As social media users questioned the arbitrary genre distinctions that pressed various artists into narrowly defined identity-based categories, they also highlighted the ambivalent power of industry bordering. The sudden visibility of long-ago naturalized musical borders is a positive and transgressive event. Yet, this visibility offered no economic or cultural reparations for the "love and theft" of Black cultural forms that have long driven the white-controlled music industry.[116]

CONCLUSION

As evidenced by the case of Adele's 2012 Grammy performance, award sweep, and subsequent online discourses, Adele's voice challenges conventional ways of understanding both authenticity and the presentations of race and gender in a way that necessitates a critical cultural vocalics analysis. As a white singer conjuring the vocal identities of Black women blues performers, including strategically placed vocal discontinuities and "fuzzy" vocal tone, Adele's Blackvoice identity simultaneously promotes intense vocal intimacy. This performance is further cemented by the content of the singer's work, which follows Black women blues stylings through the centrality of pain. The traditional performance of Blackvoice and blues pain centralizes Black bodies in both sound and story, facilitating the label of authenticity. Still, the visuality of the Grammy performance as well as the singer's album cover foregrounds Adele's glowing white face and shimmering blonde hair. The dominance of the visual thereby silences the transgressive passing performances of Blackvoice and blues pain, relegating Adele to the white feminized pop category; she can "pass" for a culturally privileged voice along the axis of race, but only when she meets generic expectations of white femininity. Adele's performance of vocal pain, intertextual struggle, and visual whiteness are intensely intertwined, succinctly demonstrated by YouTube commenter aarongluzman's poem:

> Heartfelt . . .
> A connection . . .
> Her, powerhouse voice . . .
> Softly . . .
> Suddenly, became loud . . .
> Deep, dramatic . . .
> Lighting everyone . . .
> With, her illuminating soul . . .[117]

As aarongluzman's poem illustrates, many audiences found the singer's performance to be "heartfelt," reflecting the interiority of the body and genuinely emotional in a way that "connect[ed]" the singer to themselves. This vocal intimacy was further enhanced by vocal identity in that issues of volume, depth, and power were all framed by the visual and affective performance of "illuminat[ion]." Intense visual whiteness, then, frames Adele's as a culturally privileged voice.

Adele's performance of Blackvoice illustrates a central tenet for critical cultural vocalics; although vocal identity is tied to the body, it is always socially constructed and therefore ideological. Speakers and singers learn to use our voices to particular ends. For popular singers, this process has the goal of circulation through industries with clear precedents for what is profitable and what is not. In other words, to apply the terminology I have used throughout this chapter, the cultural value of particular voices to the popular music industry is heavily influenced by the industry's borders. Furthermore, because vocal identity is constructed, it can be imitated, co-opted, adopted, and adapted to fit the demands of particular cultural contexts. Indeed, this is the goal at the core of all vocal training, both sung and spoken. Blackvoice vocal identities have been immensely profitable for the (white) music industry. Since Blackvoice is not biologically determined by the visual Blackness of the body but rather learned through available cultural contexts, the particular vocal identities tied to Black women blues singers can be adopted by white singers for profit.

Vocal identities are always complex, and this case in particular was complicated by readings of authenticity. Readings of Adele's voice as both white-performed Blackvoice and an authentic vocal identity underscore the cyclical nature of vocal identity and vocal intimacy. Adele's vocal identity draws from the presence of the body in the vocal sound, a key trait of Black women's blues stylings. Along with shaping a particular vocal identity, the way in which Adele's voice allows listeners to "hear a body"[118] in her singing also encourages intense feelings of connection between singer and listener. Adele's vocal identity not only conjured Black women performers but also encouraged and supported a deep connection between the singer and her listeners through the audible presence of spit and sinew in the voice. In other words, the particular contours of the singer's vocal identity also fed the sense of vocal intimacy, and this intensified vocal intimacy further shaped the idea that her vocal identity was "authentic." The very performance of the body that makes Black women's blues sound like Black women's blues also intensifies the connection between singer and listener. Vocal identity and vocal intimacy, then, combine to create a powerfully profitable situation for a white woman singer able to tap into these historically developed sounds. Throughout this cyclical process of singing and listening, Adele's visual whiteness supported and exacerbated the effectiveness of the Blackvoice performance, as long as her performance reflected a match with the cultural privilege of her white femininity.

CHAPTER 2

Voicing Uncle Tom

The Resonance of the South in Morgan Freeman's Films

"MORGAN FREEMAN was born in 1937. He narrated his own birth, saying, 'leaving the warm comfort of his mother's womb, I, Morgan Freeman, enter the world.'"[1] Spoken in a close aural approximation of Morgan Freeman's voice, this line opens a 2013 YouTube video that also claims that Freeman narrates the lives of "billions of [people] each day," that he dreams the sunrise into being each night, and that, by virtue of his well-known voice, "Morgan Freeman goes through four or five microphones a day because his voice turns them into bars of gold which he uses to fund his quest to create a real Santa Claus."[2] This video is only one example of Freeman's persona as an omniscient, Godlike narrator whose voice controls the movements of the Earth and its human and nonhuman life forms; a culturally privileged voice, indeed.[3] The focus, not on Freeman himself but on his voice, speaks to voices' potential as repositories for cultural understandings of identity and feelings of intimacy.

A key distinguishing feature of the discourses surrounding Freeman's voice is the actor's ability to vocally create a sense of familiarity and comfort, implying that, through his characters, audiences can gain a sense of intimacy with the actor himself. In a 2012 interview, actor Antonio Banderas remarked that the "kind of warmth that he projects is what he is . . . with Morgan it is real," and Henry Louis Gates Jr., surprised by Freeman's "extremely modest and self-effacing" demeanor, supports this assertion.[4] The actor's welcoming persona is a trademark throughout his impressive career. Speaking of Freeman's portrayal of Lucius Fox, Batman's financial and technological liaison, director Christopher Nolan not only reiterated the personable presence of Freeman on set but also stressed the actor's keen ability to forge an intimate connection with audiences: "There's a level of communication with the audience that is projected straight down the lens of the camera in an effortless way."[5] The credibility and authenticity associated with Freeman has made the actor "a dependable part of the national soundtrack," earning him the distinction of announcing the *CBS Evening News,* a position once held by Walter Cronkite, who has been called "the most trusted man in America."[6]

While both Cronkite and Freeman have earned recognition as culturally privileged US American voices, Freeman's rise to fame came in spite of an important hindrance; Freeman's status as a Black teenager in late 1950s Mississippi meant that the actor built his professional identity despite numerous racial and economic hurdles.[7] The actor denounced "Hollywood racism" over a decade ago, noting the hierarchical structures involved in hiring writers and directors, but Freeman has more recently offered himself as an example of "colorblind" casting, a practice in which actors are ostensibly cast without regard to race or ethnicity.[8] Freeman adamantly rejects being called "a *black* actor," and Arnon Milchan, who directed Freeman in *High Crimes,* similarly argues that race was irrelevant in casting decisions, adding an air of legitimacy to Freeman's recent claims that US American racism is dead.[9] Some critics support this colorblind perspective and understand Freeman's prominence in Hollywood as unrelated to his race; for Robert Eberwein, race has been irrelevant in most of the actor's roles, and biographer Kathleen Tracy boldly claims, "If Hattie McDaniel became film's enduring symbol of racism, then Morgan Freeman represents Hollywood's greatest salvation by reminding audiences that talent and style is truly color-blind."[10] Even so, many of the actor's most famous performances, including films like *Driving Miss Daisy, Glory,* and *Amistad,* have centralized both race and racial subordination, illustrating the importance of the match between racialized performers and racialized performances in the successes of speakers of color.

Complicating the question of race in Freeman's acting is the undeniable centrality of the voice in his career. Scholars and critics have called his voice "a deep growl that commands assent" and noted the "deep, lived-in texture [and] subtle variety of pitches and nuances" that the actor brings to his performances.[11] As evidenced by the fan video that opened this chapter, Freeman's powerful vocal presence has been foregrounded so consistently in popular discourses about the actor that commentary often references him as having "the voice of God," joking, for example, that Freeman first narrates documentaries "and then nature makes it so."[12] Yet, the ubiquity of references to Morgan Freeman's voice has not prompted serious consideration of the power of the actor's sound. In this chapter I approach this task, considering both the intimacy entangled in Freeman's voice and the ways that racial and gendered identity are embedded in his speech. Together, I argue, these factors demonstrate the ability for a culturally privileged voice to perform roles that depict marginalization and oppression, even when, unlike Adele's, that voice emanates from a visual body that is not culturally privileged.

Specifically, I explore the ways that vocal identity and vocal intimacy function cyclically to frame Freeman as subordinate both to white characters and to his audiences. Freeman learned to navigate vocal sound production within the threatening and violent environment of Jim Crow Mississippi. As I argue, Freeman's voice bears signs of appeasing white threats in this volatile atmosphere, and these signs emerge through subtle hints of a Mississippi accent, a whispered tonality, and the musical fluidity of his pitch patterns. So appealing were these vocal attributes to a white media industry that they became Freeman's trademark sound, a situation that led to his continual casting as a subordinate and nonthreatening figure, both vocally and narratively. As a result, Freeman's perceived "off-screen" persona is embedded with consistently subordinate attributes, shaping a vocal intimacy characterized by Freeman's servility to and ownership by his audience. Complicating the issues of Freeman's subservience is his uncanny ability to elicit feelings of intimacy from an audience, giving him power in a Hollywood context in the form of a long and consistent career and making his voice feel like a powerful draw. However, this relationship of vocal intimacy actually recoups Freeman's roles as presidents and Gods by constantly and consistently reiterating the actor's servile persona through his vocal identity, framing the actor as a figure of power but only in service to white-supremacist culture. Therefore, this chapter argues that vocal identity and vocal intimacy work together cyclically to create and then reiterate a rhetoric of racial subordination across Freeman's career.

To fully contextualize my broad argument about Freeman's long acting career, I begin with an overview of the actor's roles. Freeman's filmography has already come under fire from critical scholars for its tendency to position him as a secondary figure to white primary characters, and here I consider how this theme has both limited our understanding of the racialized voice and opened doors for further considering the same.

RACE AND FREEMAN'S HOLLYWOOD

Despite claims to colorblindness, Freeman's acting has consistently positioned the performer as a singular Black actor in a predominantly white context, a situation with both industrial and narrative functions. In a majority of his roles, the actor is cast as a "sidekick" to the film's white star, giving the film "an appearance of racial equality" while avoiding the box-office blowback that Hollywood perceives from Black men in leading roles.[13] In *The Shawshank Redemption* (1994), for example, Freeman plays a long-term inmate at a men's prison wherein he establishes a strong friendship with the wrongfully imprisoned Andy Dufresne (Tim Robbins). Although Freeman's voice-over drives the narrative, Sean O'Sullivan posits, the voice-over's content works primarily "to establish beyond doubt that Andy was/is someone special."[14] Freeman narrates the story, but Robbins's character is at the heart of the narrative.

Narratively, Freeman's role as sidekick often means he is dependent upon the primary white character who controls the movement of the story. *Unforgiven* (1992), a traditional western produced and directed by Clint Eastwood, places Freeman at the service of Eastwood's leading character. Freeman's character, whom Sally Chivers argues "appears simply helpless and in need of help from his white hero," is caught by a white sheriff, brutally murdered, and left on display in front of a saloon after deciding not to participate in a robbery.[15] Here, Freeman's character serves his white hero through sacrifice, dying to allow Eastwood's character a fiery and triumphant act of retaliation against his "obligatory dead black sidekick['s]" killers.[16] A decade later, Eastwood again casts Freeman as a white-dependent sidekick in *Million Dollar Baby* (2004). Freeman plays Scrap, a former boxer working as the janitor at Frankie's (Clint Eastwood) gym. Although, based on the character's backstory, Scrap must have at one point earned prize-fighting money, the film shows him in financial ruin and grateful for the janitorial labor at Frankie's gym. Indeed, not only does Freeman's Scrap depend upon Eastwood for a paycheck; his gambling problem also prevents the janitor from securing an independent place to live, leaving him sleeping on a cot in Frankie's gym.[17]

The subordination of Freeman's and other Black actors' characters to white leads functions as a strategy of containment. As Philippa Gates argues, Black protagonists exist in contemporary film, but often Hollywood extends "black experience to its audiences only when that 'otherness' can be contained and regulated."[18] Freeman's characters, in particular, are often contained through their professional roles as detectives through two cinematic strategies.[19] First, as Gates notes, detectives played by Black actors like Freeman are often "thinking detective[s] (rather than . . . action hero[es])," making them "identifiable for the dominant, white, middle-class audience through class and profession."[20] Second, as a symbol of law and order, the detective role contains the perceived threat of Blackness from mainstream white America. In *Seven* (1995), for example, a serial killer is committing murders inspired by the seven deadly sins. Within this setting of extreme and graphic violence, the primary "representative of law and order," Somerset, is played by Freeman.[21] A decade later, in *Million Dollar Baby*, Freeman is cast as the protector of the gym, even fighting with "a cocky young black fighter" to defend a mentally delayed young white man.[22] Throughout his career, Freeman has played regulatory roles, protecting white characters from dangerous urban forces in these films along with others including *Kiss the Girls* (1997), *Along Came a Spider* (2001), and *High Crimes* (2002). Indeed, the string of regulatory roles led Freeman to quip "What do they call me? 'The wise man who's always protecting white men?'"[23]

The structural subordination of Freeman's characters to white protagonists is not simply an issue of regulation. In many cases, Freeman's characters are built entirely from an unwavering concern for the primary white character, even at the expense of their own safety and fulfillment. Matthew Hughey and others have called this stock character "the magical Negro," a Black character whose remarkable insight, gravitas, or even supernatural powers are "used to save and transform disheveled, uncultured, lost, or broken whites."[24] This archetype has followed Freeman since his breakthrough role in *Driving Miss Daisy* (1989). Portraying Hoke, Jessica Tandy's chauffeur, Freeman's role was entirely and explicitly in service of the white woman lead. The film centralizes Hoke's mistreatment at the hands of Miss Daisy, highlighting issues of Southern racism; at the same time, Freeman's character functions as a "resource" for Tandy in her "discovery and transformation."[25] To borrow Eliza McGraw's phrasing, "the African American subordinate knows the white mistress better than she knows herself."[26] In this film, then, Freeman's character is not only subordinate to the white primary character; he is also a vehicle through which the white character is triumphantly transformed, with very little reward for the Black servant's emotional labor.

In studies of Freeman's first fifteen years of national recognition, the actor is consistently read as a secondary, supportive character designed to serve the white lead. Indeed, the token presence of a Black supporting character in films often makes the film appear, as Freeman himself has implied, "colorblind" in its casting and narrative choices. However, pairings in which the Black secondary character functions as sidekick to the white lead circulate a problematic aspect of "colorblind" culture; specifically, as Cerise Glenn and Landra Cunningham argue, "because these roles depict a utopian relationship between Blacks and Whites, Whites may believe that these ideal harmonious relationships depict current social status; therefore, racial problems only exist in the minds of Black people."[27] Freeman's characters are always secondary and nearly always in service to white characters, yet they seem happy and contented with their lives. Many white viewers have little or no contact with

Black people outside of media, and most white people still identify very few or no people of color in their social networks.[28] Freeman's roles as contented sidekicks offer an image of colorblind America in which Black people like Freeman's characters are happy to sacrifice their own success in service to their white counterparts. In other words, his roles are problematic because they encourage white viewers to understand Black men and women as, simply, happy to serve them.

Freeman's service to white characters is a persistent theme throughout his career, with the actor rarely serving as a leading character in his film and television appearances. Still, a plausible counterargument to this assertion lies in the actor's appearances in positions of power. As Gates points out, "He is a black man who's been paid millions of dollars to portray God and the president of the United States (long before we could imagine Colin Powell or Barack Obama actually occupying that office)," and this type of visibility is important for imagining a more racially equitable space in America.[29] While Gates makes an important point, such an argument is complicated by the relative lack of individual agency enjoyed by even Freeman's most powerful characters.

COMPLICATING AUTHORITY

Freeman's early tendency to be cast in secondary roles should not be symbolically underestimated. Nevertheless, as the actor has risen in prominence over the past decade he has increasingly taken roles that place him in positions of explicit authority, seemingly erasing the actor's position as sidekick and "magical Negro." Such a move parallels and supports Freeman's "colorblind" assertions, as he takes on roles as seemingly authoritative and dominant as president of the United States and God. In this section, I turn to Freeman's portrayals of authority figures from protective uncle to national leader to deity.

First, Freeman has played a number of roles in which his relationship to the primary character aligns with the protective uncle. In *Kiss the Girls,* Freeman plays a detective and "personally involved uncle" charged with tracking a serial killer who happens to target his prodigiously talented niece.[30] Where *Kiss the Girls* literally casts Freeman as an uncle, Liberato and Foster point out that films like *Driving Miss Daisy* cast him as "the obedient and caring old black man in the film, fitting nicely into the cinematic tradition of the caricature 'uncle.'"[31] Freeman's role as a kindly and vaguely paternal protector extends, too, to his role as the subordinated former boxer in *Million Dollar Baby.* In training and protecting the woman boxer, Maggie (Hillary Swank), in matters both professional and personal, he crafts "an unlikely two-father family."[32] This family establishes Eastwood as the "self-sacrificing caregiver" while Freeman hovers at a physical and emotional distance more akin to a distant father, grandfather, or uncle.[33]

Freeman's roles as a grandfather or uncle extend to implicit performances as well, even emerging through his voice alone. Present only through voice-over, the actor's narration of *March of the Penguins* (2005) has linked him with the distant paternalism of a grandfatherly presence. The film follows a group of penguins, highlighting their mating rituals and struggle against an often inhospitable environment. Freeman's narration has been praised for its ability to anthropomorphize the penguins, offering commentary that is, as Jennifer Ladino writes, "alternately serious and humorous, but always pacifying and grandfatherly."[34] Like a "combination of nature porn and bedtime story," the film uses the actor's "warm dignified narration" as a comforting, guiding presence.[35] This type of reassuring presence works in tandem with dialogue that specifically centralizes paternity through discussions of the "language games of fatherhood" and descriptions of how "the penguin fathers have a hard time leaving their chicks."[36] Given Freeman's age, gender, and his history of characters who are primarily supportive and nonthreatening, the voice-over's comforting paternity layers Freeman's spoken voice onto the paternal penguins.

Second, Freeman's paternal qualities blend with political power in his presidential demeanor. As with the actor's associations with a grandfatherly presence, Freeman's presidential qualities are both implied and explicit. When President Obama released an ad called "Challenges" a month prior to the 2012 election, his campaign tapped "Freeman's silky baritone" to deliver the message on the president's behalf.[37] The actor has also lent his voice to the Human Rights Campaign in favor of same-sex marriage, further associating his persona with the president's politics.[38] Associations between the Obama administration and Freeman's acting are likely driven by the actor's role in *Deep Impact* (1998). In the apocalyptic film that places the Earth in the trajectory of a speeding comet, Freeman's Tom Beck appears as the country's first Black president a full decade before Obama's election. Although Freeman claims not to have thought of the role as groundbreaking either for the Black community or for his own career, his portrayal in the film struck a chord with audiences; when a 2012 poll asked voters which fictional president they would elect over Obama or Romney, Freeman's President Beck placed second.[39]

Not only has Freeman portrayed fictional US American presidents, both in *Deep Impact* (1998) and briefly as a Speaker of the House turned acting president in *Olympus Has Fallen* (2013); he also famously played South

African president Nelson Mandela in *Invictus* (2009). Critical analyses of this film have been somewhat mixed. Kristin Skare Orgeret concedes that Freeman asked and received permission from Mandela to play him in the film; at the same time, she argues that the film could have more fruitfully used a South African actor "to tell one of the most important South African stories ever."[40] Conversely, Adriano Bugliani notes that the actor's treatment of Mandela is more nuanced than many Hollywood biopics, a characteristic he attributes to the "aesthetic sense of measure" in Freeman's performance.[41] Certainly, the actor's gravitas-laden performance is well aligned with US American readings of Mandela's symbolism.[42] The point is well argued by *San Francisco Gate* movie reviewer Mick LaSalle: "Morgan Freeman has become such a notable and noble presence in American film that it would seem almost as appropriate for Nelson Mandela to be playing Freeman . . . instead of the reverse."[43]

Perhaps as a result of his portrayals of Mandela and President Beck, the actor transitioned into a third character type; as Jabari Asim writes, "Freeman's performance [as President Beck] evidently earned him a promotion. In 2003 he took on the first of two performances as God in the box-office smash *Bruce Almighty*."[44] *Bruce Almighty* (2003) is a comedy about newscaster Bruce Nolan (Jim Carrey) whose constant complaining leads God (Freeman) to teach him a lesson about being grateful; for a limited time, God turns all of his power over to Nolan. As Glenn and Cunningham write, "God places himself in service roles in the movie—he appears in the form of a janitor, electrician, and an enlightening homeless person" in order to support Bruce's journey toward self-actualization.[45] Freeman's portrayal of God is decidedly New Testament.[46] The character is "all wise and all knowing . . . but more approachable," and, as the *New York Times*'s Stephen Holden argues, Freeman uses "his quiet measured drawl, which implies depths of good-humored wisdom."[47] Gates marvels at the racial progress marked by "white people . . . going to see a black God," yet such an assumption is problematized by the fact that Freeman's God exists in service to the film's white protagonist.[48]

Associations of Freeman with God, driven in part by his appearances in *Bruce Almighty* (2003) and *Evan Almighty* (2007), have lent the actor's paternal and presidential portrayals a sense of omniscient authority. Williams argues that Freeman's "god-like authority" works in *Million Dollar Baby* (2004), for example, to "table any further discussion of the relationship between women and physical violence," despite the film's potentially controversial violence and eventual euthanasia.[49] By using Freeman's implicit association with God to advance a narrative argument, the film frames Maggie's death as heaven-ordained. In *March of the Penguins* (2005), too, Freeman's association with

God justifies the intrusion of humans into the natural space of the animals' habitat. Freeman's voice-over begins with what Lauren Stephen calls "a biblical tale of paradise lost" layered over an "opening montage of breath-taking aerial shots."[50] Through this combination of language of the sacred, imagery of unadulterated nature, and links between the actor and God, the film naturalizes the presence of documentary crews and equipment as an extension of divine creation. The link between Freeman and God is so solid that the actor has even publicly stated he is "tired of playing God."[51] Unfortunately for Freeman, *The Bucket List* (2007) excluded, few other roles are available for an aging Black actor.[52]

As I have illustrated in this section, Freeman's filmography contains a number of roles in which the actor holds explicit social and natural authority. For an actor of color, such roles are important and potentially groundbreaking, given that positions like president of the United States have, until very recently, been populated entirely by white men. At the same time, Freeman's film roles speak to the "colorblindness" that the actor praises in his off-screen advocacy: rarely do Freeman's roles offer a character history that might speak to the historical and cultural patterns of discrimination and social boundaries faced by Black detectives and politicians during his characters' lives. Instead, just as Herman Gray has written about a majority of contemporary media texts, Freeman's roles in authority tend "to *ignore and repress* difference; to *conflate* it so that it becomes an expression of indifference."[53] In other words, Freeman's difference is represented as only skin-deep, as his characters' perform assimilationist, "colorblind" adaptations of white roles.

At the same time, components of Freeman's "colorblind" performance position Freeman's characters as secondary to the films' white leading roles. Even as Freeman portrays positions of authority like God and the US president, these films structurally subordinate Freeman's characters to his white onscreen counterparts, framing the former as content to serve others. In other words, it is only through their reification of Black subordination that these characters illustrate possibilities for African American men in the contemporary US. Freeman's voice is a culturally privileged one, as demonstrated not only by the longevity and range of his career but only so far as he uses that voice to perform servitude. In the remainder of this chapter, I focus on the ways that Freeman's voice contributes to this representational double bind. On one hand, combined with his filmography, his voice communicates a sense of trustworthiness and authority. On the other hand, his voice can also be understood as deeply embedded with stereotypes that cement Freeman's secondary status within his roles and, on a larger scale, limit the possibilities of Black existence.

"STEEPED IN SOUTHERN TRADITION"

Key to a critical cultural vocalic analysis is attention to the influence of social environment in the development and audience readings of speech patterns. Popular press discussions of Freeman's career, including the *Variety* article from which I drew the title of this section, occasionally reference the actor's Southern upbringing, an important component in his vocal identity.[54] Race and class have often been implicated in the types of speech that Mississippians perform; as far back as 1890, H. A. Shands's handbook of Mississippi dialects separates speech styles into discreet factions including "the cultivated white, the illiterate white, and the negro dialects."[55] On its surface, and perhaps in Shands's intention, this division seems to support a biologically deterministic perspective on race. Another approach, and the one that I advocate in this book, understands the role of social context in shaping speech acquisition just as it shapes the body and ideological perspective.

Freeman has pointed to the disparaging educational options available to Black students of the mid-twentieth century, noting that "Mississippi congressmen worked hard to keep the education of blacks at a minimum because of fear of losing the workforce."[56] Intersectional factors like economic class interact with race in active efforts to limit Black educational access, in that a lack of educational access perpetuates poverty even while poverty contributes to factors that block educational access, such as transportation and family care, excluding poor children across racial identities. Such educational limitations have material consequences for the voice; legal and de facto educational segregation means that white upper-class students receive implicit and explicit training in "proper" diction designed to hierarchically distinguish them from Black and poor white students, both solidifying the link between sonic rhetorics of power and whiteness and naturalizing the ideology of corporeal difference between Black and white communities.[57] Crossing the divide between "proper" educated speech accessible only to middle-and upper-class whites and Black dialect could also be deadly. Leon Litwack notes that a Black man "trying to act like a white man" was, in many white circles, grounds for lynching in early twentieth-century Mississippi.[58] The concept and stigma of "acting white" has been well documented as being closely linked with speech styles.[59] For families raising Black children like Freeman in 1940s Mississippi, retaining components of a socially constructed "Black sound" could function as a strategy for survival. Similarly, Hollywood has historically required that Black actors, even those who are successful in their careers, "sound Black" as a condition for employment. Although the exaggerated minstrel dialects of early sound film had eased by the 1960s when Freeman began his career, maintaining consistency between visual and vocal identities remained key to a career as a Black actor.

Freeman's remarkably consistent vocal identity reveals traces of a Black Mississippi dialect throughout his films. In *Bruce Almighty*, for example, Freeman's God once comforts the lead character, Bruce (Jim Carrey), after he has been hit by a semi and presumes himself dead. Freeman says, "Can't kneel down in the middle of a highway and live to talk about it, son," but the actor's consonants are softened to blur the words together. Placing brackets around syllables that are not individually audible, the line reads, "Can'[t] kneel down [i]n [th]e mi[dd]le o[f] a highway [a]n[d] live to talk about it, son." This line should contain several "stop-plosives," which momentarily stop the flow of air through the mouth and consequently stop the pitch resonance of the speech, such as the "k" sound in "talk" and the "t" in "it."[60] In this line Freeman replaces the stop-plosives with voiced consonants, or sounds that carry pitch vibrations and fluidly extend the continuity of the air; the "k" is replaced with its voiced cousin, "g," and the "t" with "d."

Softening consonants in this way is typical of Freeman's vocal identity. In *Invictus*, too, Freeman's Mandela sees a newspaper headline questioning whether he is ready to be president and responds, "It's a legitimate question." Freeman again softens several stop-plosives, namely the instances of "t" in "it's," "legitimate," and "question." Similarly, in *Evan Almighty*, to ask "You want to know how to change the world, son?" Freeman's God replaces "want to" with "wanna," the "t" in "to" with a more fluid "d" sound and removing the "d" at the end of "world" altogether. Reduction of consonants in clusters is common in some African American English (AAE) dialects; to borrow Wolfram's examples, speakers may substitute "lif'" up for lift up" or "bus'" up for bust up."[61] This is particularly clear when the second consonant is a stop, such as in the word "can't" at the beginning of the phrase.[62] The reduction of "and" and "in" to "n," furthermore, is consistent with less formal modes of diction including those associated with southern US American regions. Softened consonants, then, represent one consistent way that Freeman's original vocal identity remains constant throughout his career.

The softening of consonants is not specific either to Freeman or to Black or AAE dialects. In context of the moment and orientation of Freeman's original vocal-identity development, though, is the political meaning of such consonant softening. The resulting soft-spoken, nonthreatening persona attempts to appease listeners, particularly white listeners in the Jim Crow South and beyond. The figure of Uncle Tom is often used derisively for Black men who are seen as participating in racial subordination through white servitude, but the performance of subordination to white supremacy has, at times, been a necessary condition of survival.⁶³ Litwack writes that "victims of lynch mobs, more often than not, had challenged or unintentionally violated the prevailing norms of white supremacy," and many common violations include "improper" use of language or speech.⁶⁴ In mixed company, then, it behooved Black Mississippians, even and perhaps especially those with higher economic statuses, to speak loud enough to be heard but not so loud as to appear insubordinate or prideful. Black families knew this and instructed their children about which behaviors to avoid to increase their chances of arriving home safely.⁶⁵ In a particularly chilling reminder of this morbid form of instruction, Emmett Till, the Black fourteen-year-old Chicago boy who was brutally murdered in Mississippi in 1955 for purportedly flirting with a white woman, had been warned by his mother, "[Do] not hesitate to humble yourself, . . . [even] if you [have] to get down on your knees."⁶⁶ Black families in the South knew all too well the importance of a soft-spoken and subordinate vocal rhetoric.

This context speaks to the necessity for adjusting vocal identity based on likely listener perception. Adjusting in this way is not only necessary for survival; it also allows actors like Freeman to navigate white-dominated Hollywood and to emerge as culturally privileged voices. As *New York Times* reviewer Stephen Holden writes, Freeman's "quiet measured drawl . . . implies depths of good-humored wisdom," subtly drawing out his Mississippi roots to access the safety of servility represented by an "Uncle Tom" archetype in minstrelsy and beyond.⁶⁷ In this case, Freeman's softening of particular consonants and syllables in a way that is consistent with a Black Mississippi dialect points to his place as a marginalized actor, raised in the mid-twentieth-century South. Freeman's vocal identity is not a bold declaration of unapologetic Blackness but rather a way of navigating a mainstream film and television career. Consistent with AAE forms common in his home state of Mississippi, Freeman's vocal identity helped him rise to and maintain a successful acting career by inviting a particular kind of vocal intimacy with mainstream white audiences.

This analysis of Freeman's vocal identity speaks to the synergy of identity and intimacy. The actor's vocal identity consistently features the use of quieter speech patterns, a trait that speaks to subservience learned in speech development and maintained to navigate Hollywood's racial expectations. This serves vocal intimacy as well, since quieter speech patterns make the passage of air through the vocal cords more audible because less vocal tone is present to obfuscate the sound of exhaled breath. For Barthes, the audible presence of air in the voice foregrounds the presence of a body, inviting a more intimate connection between the bodies of speaker and listener.⁶⁸ Additionally, the particular qualities of mediated voices invite listeners/viewers to interact with programming in specific, structured ways. A quieter speech pattern encourages listeners/viewers to lean in toward the screen, lest they miss a portion of dialogue.[69] Whispering amplifies this effect, since the additional breath captured by microphones adds a subtle static to a film's or television show's soundtrack. In other words, the corporeal sounds added through a whispered delivery make listeners/viewers work harder to decode the linguistic rhetoric of a media text while foregrounding the body of the speaker. Freeman's brand of Black Mississippi vocal identity not only allows him to navigate racially hostile spaces but also foregrounds his body in performance, encouraging vocal intimacy. While doing so in the context of extreme marginalization is difficult and therefore rare, Freeman synthesizes vocal identity and intimacy to create a culturally privileged voice from experiences of cultural oppression.

Freeman's soft-spoken vocal identity is readily apparent in *The Shawshank Redemption*.[70] Freeman's character, Red, is serving a prison sentence for murder. Several times throughout the film, prisoners are called in for a probationary hearing in which they must address whether they have been rehabilitated. In Red's final probationary hearing, the character laments his previous criminal actions and wishes he could "try and talk some sense into" his younger self. During this monologue Freeman often pauses, leaving silences as long as 3.8 seconds between utterances; during the sixty-four-second monologue, Freeman is silent for a full thirty-six seconds, or more than half the pivotal scene. When the character does speak, he gets progressively quieter. Compared with the conversational level at the beginning of the scene, the decibel level at the end of Freeman's monologue is reduced by 23 percent, or nearly one-quarter.

Particularly at the quietest parts of this monologue, Freeman's voice grows noticeably breathy, as air escapes the vocal cords without engaging them to form pitch. The audible exhale can be read as a whisper, but it is additionally the injection of body into the voice or, in Barthes's terms, a spoken vocal "grain." For Barthes, this type of vocal quality allows the body to be heard in the voice, inviting a sensual connection felt between speaker and listener. As he explains, the voice is produced by the abject body's incorporation of "the cavities, the muscles, the membranes, the cartilages," and this abjection produces a raw, erotic, affective elation in the listener that enhances the affective rhetoric of the text.[71] In this case, Freeman's character performs the literal subordination of prisoner to parole board, and this soft-spoken vocal identity simultaneously foregrounds the body in his speech. Through necessity to hear the lines, this encourages the audience to listen harder. The situation of subordination that shaped Freeman's original speech acquisition and continued success in the industry also invites audience connection.

Any whispered performance amplifies vocal intimacy. Freeman's use of this technique is important not only because it further solidifies the subordination at the center of his vocal identity but also because such whispered dialogue is consistent across his characters and their narratives. Ten years after *The Shawshank Redemption*, Freeman appeared in an award-winning role in Clint Eastwood's *Million Dollar Baby*. As narrator, as well as a trainer and custodian at a gym, Freeman provides a voice-over peppered with whispered and breathy text. In his opening voice-over monologue, for example, Freeman's vocal rhetoric is interspersed with sounds of a boxing match during a break in the fight, and the audible breathing of the resting athlete underscores the breathiness of the voice-over in several places, for example:

FREEMAN: Only ever met one man I wouldn't wanna fight.
BOXER: (breathing) hhh—hhh—hhh
FREEMAN: . . . Started training and managing in the sixties but
BOXER: (breathing) hhh
FREEMAN: never lost his skill

In a close reading of this sound bite, Freeman's breathy tone is difficult to distinguish from the boxer's breathing in the background track. The frequencies of the breathing are very similar to Freeman's pitch in the monologue and throughout the film,[72] but more importantly, the timbre of Freeman's voice is so breathy that it blends in with the boxer's panting.

Just as in *The Shawshank Redemption*, Freeman's performance in *Million Dollar Baby* places subordination at the intersection of vocal identity and vocal intimacy. Freeman's breath foregrounds his Black body, which is narratively subordinate to Eastwood's white character, and that corporeal breathiness produces a distinct "grain." For Barthes, voices like Freeman's breathy whisper invite an "erotic" relationship between speaker and listener.[73] In *Shawshank* and *Million Dollar Baby*, I have chosen examples that make the breathiness of Freeman's performance obvious and explicit, but the breathy whisper of Freeman's delivery is built into his trademark vocal identity and also features in interviews and ads in which the actor effectively plays himself. It is one of the most consistent components of his vocal identity. It is, like all vocal identities, clearly shaped by his perceptions of what will be most successful in his contexts of speech, and these perceptions are developed by the cyclical disciplining processes both specific to Freeman's upbringing and general to my conception of vocal intimacy and identity. In short, Freeman's voice bears the markings of the context of his speech acquisition, including both real threats of violence and the perception of what type of sound is marketable. Vocal identities, then, are always based in part on context and in part on perception, a trait that creates similarities between speakers with similar upbringings and differences based on the uniqueness of individual bodies and perceptions.

Freeman's performance of vocal identity contains one final signature element; his voice moves in a consistently tonal musical pattern that joins the comforting deference with the corporeal subordination of the whispered body in speech. Voices most often move through spoken phrases stepwise, rather than leaping between extremely varying pitches, but most vary in their pitch patterns depending on factors like the content of the speech and the underlying affect behind the utterance.[74] This type of variance is limited in Freeman's vocal patterns, which have a particularly recognizable and predictable movement, both in their pitch patterns and in their rhythmic structure. Across the sections of dialogue and monologue I transcribed, Freeman uses a regular pattern of pitches best described as ostinato movements. The term *ostinato* refers to a repetitive pattern in a bass, or low-pitched, instrument that is designed to provide stability through its constant, comforting repetition. Ostinato is, by definition, a secondary accompaniment to a primary melody. In short, an ostinato, like the Uncle Tom archetype and epithet, supports and comforts but never overshadows the musical star.

The musicality of Freeman's vocal rhetoric takes the form of a consistent and repetitive ostinato pattern that cycles through one lower pitch followed by a series of higher pitches. In *Million Dollar Baby*, for example, Freeman's line "and no matter how hard you work at it, you just can't stop the bleeding" uses the first and fourth pitches in the diagram in figure 2.1, properly notated as G2 and E3,[75] as set points. In the sixth measure of this excerpt, the pattern is particularly clear.

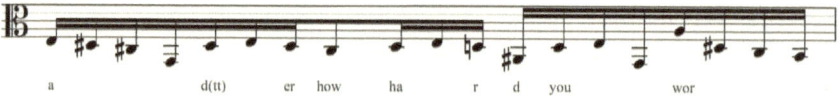

FIGURE 2.1. "[m]atter how hard you work," *Million Dollar Baby*.

Freeman's voice begins just below the staff at an E3 (the first pitch in figure 2.1) with the word "at," which wavers in a cluster of pitches. The fourth pitch, then, drops down to a G2 (the pitch hanging three lines below the staff), which is nine half-steps lower than his starting pitch. Following this drop, Freeman's voice returns to its approximate starting pitch and the pattern repeats, with a decline in pitch on every fourth note or, in the fourth series, the third note. Just as in a classical music ostinato pattern, this series of pitches creates a subtle but soothing wavelike sound. This pitch pattern is supplemented with

FIGURE 2.2. "This is the crew," *Deep Impact.*

FIGURE 2.3. "Don't know how to begin," *Evan Almighty.*

the whispered breathiness and softened consonant patterns I discussed above (in this case, the "tt" in "matter" is a soft "d" sound and the "k" in "work" at the end of the diagram is replaced by a "g"). His voice, then, contains a softened Mississippi accent that spans his Southern heritage and white expectations of how a Black voice *should* sound. Simultaneously, Freeman's vocal identity centralizing his Black body through whispered tone and the comforting repetition of tonal musicality. Freeman's voice, in short, is structured to reassure white listeners of his deference.

Freeman's vocal patterns are not always as perfectly ostinato as in *Million Dollar Baby,* but his voice is consistently musical and therefore soothing to the ear. Freeman's President Beck similarly pitches his voice in a wavelike pattern when he announces that "this is the crew" that will save the world from the impending comet crash (figure 2.2). Even years later in *Evan Almighty,* the same pattern emerges as Freeman's God laments that people want to change the world but "don't know where to begin" (figure 2.3). This pattern reemerges, then, not only within a single film, but also across Freeman's career. In musical composition, an ostinato is often used in the bass line to allow composers to be more inventive with the primary melody of a piece, since the ostinato's repetitiveness grounds the music's tonality.[76] It could be argued that characters like Red in *Shawshank* or even a servant God in the *Almighty* films represent Freeman's active characterization as subservient characters, but the constant presence of these features across his filmography belies that assumption. Instead, the general movement of Freeman's vocal rhetoric mimics typical ostinato patterns through its wavelike ebb and flow, building familiarity, approachability, and the comforting tone of servile complicity.

THE SOFT-SPOKEN SERVANT

Across Freeman's remarkably consistent body of work, in roles explicitly servile and those with presumably more social power, the actor performs deference not only through what the audience hears but also through what we do not hear. These rhetorical features, including direct address, breathiness, and silence, common to Freeman's speech underscore the interaction between vocal identity and vocal intimacy. Freeman's continued reputation as an actor who solicits intense audience investment in his characters, alongside his experiences of speech acquisition, elevates the actor's voice to a position of cultural privilege. As that of a soothing, deferent figure, Freeman's voice is both comforting and reaffirming for white audiences, and this affect paved the way for further casting in roles supporting white primary characters. In these roles, Freeman's subordination is reinforced not only by the qualities of his voice but also by the limited agency of his characters. Freeman's consistent subordination makes him a good fit for roles that feature forms of sonic subordination like silence and containment through musical accompaniment, and these features cyclically limit his potential approaches to identity and intimacy if he would maintain the economic and cultural benefits of voice widely understood as culturally privileged.

Freeman's whispered, subordinate vocal rhetoric is underscored by the frequent silences that many of his roles require. Silence, like whispered delivery, can be understood as a mode of vocal containment.[77] Whereas the whisper foregrounds the body through audible breath, silence foregrounds the body through an expectation of speech, and both of these techniques straddle issues of containment and an adept ability to incite audience affect. Speaking of media intimacy, Misha Kavka offers the term *proximity* to describe the way the television camera is "both not there, accentuating immediacy, and palpably present, since it is a material stand-in for the cameraman's body that is bounced or pushed around."[78] Freeman's frequent silences and whispers, which I examine in this section, further illustrate this concept's relation to sound. Audience expectation of speech prompted by characters' extended silences or the difficulty to hear and understand caused by very quiet or breathy whispers highlight the divide established "between the origin of a sound and its listener"; in essence, the audience wants to hear what the character is saying but, particularly in a movie theater, has little control over onscreen voices' audibility.[79] Affectively, this *parole-emanation,* Chion's term for cinema sound that is difficult to hear, compels us to strain to understand the speech or to "lean in" to the screen.[80] Audiences, in other words, put forth effort to create proximity or intimacy with the character. At the same time, this type of performance is both culturally subjugated, as I described above, and narratively subordinated by characters who speak out and over the silence of Freeman's characters.

The narrative subjugation of silence is exemplified by Freeman's role in *Amistad.* In this film, Freeman plays a free Black man named Theodore Joadson in the midst of a heated trial about the morality of slave trade and ownership. Although Joadson's white companions are abolitionists who treat him as a social equal, the character rarely speaks throughout the film, more often demonstrating attentive listening by leaning in to conversations, nodding, and glancing down in apparent thought. Indeed, Freeman is visibly present throughout the film, but based on his level of participation in conversation, he is a relatively minor character. At various times in *Amistad,* Freeman is shown listening as white characters explain their various plans for freeing a group of African women and men who took over the ship transporting them to America to be sold as slaves. These moments of listening feature close-up images of Freeman's face as he leans in, performs confusion or shock, and, in a dinner scene, chews his food thoughtfully. He is, as the idiom about good children goes, "seen but not heard."

Such an idiom is appropriate, given the roles of silence and infantilization in subordination. Freeman is so frequently subordinated in his films that his persona seems to dictate casting as a silent bystander, even when silence and subordination seem incongruent with his characters' roles. As I have noted, Freeman's *Amistad* character, Joadson, has relatively few lines despite his frequent presence on camera, and being "seen but not heard" is even more egregious given the experiences we can assume this free Black man would have had with issues of racism and dehumanization.[81] During one particularly salient scene, Joadson visits John Quincy Adams (Anthony Hopkins) to discuss the Africans' grim fate. Just as all seems lost and Joadson turns to leave, Adams asks, "What is their story, by the way?" Joadson has no answer, other than to note, in confusion, that "they're from West Africa," an observation he follows with an audible sigh. Adams's point in this scene is that the abolitionists must spend more time learning about who these slaves are as humans, and the film's emphasis on Freeman's surprised face frames Adams as a savvier humanist than Joadson; the free Black man seems not to have considered the possibility that the slaves have background stories at all. As that of a former slave himself, Joadson's oppressed standpoint might allow Freeman's character a richer perspective than Adams in terms of the slaves' histories and experiences. However, the film instead emphasizes Joadson's ignorance and lack of understanding of the slaves' humanity. Adams must explain to Joadson, who stands in silent consideration, that this group of slaves might have the same kind of story as the two abolitionists. In other words, Freeman is, as usual, a guide, this time silently facilitating the white characters' revelatory ideas. Here, silence contains Freeman's agency just as much as the narrative structure of the film. For this type of role, Freeman is a natural fit, particularly compared with the noisy and forceful performance of the film's other Black leading character, Cinque (Djimon Hounsou). At the same time, Freeman's silence in *Amistad* reinforces the quiet subordination in his voice.

While Freeman's relative silence in *Amistad* subordinates him to his white costars, the actor's portrayals of presidents are marked by a dearth of dialogue that is more ambivalent. Freeman's character in *Olympus Has Fallen* is a Speaker of the House who is promoted following the kidnapping of both president and vice president. Freeman is featured prominently during the film's frequent administrative briefings, in which legislative and military administration members work remotely with Mike Banning (Gerard Butler), a rogue former soldier tasked with saving the president and the country from a massive North Korean terrorist attack. Freeman sits at the head of the table, and the camera frequently captures shots of him appearing worried and overwhelmed. Yet the acting president rarely speaks. In the first briefing, Freeman does not speak at all, and in several other scenes, his character announces a decision that is immediately refuted and rejected by Banning, rendering it moot.

In the world of *Olympus Has Fallen,* Freeman is not overtly constructed as an inept president; narratively, listeners/viewers are given no reason to suspect his leadership will be weak. Rather, his presidential role is to listen. He listens to the overbearing general's (Robert Forster) intelligence, to the terrorists' threats, and to the soldier's barked demands, all with a grimace of uncertainty and fear. Indeed, frequent shots of Freeman worrying or thinking create an expectation that the character *will* speak, if only given an opportunity. This framing is illustrative of Kavka's *simultaneity,* which posits that media intimacy is elicited when characters and audiences experience similar emotions concurrently.[82] For Kavka, this type of situation aligns audience and actor through affective identification; listeners/viewers understand what the character must be feeling, because they feel it too.[83] Shots of Freeman looking overwhelmed and uncertain are often accompanied by dramatic conflict of other characters in the scene and a rising musical underscore. This type of narrative structure, common to action movies and thrillers, is designed to create tension and anxiety in the audience, and, indeed, these same emotions appear as Freeman furrows his brow or drops his jaw slightly to show surprise and fear. In a pivotal scene later in the film, for example, Banning discovers that the White House security has been breached and yells through an intercom, "Do not launch anything until I do some recon." The acting president silently nods with a look of confusion and shock, as the music rises to signal the upcoming climactic action scene. Indeed, the revelation that the enemy has infiltrated the White House is presented as an issue of grave concern. Freeman's silence, then, is used as a way to invite the audience to share his uncertainty and discomfort, soliciting affective simultaneity. As Freeman's silence invites affective intimacy with his audience, it simultaneously reiterates the subordinating associations of the Uncle Tom figure in literature and media. So prevalent is the actor's silence in this film, his presence is consistently seen but not heard, speaking rarely and only to enable white men to usurp his role as acting commander in chief. Freeman's vocal subordination couples with his ability to solicit intense feelings of intimacy with his audience, and these are layered into his frequent silences.

Freeman's presidential roles are contained not only through silence but also through the structure of the soundtrack. In *Deep Impact,* not only does the president (Freeman) appear very rarely, his pivotal address is incorporated into the fabric of the musical score. *Deep Impact* features Freeman as president during an impending meteor strike, and it ends as many cinematic dramas conclude: with rich, majestic orchestral music and a triumphant voice-over. Both of these techniques are commonly used to deliver catharsis in the finales of movies like *Deep Impact,* but this film offers a unique scenario in that the two sound files play simultaneously. As a timpani roll gives way to the soaring melody of violins, the spacecraft sent to destroy the comet collides with its target above the horizon, providing a backdrop for the white main characters to hug and celebrate. After ten seconds of the violin theme, Freeman's voice cuts in with a presidential address, but the orchestra continues, interjecting a timpani roll in the middle of Freeman's first phrase. Even excluding the loudest point in the orchestral underscore, the timpani, the violin theme is approximately 20 percent louder, in decibels, than Freeman's voice.[84] As Freeman continues speaking, the violins continue alongside his voice, until both the strings and the actor's speech rest, with Freeman pausing between phrases, and the strings simultaneously growing about one-third quieter. When the presidential address resumes, so too does the orchestra, this time passing the triumphant melody to the french horns, again at a volume slightly above Freeman's voice. In the speech's final phrase, the orchestral accompaniment grows nearly twice as loud, transitioning into closing credit music.

This scenario offers three insights into Freeman's voice as a musical element; first, in the climax of the film, the symbolic importance of Freeman's voice is designated as less than or equal to that of the orchestral underscore. In short, Freeman's voice is the accompaniment, supporting the instrumental score, rather than the reverse. Musical underscoring as a supplement to voices in film is not unique; music overpowering an actor's voice is much more unusual. Sound-film music conventions developed specifically as a supplement to actors' voices. For example, woodwinds like clarinet and bassoon are rarely used in film scoring to be played under dialogue, as they tend to blend too closely with the spoken voice, and film music is specifically mastered with lowered volume and simple rhythms when dialogue or monologue is to occur simultaneously. Violating conventions generally points to a particular narrative or affective effect, and in this case, *Deep Impact* seems to imply through the overshadowing of Freeman's voice by the score and by its slow zoom out that humans are a much smaller part of the universe than we might like to believe.[85] This thematic maneuver occurs only during Freeman's presidential address. In the same montage that ends by zooming out to minimize Freeman's prowess behind the presidential podium, the camera zooms in on and tilts up toward the white main characters as they celebrate their survival. In this case, Freeman's voice and physical presence are absorbed into the fabric of the orchestral music, positioning him as a literal part of the film's underscore.

Second, and relatedly, Freeman's speech is redundant as a message. When the speech begins, the audience can see that the comet has been destroyed not only directly, through the explosion in the sky, but also indirectly through the white characters' relieved physical reactions to the comet explosion. The content of Freeman's speech, then, which retells the story of the comet's destruction through phrases like "the bombs shattered the second comet into a million pieces of ice and rock," is not particularly useful in advancing the narrative. Instead, his speech is used here as a layer in the triumphant musical catharsis. Whereas in the other films I have analyzed in this chapter, Freeman's voice-overs are often necessary to reveal the inner thoughts and feelings of his white costars, in this case his voice is narratively redundant; the white characters' visual performance tells a story and his character retells that narrative from behind the blaring musical score. Freeman's role in the film is to facilitate the white heroes in their quest to save the world. Once that goal is complete, Freeman's voice is needed only as a musical accompaniment and can be discarded to blend into the fabric of the story.

Finally, Freeman's voice makes him a particularly strong fit for this moment, as the film invites a cathartic emotional release from the tension of the impending comet built throughout the narrative that is mirrored in Freeman's address. Not only does the ostinato pattern of Freeman's voice lend credence both to his vocal subordination and to his containment within the music of *Deep Impact*'s score; it also adds a human layer to the soaring musical underscore. At this moment in the film, the music is designed to envelop the audience and to solicit an intense emotional catharsis.[86] Simultaneously, just as in *Olympus Has Fallen*, Freeman's president performs the emotional release invited from the audience, encouraging listeners/viewers not only to sigh in relief but to do so alongside Freeman. Kavka writes that this type of simultaneity encourages feelings of intimacy and connectedness between actors and audiences, and, since listeners/viewers would also need to strain to clearly make out Freeman's words, such an impact is strengthened by the added tenet of proximity.[87] In other words, it is Freeman's subordinated identity, and the aural traits of silence and whispered service that accompany it, that helps to build the sensation of vocal intimacy that is key to his performance of a culturally privileged voice.

The subordination built in to Freeman's voice makes him a good fit for roles that centralize the support of white characters while encouraging a sense of vocal intimacy from the audience. Put another way, Freeman's vocal identity is a driving factor in his incredibly marketable vocal intimacy. In satisfying his brand as an actor who projects warmth and comfort, he must play on his skill in soliciting heightened vocal intimacy. For Freeman, vocal intimacy is directly connected to vocal identity; the servitude built into this voice makes him a natural fit for the kinds of deference and invisibility at the heart of the narratives for which he is best known. Importantly, this type of subordination supersedes assumptions about the power of Freeman's most authoritative characters, replacing narrative and political power with the power to invite connections from the audience. In other words, it is the subordinate performance of vocal identity and vocal intimacy that synergistically build Freeman's culturally privileged voice.

CONSISTENCY AND SUBORDINATION

The consistency of Freeman's vocal and narrative subordination makes his vocal identity particularly clear, centering his vocal body in each role he plays. Through this process, the voice I have described as growing from the tumultuous environment of the Jim Crow South becomes popularly attached to Freeman's body, which, in turn, is attached to his consistent characterizations. This consistency feeds vocal intimacy, since the expectation of familiarity is never violated, even in cases when a deviation from Freeman's normative vocal identity might be expected.

A particularly salient example of Freeman's remarkably consistent vocal identity, illustrating the way this identity bubbles beneath the surface of his characters and emerges even at unexpected times, is in his portrayal of Nelson Mandela in *Invictus*. One might assume that Freeman's vocal sound deviated from his consistent sound for a role like this, at least replacing the actor's Southern US American sounds with the late politician's South African dialect. Instead, Freeman resists changing his voice to play this particular role. Even in the face of criticism, Freeman allows his trademark vocal sound to lurk beneath the sounds of his characters, disrupting his Mandela characterization with his own sonic brand; the actor was adamant that he would perform Mandela as an interpretation rather than an impression, resulting in a noticeably inconsistent South African dialect interspersed with frequent notes of Freeman's Mississippi vocal identity.[88] Critics attributed this to a weakness in Freeman's performance, but the inconsistent accent is better understood as a way for Freeman's vocal identity to blend into the character of Mandela.[89]

Often in *Invictus* Freeman begins with a nod to Mandela's South African dialect, but, in a move that may be counterintuitive for his listeners/viewers, shifts seamlessly into his typical vocal sound. In a scene marked as pivotal through its soundtracks' use of the soaring anthem "Colorblind," for example, Freeman greets the members of the white South African rugby team. The scene focuses on Mandela's personable presentation, as he smiles and shakes each player's hand, sharing brief phrases of encouragement as he moves down the line of players. The scene opens with Mandela explaining, "I just wanted to come and wish you good luck in person. Sometimes . . . as president, I am allowed to do what I want." Freeman uses an affected pitch movement that shifts somewhat choppily from high to low register, so that the phrase "do what I want" begins with a high "do" and drops to a lower "what I want," and rolls the "r" in "president." Such characteristics are cornerstones of a South African, Afrikaans, dialect.[90] However, as the scene continues, Freeman's speech mannerisms shift to his trademark speech patterns; specifically, where the "r" in "president" is overtly rolled, the "r" in "Brendan" is minimized, and the Mandela character even wishes one player "good luck, son," adding the address "son" that Freeman has frequently included in dialogue from *The Shawshank Redemption*, *Million Dollar Baby*, *Evan* and *Bruce Almighty*, and other films.[91] Freeman's portrayal of Mandela, then, contains fissures in which the actor's Southern-rooted vocal identity emerges to mark the actor as Freeman rather than allowing him to become completely immersed in the character he is creating in the film. Such layering functions to remind the audience that they are watching Freeman and not Mandela. In other words, Freeman-the-actor is audibly present within even his most diverse characters.

Freeman's vocal consistency is particularly marked within his portrayal of Mandela when *Invictus* draws dialogue from real events, facilitating comparison. Early in the film, Freeman appears as Mandela being sworn in as South African president. This scene can be directly compared with Mandela's own swearing in, archived by the *BBC*, since both men utter the statement "I, Nelson Rolihlahla Mandela, do hereby swear to be faithful to the Republic of South Africa," and the comparison reveals several differences. First, both men drop their pitch at the end of the president's name, but Mandela clearly and intentionally articulates the "uh" sound whereas Freeman does not; the actor's pitch and volume drop so low at the end of the name that the "uh" is subsumed by a breathy exhale. This breathiness is a consistent trait of Freeman's, as he frequently tapers off in volume and pitch at the end of phrases, replacing articulated final syllables with audible sighs.

Second, while Freeman pays some lip service to a South African dialect in this clip, the accent is used only as an infrequent adornment and not as an overall characteristic of his portrayal of Mandela. In this statement, for example, Freeman breaks his consistent vocal sound only twice: with a dramatic roll of the "r" on "Republic" and in the replacement of the "t" in "to be" with a softer "d" sound. The rolling of the "r" sound here is particularly important since both Mississippi and South African dialects have particular formations of the "r" sound. An "r" at the beginning of a word is not rolled in any US American dialect, and the "r" at the end of a word is generally dropped in the Mississippi dialect, so that it sounds more like a schwa (ə) or soft, unaccented "uh" sound. As demonstrated in Mandela's speech, the "r" sound in some South African dialects borrows from early British colonizers and is characterized by a rolled (technically, alveolar trilled) "r" sound at the beginning of words and a more pronounced "EE-yah" sound at the end of words. These differences play out fully in a comparison of these two men's oaths. Mandela's pronunciation of "hereby" is sharply accented and crisp and borrows from the British linguistic influence on South African speech: "Hee-YAH-BY." Freeman's pronunciation, on the other hand, reverses the accent pattern to de-emphasize the "r" sound, just as one might expect from a native Mississippian: "HEE-yuh-by." Despite, of course, Mandela never employing a Mississippi accent, Freeman's speech throughout the clip consistently points to his Southern US upbringing, making the actor's speech recognizable and distinct from Mandela's throughout this clip and the larger film. In other words, Freeman's vocal identity is consistent in his films, even when he portrays someone whose speech should sound quite different.

Freeman's personal sonic rhetoric extends beyond overt markers like consonant pronunciation and forms of address; one of the particularly consistent elements that make Freeman's voice unique and identifiable is the audible presence of the body in the actor's voice. Across his filmography, Freeman often ends phrases with a low but audible exhale. In an early conversation during *Evan Almighty*, for example, Freeman's God explains to the main character, Evan, that changing the world must be done incrementally. A close transcription of the line reads, "People wanna change the world [exhale]. Don't know how to begin [exhale]." Each of these two sentences ends with the same pitch and breath pattern. The phrases end on very low pitches; the first phrase concludes on C_2 (indicated as the last pitch on the second staff), which represents a frequency of approximately 65 hertz, and the second phrase ends on E_2 (the last pitch on this diagram) indicating 82 hertz. Compared with the average adult man's speech frequency of 120 hertz, nearly an octave higher at just below C_3, these pitches are quite low. Add to this the tendency for men's voices to rise in pitch as they age, and Freeman's pitch dips into remarkably low pitch ranges. Simultaneously, the volume of the speech dips, likely necessitated by the pitch drop, giving way to a subtle but audible exhaling sound that flows directly from the previous consonant sound, and replicating the pattern I described in the actor's portrayal of Mandela. In the first sentence, as figure 2.4 demonstrates, Freeman moves from an elongated "world" into a 0.15-second audible exhale. While such an exhale represents a short amount of time, 0.15 seconds is longer than the time Freeman uses to pronounce the word "people" in his first sentence.

This pattern of breath at the end of phrases was present in nearly every sample I transcribed, changing very little as the actor aged and remaining stable across characters and character types.[92] It offers a way of hearing Freeman's body through his spoken performance. The audible breath, Barthes specifically notes, offers a particularly bodily presentation of the voice, since the breath incorporates deep pulmonary movements separate from language.[93] In Freeman's example, the actor's breath transcends language. Examples as diverse as Freeman's President Beck in *Deep Impact*, the actor's God in *Bruce* and *Evan Almighty*, and his role as an inmate in *The Shawshank Redemption* demonstrate how Freeman's breath is peppered throughout his performances, injecting the sounds of his body into the films' dialogue. As a primary indicator of Freeman's vocal identity, the whispered breath at the heart of this example is an important link, tying together all of the actor's performances into one consistent persona that simultaneously invites vocal intimacy.

I have demonstrated that Freeman's vocal identity is marked in its consistency across his long acting career. Even in instances when we might expect

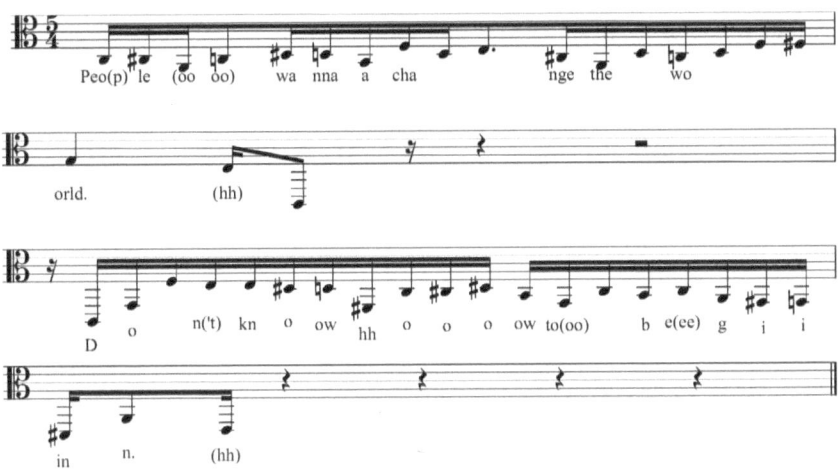

FIGURE 2.4. "People want to change the world," *Evan Almighty*.

variation, for example as the actor aged or in different character roles, his vocal identity is remarkably stable. By performing such a consistent vocal sound throughout his characters, Freeman continually reiterates his presence within his roles. This consistency carries a corporeal subordination through all of his work; since Freeman's vocal identity never changes substantially even in portrayals of real people like Mandela, Freeman's entire filmography is marked by consistent themes of subordination, whether these are coded into individual narratives or not. As I discuss in the next section, the most important implication for this consistency lies in Freeman's framing as a supportive guide for white characters and audiences.

"GUIDE MY PATH"

Freeman's career is characterized by his iconic voice-over work, branding him as an omniscient narrator through his soothing but subservient vocal identity and the consequent vocal intimacy that it encourages. Many of the actor's characters have provided voice-over for their films' larger narratives, with *Million Dollar Baby* and *The Shawshank Redemption* serving as notable examples, and Freeman has also offered his voice to advertising and political campaigns for Visa and for President Obama's election. For issues of vocal intimacy, voice-over is a particularly important consideration, since, as Mary Anne Doane points out, "as a form of direct address, [voice-over] speaks without mediation to the audience, bypassing the 'characters' and establishing a complicity between itself and the spectator."[94] Here, Doane assumes that the voice-over is somewhat anonymous; the voice represents an "itself" rather than a "herself," "himself," or "themself." In the case of Freeman's voice-overs, the actor is constantly linked back to the voice; not only does he appear visually in films like *The Shawshank Redemption* and *Million Dollar Baby*, two of his better-known voice-over roles, but his voice-overs have become so ubiquitous as to be widely recognizable. The "complicity between [the voice-over] and the spectator" that Doane describes, then, becomes a form of intimate connection between the audience and an actor who, as I have argued throughout this chapter, is so remarkably consistent as to seem familiar and intimately knowable, even by audiences who will never meet the man.[95]

A particularly intimate aspect of voice-over rests in its perceived revelatory qualities. Many scholars focus on the ways that voice-over distances voice from body,[96] but a more salient aspect of Freeman's voice-overs is the implication that he is speaking to the audience personally, establishing the kind of "complicity" that Doane describes.[97] In *The Shawshank Redemption*, for example, the camera often zooms in on the actor's face just before the voice-over begins, implying that the ensuing monologue reveals a glimpse into the character's private thoughts and feelings. These voice-overs often contain particularly intimate information, as well, such as when Freeman's character laments that he "misses his friend" or notes that he has "been asking permission to piss" for forty years and "can't squeeze a drop without say so." During these and other personal revelations, the character's voice floats above the narrative, inviting the audience into an intimate relationship with the character. In *Shawshank*, in particular, such revelations are striking, as they contrast with the rough, street-smart masculine veneer common among the other prison inmates. Freeman's voice-over, then, appears to allow a glimpse into his character Red's true feelings, positioning the audience as a confidante for the emotions behind the character's façade and making Freeman seem more accessible to the audience he is addressing.

Freeman's positioning as a guiding voice invites a particular vocal intimacy. Specifically, his role as supportive guide, both for the leading characters in his films and for audiences, is often evidenced through comments that point to issues of ownership, a way of recouping the threat to white-supremacist culture posed by a Black man being portrayed as president and God. I have thus far suggested that many attributes of Freeman's vocal identity speak to the role of Uncle Tom, a way of speaking that navigates racist and threatening systems of life and work. The consistency of these attributes, paired with Freeman's resultant casting in roles featuring subordination and servile voice-over and direct address, has led audiences to comment on the ways they "use" Freeman's voice for pleasure as well as instances in which they are "disappointed" in his personal actions. In both cases, audience interaction with the actor's voice reins in the power attributed to Freeman through his most authoritative roles. As I discuss in this section, the same sense of audience accessibility that supports the cultural privileging of Freeman's voice symbolically undercuts his vocal privilege.

This type of language emerged across online fan comments. Writing on Freeman's fanpop.com site, missycottman reveals, "i sometime wish your [sic] were my grandfather,"[98] and replying to a profile picture on Freeman's official Facebook page, Vee Sutton notes, "It does seem that you have always been there to help guide my path."[99] Such comments go beyond open-source fan boards. *Slate* writer April Son's compilation of inspirational quotes was titled "Morgan Freeman Being Inspirational Will Get You Through Another Week."[100] These phrases demonstrate the kinds of intimacy that John L. Caughey describes, implying that both online commenters and professional cultural critics feel a relationship with Freeman.[101] At the same time, comments like these frame Freeman as a secondary guide in service to the audience of commenters. Missycottman appreciates that Freeman "make[s her] smile," Sutton uses Freeman as a "guide," and Son invites her readers to draw inspiration for their weekly grinds. In each of these scenarios, just as in his film roles, Freeman is cast as the "magical Negro" in that he is discursively endowed with the power to reach through listeners'/viewers' speakers to give them what they need.[102] At the same time, Freeman's almighty power is reserved for servitude as he is imagined to bend to the whims of his audience members' needs.

Freeman's consistent portrayal as servant, through both the subordinate qualities of his voice and the consistent development of his servile persona, offers one lens for understanding the secondary role that the actor plays in audience fantasies. Drawing from Brian Massumi's affect scholarship, Lisa Blackman pushes identification theories like Caughey's further, arguing that the presence of bodies onscreen, and I would add through audio equipment, urges audiences to connect with media by conjuring memories of their own emotional experiences.[103] In Freeman's case, such relationships are complicated by his consistent persona as a servant to both white characters and audiences, particularly through his voice-overs. Frequently, for example, online audience comments centralize reading various phrases in Freeman's voice. When Freeman's official Facebook account posted the statement "Can't believe another year is almost over. Make it count" on December 29, 2014, within two minutes the post had numerous replies of this sort. Jenny Medina Jimenez remarked, "I read it in your voice"; Kyle Hardman replied, "Still read it in his voice"; and Dimitris Dimarelos responded, "I will because I heard it in your voice. . . ."

Just as with the comments that positioned Freeman as a "magical Negro," these comments illustrate the ways that audiences use Freeman not to recall their own emotional memories, as Blackman asserts, but to recall the actor's vocal identity.

While reading Freeman's own text in his own voice seems reasonable, discussions of reading lines in the actor's voice for personal amusement are even more prevalent. A forum on Bungie.net began a thread in which users could post particular phrases that would be read by other users "in Morgan Freeman's voice."[104] The thread features comments like "Everyone loves big booty bxtches [sic]. I love them in every color, but I prefer a Chinese woman," and "Giant. Throbbing. Cock," to which a poster responded "please don't" under the user handle Morgan Freeman.[105] As an explanation for this type of behavior, the webcomic xkcd.com coined the term *Fremanic Paracusia* to reference "a disorder wherein you hear everything you read in the comforting voice of Morgan Freeman."[106] In this comic the "disorder" was illustrated with a cartoon of a stick figure reading about penis enlargement on the internet. Like Freeman's breathy, musical voice, the online behaviors of these commenters subtly reiterate the contours of racial domination in the Jim Crow South and beyond. As Litwack points out, acts of public humiliation run alongside lynching as a way of "underscor[ing] the unmistakable limits placed on [African Americans'] aspirations and rewards in a white man's society."[107] By casting these vulgar remarks in Freeman's voice, specifically without the actor's permission or consent, online communities essentially reinscribe Jim Crow–era public humiliation onto the digital age, forcing embarrassing and hypersexual lines into Freeman's voice. That these lines are exaggeratedly sexualized, then, is not accidental. Instead, these dialogic choices speak to the historical hypersexualization of Black men and the practice of using this stereotype for public degradation to enforce racial domination.

Yet not all references to reading in Freeman's voice are as vulgar or hypersexualized; bitteranagram simply tweeted, "Great, even my internal monologue is in Morgan Freeman's voice,"[108] and one meme encouraged users to "read" the silly, if vaguely sexualized, phrase "titty sprinkles" in the actor's voice.[109] My point here is to suggest that Freeman's audiences freely use the actor's voice, often in ways that seem explicitly incongruous with the "gravitas" that Freeman tries to convey in his roles.[110] Such online play reinforces the subordination so common in Freeman's roles by positioning the actor as a pawn of the will of his audiences. This positioning requires that the imposed lines deviate sharply from Freeman's typical characterization, since it is the contrast between the two styles of vocal rhetorical content that highlights the power of the audience over Freeman's culturally privileged voice. In other words, that these phrases would not typically be uttered by the actor is what marks them both as humorous and as a demonstration of Freeman's subordination. While such online activities represent little harm to the actor directly, they crystalize the ways that Freeman's voice is separated from his body to enact performances purely in service to audience pleasure.

Relationships in which Freeman represents a grandfather or guide and those in which the actor's voice is in service of audience humor exist alongside a somewhat darker understanding of Freeman's life in relation to his audience. Although a widely circulated meme depicts Freeman's face alongside his urging that to end racism we should "stop talking about it," the actor took a very different stance in response to Tea Party politics and race.[111] In a 2011 Piers Morgan interview, Freeman called the Tea Party's vendetta against President Obama "a racist thing," and many fans took to sites to contrast their now defunct love of Freeman with their disdain for his politics.[112] Writing on MorganFreeman.net, for example, Linda F. noted, "I am so disappointed that I just have to comment . . . You are my most favorite actor! But you are wrong about the tea party," and Mary wrote, "This is the first time I ever wrote to any celebrity. So many of them are young and have such slanted views. I hope you will give this matter further thought . . . you do have the carriage of a wise and thoughtful man . . . For a lot of us it's not about color." The disappointment these commenters reference points to their expectations of knowing and understanding Freeman's politics, seeming to draw from the actor's persona as "a wise and thoughtful man." Freeman's persona as a deferent, supporting character is important here, as his film roles invite an expectation that the actor's subordination and service to white leading characters and audiences should translate off-screen as well. In this case, Freeman fails to guide and grandfather, and instead he disappoints those with whom he has established a relationship of servility. The cultural privilege of Freeman's voice, then, is rejected when it fails to serve audience political perspectives completely and selflessly.

Freeman's discussions of racial politics have also led commenters to bargain their fandom, assuming, as Lawrence indicates, that the voice behind the voice-overs had established a reciprocal ethic of exchange with his fans. Commenting on fanpop.com, for example, a self-proclaimed Republican and "early TEA party person," ItsthePolicies, demanded, "I have supported you in all your movies but that stops till you get copies of the Democratic . . . [and] Republican party platforms . . . and read them thru."[113] In this case, the fan writes directly to Freeman, offering to re-establish their relationship only on the condition that the actor learns about, and presumably adopts, Republican policies. This type of demand continued following Freeman's voice-overs for

Obama's 2012 re-election campaign; addressing the actor by his first name, commenter bebeep53 remarked, "Well Morgan you lost a life long fan because of your recent voice over for Obama. I will never listen, watch, or buy anything with you in it for the rest off [sic] my natural life. I hope many will follow me."[114] Again, this comment reiterates the former fan's loyalty before disciplining the actor for not aligning his actions with bebeep53's political views. This type of bargaining and disciplinary discourse demonstrates the role of Freeman's consistent subordination in shaping particular types of vocal intimacy between the actor and his audiences. That this last commenter speaks directly to an issue of voice-over is telling; whereas Freeman's frequent appearances in subordinated roles have framed the actor in service to his audiences, his voice-over for Obama elicited a sense of betrayal from those positioned against the president.

The consistency of Freeman's appearances as a comforting guide for white characters and audiences alike builds a dark underbelly among the majority of appreciative fans. Namely, because Freeman's voice is understood to be one of subordination and servitude, the actor's vocal sound emerges as an object of ownership, breaking expectations of servility when Freeman communicates policies disagreeable to facets of his conservative white audience. In other words, instead of taking on the values of the celebrity they admire, particular fans expect that Freeman will instead maintain or take on *their* political positions. Such audience usage illustrates the racial paradox in Freeman's casting as presidential and almighty figures. While the presence of a Black man in media representations of presidents and gods offers images of a racially equal society, these representations of power are undercut by Freeman's subordinating persona. The *Maclean's* author Jordan Timm writes, "And there is, I think, an unspoken racial joke there: that God should finally be black—but, if he's black, then of course he must be Morgan Freeman."[115]

CONCLUSION

Throughout Freeman's career, the actor's voice has played an important role in reinforcing and solidifying his position as a deferent character who soothes, rather than disrupts, white-supremacist representational systems. As I have argued, Freeman's voice carries traces of his Mississippi heritage, weaving through hints of the type of subordination necessary for Black boys and men to survive in the violent conditions of the Jim Crow South. Since the hypersexualization of Black masculinity was framed as particularly violent and dangerous during this period, Freeman's identity as a Black man meant that navigating the politics of the South required a particular attitude of subordination. When this servile identity is layered into the remarkable sonic consistency of Freeman's long media career, the actor's constant and constantly audible vocal identity weaves attributes of subordination throughout his roles, even those in which he appears most powerful. In this way, the political and cultural power afforded to Freeman as a Black man playing presidential and almighty roles is tempered and undercut both by the ways that Freeman's characters are positioned as servile and by the actor's ability to seem intimately connected with audience members. Finally, the structure of the actor's roles, including his trademark voice-overs, exacerbates the sense of vocal intimacy from the audience. While such intimacy should not be dismissed or pathologized, in Freeman's case, some factions of his audience seem to read the actor's voice through a lens of ownership, reinforcing and recirculating themes of subordination present within the actor's voice.

The racial undertones that bubble beneath the surface of Freeman's performances speak to the importance of repetition and recirculation in discussions of vocal identity; despite an acting career spanning several decades, Freeman's vocal identity remains not only stable but stably reminiscent of 1940s Mississippi. Freeman's voice demonstrates how history can be subtly built into the vocal identities of the culture's most privileged voices. In Freeman's case, the historical power relations between white cultural supremacy and representations of Black masculinity as dangerous and necessarily contained are marked on the voice. Issues of race and gender, then, are communicated through the voice as references to power relationships built into the particular delivery of the actor's speech patterns. As I have argued here, much of Freeman's performance career has been built on the backbone of his voice-over narrations. In this work, Freeman's vocal identity is one of racialized support of both the white characters in the diegetic world and the audience in the theater. Such a career is feasible given Freeman's vocal identity as a figure of deference, prominently featuring sonic traits like subordination, servitude, and silence that soften perceived threats of Black masculinity. The race and gender of Freeman's voice, then, emerges through his support of white leading characters and audiences through the subtly racialized channel of the voice.

The cyclical nature of Freeman's Southern Black masculine vocal identity and the subordinating vocal intimacy developed between the actor and some members of his audience reinforce themes of racial servitude and marginalization coded into Freeman's voice. Freeman's vocal intimacy *is* his power. Since the actor is so easily able to forge intimate connections with listeners/viewers, his voice is understood as powerful, but through processes of containment, his vocal prowess is recouped to contribute to the defining subordination of his vocal identity. Specifically, Freeman's voice is often featured as voice-over and direct address, making the servile qualities of his voice appear to reach through the film or television text to invite white audiences into a relationship of vocal intimacy. That relationship is easily perverted to reinforce the servile nature of many of Freeman's roles. Certainly the comments I collected for this chapter are not representative of all of Freeman's fans; they demonstrate the potential of a voice to replicate and strengthen cultural racial hierarchies as performed through the speaker–listener relationship of vocal intimacy. The structure of vocal rhetoric here, then, encourages vocal intimacy both through consistency of vocal identity and through the voice-over and direct address format, particularly in conversation with narrative and vocal subordination.

CHAPTER 3

Sounding Presidential

Saturday Night Live *and the Politics of Impersonation*

ALONGSIDE PICTURES of Sarah Palin, the phrase "I can see Russia from my house" has graced merchandise ranging from T-shirts to coffee mugs to refrigerator magnets. The phrase currently serves as the title of an anti-Palin Facebook page, and a July 29, 2014, episode of *Nightline*, six years after Palin's vice presidential run, described the former politician as the "woman who says she can see Russia from her house." Although the line has taken hold in the pop-culture sphere as a way of mocking Palin's political inadequacy, it reveals more about the power of late-night comedy to shape political deliberation than about the GOP's 2008 vice presidential nominee. While Palin did mention being able to see part of Russia from Alaska, it was Tina Fey, not Palin, who spoke the iconic phrase "I can see Russia from my house," during a 2008 impersonation of the politician on *Saturday Night Live* (*SNL*).[1] Still, over the next six years, the phrase became so widely attributed to the conservative political voice that Representative Louie Gohmert (R-TX) was driven to "set the record straight," adding a clarification to the Congressional Record in March 2014 that Palin had not used this phrase during her campaign.[2] The widespread confusion that attributed Fey's line to Palin underscores the potential for impersonation, which layers the vocal and visual attributes of one body onto another, to influence public political deliberations.

In political impersonations, audience familiarity with political figures intersects with comic media conventions, creating layers of intertextual familiarity. Scholars like Jonathan Gray, Jeffrey P. Jones, and Jeff Smith have examined the importance of cultural foreknowledge in political satire, noting that an important component of presidential impersonations involves the audience's intertextual understanding of both the politician being mimicked and the comedian mimicking that politician.[3] As Linda Hutcheon points out, parody involves "the structural superimposition of texts," so that, in the case of comic impersonation, the comedic performance makes constant vocal and visual reference to a familiar politician.[4] To be in on the joke, the audience must draw comparisons between their knowledge of the political persona and the impersonation on the screen. The layering of politician and comedian also reflects back onto the impersonator. Whereas Fey's persona was well-defined prior to her Palin impression, *SNL* often uses political impersonations to define particular cast members' "brands."[5] In other words, Palin's image was influenced by Fey's impersonation, but Fey's comic persona was also defined, at least in part, by her iconic portrayal of the conservative politician. Political impersonations, then, layer one familiar body over another, reshaping the sonic rhetoric of the impersonated and impersonating bodies.

By layering the bodies of politicians and comedians, political impersonations draw from audience familiarity, and, in doing so, they use comedy to discipline differences in the vocal and visual identities of marginalized groups. *SNL*'s impersonations first portray a politician's personality quirks or salient stances before comically exaggerating these attributes. In other words, these impersonations use comedy to isolate atypical aspects of the voice and body, disciplining difference, as Jacob Smith observes, through laughter.[6] This process is not limited to *SNL*'s impersonations. Indeed, as Jones argues, "Caricature is about essence, reducing numerous competing narratives to a particularly arresting one."[7] As a means of essentializing and disciplining political figures, impersonations carry the potential not only for redefining individual politicians but also for Othering marginalized groups through particular visual and vocal identifiers. Moreover, in the cases I examine here, through the mimicry of impersonations, these disciplining essentialisms are layered onto already marginalized women and minority politicians, satirizing public figures' racialized and gendered identifiers rather than their political views and actions.

Despite the potential for further marginalizing women and gender minorities of all races and other people of color in the public sphere, popular cultural parody and satire are often lauded for their power to bring political deliberation to a broader audience. Gray notes that political parody can "energize civic culture, engaging citizen-audiences . . . inspiring public political discussion, and drawing citizens enthusiastically into the realm of the political with deft and dazzling ease."[8] As a specific example of this process at work, "the

SNL effect" has been used to describe the shifts in both interest and opinion that follow the show's political parodies.[9] SNL's influence can be explained by a combination of the simplification of complex political issues on television comedy shows and contemporary audiences' abilities to share short clips through social media.[10] Together, Jones argues, these factors translate SNL's impersonations into "water-cooler moments," channeling both the audience's familiarity with parodied politicians and the particular identity traits at the heart of the impersonation.[11] While political satire has been examined as a mechanism of producing and challenging intimacy with particular politicians and comedians, these discussions rarely centralize sound.

In this chapter I tease apart how the act of imitation in political satire layers culturally privileged voices, encouraging marginalization on the basis of race and gender despite its ostensibly progressive politics. Beginning with Tina Fey's impression of Sarah Palin in the 2008 season of SNL, I explore the way that pitch patterns mark particular bodies as exaggeratedly gendered. Whereas the development of Morgan Freeman's speaking voice was, in part, a product of his environment, I argue that Fey's performance of Palin was an amalgam of Fey's more typical vocal pitch and the comedian's reading of Palin. Fey's performance of Palin furthermore layered the two white women's bodies together, blurring the lines between Palin's vocal sound, Fey's vocal sound, and Fey's spoken impression of Palin. Slightly higher in pitch, Fey's voice projected exaggerated white femininity onto the politician, making her appear less fit for a political office held exclusively by men. On the other side of the same coin, in impersonations of Barack Obama, the president's lower pitch made him appear more suitable for the presidency, given patriarchal culture's alignment between authority and lower, masculine pitches.[12] The racial stereotypes that exaggerate masculinity and heterosexuality in Black men further this goal, making Obama seem more authoritative and consequently more presidential. Finally, in the cases of both Fey and Obama, vocal intimacy plays an important role; since Fey was much more familiar to audiences than Palin prior to the 2008 election season, audiences interpreted the Fey-Palin impression through a lens of Fey, whereas Obama quickly grew more popular than his impressionists. This allowed Fey to layer exaggeratedly racialized and gendered performances onto Palin's body but restricted the level of influence that Fred Armisen, Jay Pharoah, or Dwayne Johnson could exert on their readings of the president's persona. The relative cultural privilege of these political and comedic voices, then, was contextual and unsettled, shifting in the moment even while drawing from deep-seated historical stereotypes.

As part of a long-running television program that has historically engaged in topical and political humor, SNL's political impersonations should be understood within the general context of television satire and the more specific context of broadcast television's political constraints. Therefore, this chapter begins by historicizing the politics of televised political critique before tracing *SNL*'s historical engagement with presidential politics. I then examine the mechanisms of vocal intimacy in the show's political impersonations, followed by an exploration of the vocal identities of Palin, Obama, and their impersonators. I conclude the chapter by drawing these cases back to the larger issue of vocal identity and intimacy.

BROADCASTING SATIRE

Televising satire comes with inherent risks, which have limited presidential satire like that of *SNL*. As George A. Test points out, satire is built on "the special mixture of aggression, play, laughter, and judgment."[13] Depending on the program's brand of commentary, this type of programming may uncomfortably challenge audience knowledge, opinions, and deeply held cultural beliefs. Given satire's critical format, network television has often been resistant to the potential alienation of both audiences and advertisers threatened by biting political critique. The contemporary proliferation of satirical shows like *The Daily Show* was made possible through the changing structure of television distribution, including increased online formats like YouTube and Hulu as well as the marked change from a three-network system to cable narrowcasting.[14] During the decades leading up to *SNL*'s 1975 debut, when a network's financial viability depended on appealing to a broad audience, television was hesitant to embrace explicitly political content.

Against a backdrop of growing social upheaval, 1950s and 1960s television worked to reconcile its roots in lighthearted entertainment with its massive potential for social and political commentary. Growing from radio's early adoption of live vaudevillian performance, television's 1950s programming was dominated by the live variety format.[15] In the decade's early years, network television offered more than forty weekly variety shows, featuring popular musical guests, sketches, and stand-up comedy tied together with a familiar emcee or host. Propelled by the popularity of the variety format and Britain's 1960s surge in satirical media, one early US precursor to *SNL* was ABC's adaptation of the BBC's *That Was the Week That Was*. During the show's short run, *TW3*, as it was popularly called, "was satiric and often quite caustic," leading to multiple battles with network executives, a temporary removal from the air prior to the Johnson-Goldwater election, and the show's eventual cancellation.[16] As Gray points out, *TW3* was a rare exception to the era's resistance to satirical television that "ultimately proved the rule."[17]

Despite its early cancellation, *TW3* paved the way for satirical variety shows, carving out television's role as a participant in the volatile era's public political deliberation. Two such shows dominated the airwaves in the mid- to late 1960s: the controversial *The Smothers Brothers Comedy Hour* and the more broadly popular *Rowan and Martin's Laugh-In*. The first of these built on *TW3*'s biting political commentary to explicitly critique powerful political figures, including President Johnson.[18] Flying in the face of assumptions that controversial programming alienated and distanced audiences, *The Smothers Brothers* maintained high ratings. Still, as Hilmes notes, the network shut down the show's bold and brash political commentary midseason, delineating "what networks deemed permissible in terms of incorporating the more political elements of 1960s youth culture into network television during the prime-time hours."[19] Although the network blamed the writers, citing failure to submit a script prior to the contracted deadline, the episodes' writers, including Rob Reiner and Steve Martin, maintain that the show was a casualty of network and cultural politics.[20]

Whereas *The Smothers Brothers* prioritized biting political substance, *Laugh-In* incorporated its commentary into a more easily digestible format. The show, which in Henry Jenkins's terms "snared the decade's flamboyance, its anarchic energy, and its pop aesthetic, combining the Blackout comedy of the vaudeville tradition with a 1960s-style 'happening,'" was in many ways a direct predecessor to *SNL*.[21] First, *Laugh-In* created space for a milder brand of topical humor that *The Smothers Brothers* had demonstrated was unsustainable. Second, the show had a standardized format similar to that adopted by *SNL* in the 1970s, incorporating not only politically based sketches but also a "fake news" segment similar to *SNL*'s signature "Weekend Update."[22] Finally and most directly, as a writer for *Laugh-In*, Lorne Michaels began to imagine a new show that would adapt the 1960s aesthetic at the heart of *Laugh-In* for the up-and-coming baby boomer generation. That show, which Michaels would later create and produce with Dick Ebersol and NBC's president Herb Schlosser, was *SNL*, and it boasted "the presentation of authentic selves, unfiltered, and uncensored."[23] In other words, *Laugh-In* defined a safer format for satirical variety during a cultural moment hungry to reach the youth market, paving the way for *SNL*'s signature political commentary.

THE POLITICS OF SATURDAY NIGHT

When *Saturday Night*, as it was originally called, first aired in 1975, it shifted the politically charged commentary and variety-show format popularized by *Laugh-In* and *The Smothers Brothers* to appeal to the up-and-coming power of the baby boom generation. As Nick Marx, Matt Sienkiewicz, and Ron Becker note, an important aspect of *SNL*'s conceptualization was its situation in the heart of network-era television, "a time during which powerhouses NBC, CBS, and ABC fought to win a bigger piece of what was essentially a three-slice pie."[24] From the show's first airing, showrunner Lorne Michaels aimed to develop an alternative iteration of television comedy, balancing, as *Laugh-In* and *The Smothers Brothers* had both attempted, a voice in public political deliberation with a type of humor suitable to the television medium. In a network-era context, Michaels opted to select material for its comic potential first and its social meaning second, crafting a program that walked the line between countercultural icon and entertainment for the masses.[25]

An important element of Michaels's strategy involved the baby boom generation. This youth market was not only growing in its spending power, it was also developing a voice as the generation of water-cooler politics. That moment was one of cynicism, characterized by Watergate, the fall of Saigon, and the dark progression of the Patty Hearst story, reflecting a moment ripe for dark satirical rhetoric.[26] Furthermore, as "the first network series produced by and for the television generation," *SNL* was among the first television series to target baby boomers.[27] This marketing strategy did not initially pay off, as the show began with ratings similar to the reruns of Johnny Carson that NBC had previously aired in its time slot. However, the baby boom generation soon proved to be both a market interested in the lighthearted political comedy that Michaels imagined for *SNL* and a loyal fan base. While the show's ratings have steadily declined since its peak in the early 1980s, an effect that can be at least partially attributed to the proliferation of programming in the post-network-television era, *SNL*'s cultural importance has been consistently lauded.[28] Not only is the show often considered "the nation's primary launching pad for comics,"[29] *SNL* has also been shown to influence US American electoral politics through its staple political impressions.[30]

A particularly important aspect of *SNL*'s political branding was the inclusion of overt imitations of presidential candidates and figures. Shows like *Laugh-In* and *The Smothers Brothers* had opened a space for political humor as an element of the televised variety show, but presidential impersonations would mark *SNL*'s unique contribution to satirical television. Before the 1970s very few television comedy shows risked impersonating US presidents.[31] *SNL* entered this arena on its fourth episode shortly after Gerald Ford tripped and fell down the steps of Air Force One; the show featured Chevy Chase as a "stumblebum . . . slapstick" version of the president that helped build Ford's reputation as a klutz.[32] Chase's performance of Ford was remarkable for two reasons. First, *SNL* marked one of the first times a president was criticized not for his policies but for his "sheer physical clumsiness," an interpretation made even more remarkable by Ford's past athletic success.[33] Second, Chase caricatured Ford's physical movement, but he made no other efforts to sound or look like Ford; as Diane Holloway recalls, Chase "just said he was Ford, and he was. He was playing an attitude."[34] Together, these two features created a performance of Ford that attempted to discredit the president through a type of physical ad hominem, arguing that, in Chase's terms, Ford "had never been elected, period, so I never felt he deserved to be [in office] to begin with."[35]

Building on the popularity of Chase's Ford sketches, Dan Aykroyd debuted impressions of both Jimmy Carter and Richard Nixon in 1976, moving *SNL*'s presidential impersonations to a mimetic accuracy laced with biting political rhetoric. During the Carter presidency, Aykroyd impersonated the president in nearly every sketch. Aykroyd was lauded as Carter's most successful impersonator, Tony Hendra recalls, using "the gluey sanctimoniousness"[36] of the president's persona to critique the "go-it-alone, smarter-than-thou persona" that would ultimately cause Carter's decline in popularity.[37] During the mid-1970s, too, Aykroyd took on an even more popular impression of former president Nixon, whose presence on the show was necessitated by continued scandal following Watergate, Ford's controversial pardon of the disgraced politician, and Nixon's continued attempts to regain footing in domestic and international politics. Nodding toward "Nixon's gravely [sic] voiced speech, hunchback posture, and furrowed brow," Aykroyd's impersonation criticized Nixon's mental stability.[38] In the May 1976 sketch "The Final Days," the comedian represented Nixon as "a half-crazy, anti-Semitic racist," driving home the cast's and writers' disdain for Nixon and problematizing Ford's controversial pardon of his predecessor in the final months of the president's ill-fated re-election campaign.[39]

If the Nixon and Carter presidencies corresponded with what many call "the golden years of *SNL*," the Reagan years saw a sharp and steady decline in the popularity and satirical bite of the show's presidential comedy.[40] Citing Reagan's perceived popularity with the *SNL* audience, Lorne Michaels recalls, "We didn't do Reagan very often because there wasn't much to do. He was an actor, and people liked him."[41] More importantly, *SNL* struggled to find an actor who could humorously impersonate the president; the show cast six different actors as Reagan, each falling short of the popularity and poignant political rhetoric that Chase and Aykroyd captured in their roles as Ford, Carter, and Nixon. *SNL* had gained popularity at least in part from its hard-hitting political satire, but as the show became increasingly mainstream in its target audience, that same political satire had to be tempered.

The George H. W. Bush and Clinton presidencies seemed to be the nail in *SNL*'s satirical coffin, as presidential impersonations decreased in political punch as they increased in mimetic accuracy. As Matviko points out, Dana Carvey's impression of Bush focused primarily on catchphrases like "I'm not a wimp," and Phil Hartman's Clinton impersonation foregrounded the president's affinity for junk food.[42] *SNL*'s commitment to political commentary seemed so light during this era that impersonations actually rendered political figures more endearing, covering legitimately flawed politics with menial personal shortcomings. In fact, while Chase and Aykroyd's portrayals had often been understood as countercultural, antiestablishment satire, impersonations of Bush and Clinton appeared so harmlessly complementary that Bush arranged for Carvey to present his impression at the White House during his last days in office, and Darrell Hammond was invited to Clinton's second inauguration.

Simultaneously, the Bush and Clinton administrations coincided with *SNL*'s development of a mimetic aesthetic for their political impersonations. Departing dramatically from Chase's early Ford impersonations, Carvey aimed to imitate Bush as accurately as possible, "mimicking his patrician attitude, nasally voice, [and] overused hand movements."[43] Jones argues that it was this precise imitation of the president's personal delivery style that left little room for the type of political satire at the heart of 1970s *SNL*. Similarly, Hartman's Clinton focused on precisely matching the president's sound and appearance, replaced by Darrell Hammond's even more striking verbal and visual resemblance to the president after Hartman left the show.

As I have discussed in this section, previous analyses of *SNL* have tended to align the decline in the show's presidential impersonations as political satire with their increased focus on mimetic accuracy. Jones, in particular, draws a sharp division between *SNL*'s 1970s biting political commentary and the later, more physically accurate portrayals of Bush and Clinton,[44] and Day and Thompson assert that the show's later impersonations attend only to "personality quirks and physical flaws" at the expense of any real political intervention.[45] The show's presidential impersonation aesthetic has certainly evolved (or devolved, as the case may be), with previous research often labelling its broadly appealing content as rhetorically empty. Missing from these analyses is the slipperiness of sonic impersonation. As the ideologically shaped aural projection of the body, the voice offers insight into the role of identity in the political sphere. A vocal impersonation is always a reading of this vocal identity, layering the meanings of the politician's voice for speaker and audience onto the impersonators' voice. Such a performance, then, is a reflection of vocal intimacy. This cyclical process of intimacy and identity, channeled through the network television format, is clear in *SNL*'s impersonations of Sarah Palin and Barack Obama.

VOCAL POLITICS AND THE IMPERSONATED NOMINEE

Following Fey's early *SNL* appearances as Palin, a 2008 *New York Daily News* article remarked, "*Saturday Night Live* is buzzworthy again, thanks to Tina Fey as Sarah Palin."[46] Fey's impression was a cultural and political hit, boosting the show's ratings 76 percent compared with the previous season[47] and leading many journalists to turn on Palin, blaming her, rather than the McCain campaign advisers they had previously censured, for her string of disastrous media appearances.[48] In contrast to previous *SNL* political impressions, Fey's Palin impersonation was lauded for its purportedly uncanny and "particularly brutal" satirical effect.[49] In fact, contrasting Fey's performance with Chevy Chase's intentionally physically and vocally inaccurate impersonation of Ford in the 1970s, Gray, Jones, and Thompson note that the satire of Palin's vice presidential campaign "bristled with judgment and aggression . . . something important was being said."[50] Although Fey's performance differed wildly from Chase's in its level of mimetic accuracy, and despite the 2008 performance's placement during a cultural moment in which many believed "*SNL*'s counterculture roots ha[d] withered," Fey's impression of Palin gained power both as a popular culture phenomenon and as a political critique.[51]

Once *SNL* had aired several sketches featuring Fey as Palin, discussion of the comedian's physical and vocal resemblance to the politician flooded the internet. Much of this commentary focused on the intersection of Fey and Palin, specifically highlighting the unique aspects of the white women's voices through comparison. Given the slipperiness of the voice and cultural difficulties with precisely describing vocal sound, these comparisons offer two important contours of vocal mimicry. First, the abstract quality of vocal sound makes voices difficult to describe. In the case of Fey's Palin impression, both of the women's voices were ubiquitous on online and televised sources, allowing listeners to regularly hear both versions of Palin's voice and compare them with one another. As I discuss further in this section, many consumers offered concrete comparisons of Palin's voice and Fey's Palin voice, detailing the vocal intimacy through which listeners/viewers heard these two culturally privileged voices.

Second, ubiquitous discussions of Fey's impression led some commenters to highlight an important but often overlooked aspect of mimicry: namely, Fey's necessary role as an audience member for Palin's political performances and Palin's probable role as an audience for Fey's impressions. Impressions necessarily illustrate the cyclical nature of vocal production, since the performer must gain an intimate knowledge of their target in order to replicate that person's speech and movements. By listening to readily accessible footage of Palin's interviews with Charlie Gibson and Katie Couric, Fey writes, she worked particularly hard to perfect an imitation of the vocal identity she describes as "'Alaskan wind song' with a blend of 'Fargo,' Reese Witherspoon in 'Election' and a Midwestern accent borrowed from a friend's grandmother."[52] This description points to an important contour of vocal impersonation. A vocal impersonation is not a copy of a vocal original. Instead, the impression is a reperformance of the impressionist's reading as an audience member, and that reading, like any other reading, is filtered through the impressionist's experiences with other, often hidden intertextual discourses. It is a citation, in Butler's terms, but not only a citation of the politician. Fey did not simply repeat Palin's voice. She performed Palin's voice *as she heard it*, which was impacted by various named and unnamed cultural influences that shaped Fey's vocal intimacy with Palin.

The voice that emerged from Fey's lips was an amalgam of Palin's voice and other vaguely northern popular culture artifacts that highlighted the candidate's dialect. The former Alaskan governor's accent is a particularly salient point of her persona that both draws from and reinforces the racially problematic misconception of Alaska as a white northern state. As *Slate* wrote,[53] Palin's accent is representative of her childhood in the Anchorage area, a city whose culture dominates popular representation of a very rural state.[54] The Anchorage area contains 40 percent of the state's population, but Alaska Natives make up only 8.8 percent of the municipality's population compared with at least 15.3 percent in the state as a whole.[55] Palin's hometown, Wasila, a commuter suburb of Anchorage, is composed largely of the descendants of northern midwestern US farmers who migrated to Alaska during the Great Depression, so its population is not representative of the state or the state's history as a whole.[56] Alaska, like other profoundly segregated regions, has residents with widely varying accents, with the white northern US accent dominating media, politics, and other sites of representational power.[57] The state is only 66 percent white, but Palin's white Alaskan voice is the most widely circulated representation of the state, a fact that hides histories of slavery, colonialism, and profound and lasting discrimination against Alaska Natives by characterizing the state as white.[58] By highlighting Palin's as "a distinctive Alaskan accent,"[59] news and commentary effectively centralized the colonizer's voice, obfuscating the dialects of Alaska Natives. The fact that Palin's is perhaps the only culturally privileged voice connected to Alaska, in other words, both draws from and exacerbates the oppression of Alaska Natives at the hands of white settlers.

The accent became a trademark of Palin's candidacy, later marking her political television commentary, in part because of how frequently it was discussed online. Palin's white northern dialect solicited commentary not only in feature articles on *NPR* and *Slate* but also in numerous discussion forums.[60] So exaggerated is Palin's accent that Fey recollects thinking "how hard could that voice be?"[61] Furthermore, she discusses focusing explicitly on developing a version of the former governor's dialect over other aspects of vocal sound. Fey's impression did not disappoint and, indeed, drew focus from internet commentators who often reacted to the "flat" accent that the comedian developed for her impression. Calling it a "flat, Francis[sic]-McDormand-in-Fargo voice,"[62] a "flat northern accent,"[63] and even a "flat Palin-esque accent,"[64] a comment that uses circular attribution to tautologize Palin and the sound of her accent, listeners/viewers often used discussion of Fey's accent to praise the accuracy of her Palin impression and, through an accent associated with the whiteness of the northern US, to underscore the white in Palin's white femininity. Fey's Palin voice, then, was marked by a focus on racialized ornamentation, foregrounding the accent as the voice's singular trait and ignoring other complexities of Palin's vocal sound.

Lurking behind the exaggerated accents at the heart of both Palin's personality campaign and Fey's Palin impersonation is an explicitly feminized and explicitly white component of vocal pitch. Issues of pitch and pitch variation are important considerations when studying white women politicians since, as Sally McConnell-Ginet notes, higher and widely fluctuating pitches are often associated with emotional instability, a trait that has been used to discredit women of all races in positions of power.[65] Where Black and Latina women are often coded as emotionally excessive and therefore aggressive, as in stereotypes of the "angry Black woman" or the "Latina spitfire," white women are often discredited through emotional excess coded as weakness and instability.[66] Speaking with a high, widely fluctuating pitch range can result in white women being coded as emotionally unstable, but as I have argued elsewhere, this process can also be reversed. A woman need not begin with a particular vocal identity to be discredited. Rather, since ideological context plays such an important role in the interpretation of vocal identity by listeners/viewers, commentators may project a hypothetically high-pitched voice onto a white woman to foreground and discredit her feminized body.[67] Attaching an adjective to a voice often makes us hear it differently.

Internet commenters who pointed to "Palin's high-pitched squeak"[68] as a particularly accurate aspect of Fey's impersonation illustrated the power of a vocal description to shift the way that the original vocal identity is heard. In the two media interviews Fey reports studying, Palin's voice clusters around pitches lower than what is generally assumed to be the "average" woman's voice.[69] During the Charlie Gibson and Katie Couric interviews explicitly referenced in several of Fey's sketches, Palin's voice clusters around an F3 and often dips down to a C3 (see figure 3.1), well below the feminine voice averages that range from the much higher C4 to E3.[70] Palin's average speaking voice is simply not high-pitched. Perhaps this is a factor of the physiological and cultural influence surrounding Palin's vocal development; the politician has frequently referenced her interest in activities stereotyped as masculine, including sports and outdoorsperson activities like hunting and fishing.[71] The pressure to fit in to culturally masculinized activities may have shaped Palin's average speaking voice, or perhaps this is a result of pressing the voice downward to seem more masculine and therefore more credible in a political context dominated by cisgender men. Whatever the reason, as Palin rose in political prominence, her voice did not reflect its popular characterization as "the high pitched voice of a teenage girl."[72]

FIGURE 3.1. "A seven hundred billion dollar [bailout]," Palin in Charlie Gibson interview.

Palin's voice is lower than the average woman's. However, Fey's impersonation of the vice presidential nominee, and Fey's typical vocal pitch, clusters at the high end of the average woman's vocal pitch range and extends well above that average level.[73] Impersonations are always an amalgam of the impersonator and the impersonated. Thus, although Fey employed a vocal identity convincingly similar to Palin's, Fey's voice functioned as a conduit for the performed vocal identity and was therefore imprinted on the impression alongside her reading of Palin. Fey's voice is markedly higher than Palin's. In a 2014 appearance on *Late Night with Seth Meyers*, for example, the comedian's voice clustered around the high end of the average woman's vocal range[74] and, at several points, extended above that range (figure 3.2). Since Fey's voice is typically higher than Palin's, her impression of the politician could be expected to resonate at slightly higher and therefore more stereotypically feminized pitches than Palin's actual voice.

FIGURE 3.2. "Pretty amazing, too, to look in the audience was," Fey on *Late Night*.

The differences between Fey's and Palin's typical ranges emerge to mark Palin's public appearance as exaggeratedly feminine. In a 2008 episode of *SNL* three days after Palin's first interview with Katie Couric, Fey spoke a line lifted directly from the real Couric-Palin interview: "Ultimately what the bailout does is help those that are concerned about the healthcare reform that is needed to help shore up our economy to help—it's got to be all about job creation." As figures 3.3 and 3.4 demonstrate, Fey's performance of this line is consistently higher-pitched. On the syllable "ult" at the beginning of the phrase, Palin's voice reaches its peak of E4 (the second line from the top of the staff), and Fey stretches three-and-a-half steps higher to reach a G#4 (the top line of the staff). Following the first word of the utterance, Palin's voice regains its lower pitch, hovering around the bottom of the staff, whereas Fey's Palin impression remains in the center of the staff. In this way Fey's impression is consistent with her typical pitch range but higher than Palin's. This comparison illustrates how Fey's voice is etched into Palin's vocal range through imitation. Fey uses Palin's exact dialogue, giving her impression a mark of authenticity; however, the comedian's voice is subtly but identifiably higher in pitch. Such subtlety is difficult to detect by listening alone, but it notably reframes Palin's pitch as higher than average, distancing her performance from the typically lower voices associated with governmental leadership.

While Fey's naturally higher voice contributes to the increased white feminization of Palin's persona in her impression, the comedian's typical pitch range falls short of explaining the dramatically shifted pitch range of Fey's Palin impression. In the first episode of *SNL*'s 2008 season, Fey introduced her Palin impression with "A Non-Partisan Message." In this sketch, Amy Poehler joins Fey as Hillary Clinton, and the two white female politicians decry the rampant media sexism of the 2008 presidential election. In this sketch Fey's voice soars above the feminine vocal average, and in Fey's most quoted two-second-long line, "I can see Russia from my house," her voice is not only much higher than Palin's, it also shifts pitches up and down a full octave scale

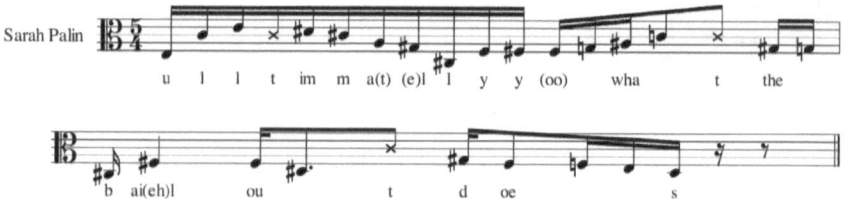

FIGURE 3.3. "Ultimately what the bailout does," Palin in Katie Couric interview.

FIGURE 3.4. "Ultimately what the bailout does," Fey on *Saturday Night Live*.

three times, with each melisma, or movement up and down the staff, taking less than half of one second. Higher pitch ranges and wider, faster fluctuation are cultural markers of infantilized femininity, often used to stereotype white women as incompetent, overly emotional, and weak.

Representations of Black and white women have developed as a binary. Stereotypes about Black women position them as sturdier and more masculine, a controlling image used to justify Black women's enslavement and labor in physically demanding tasks during chattel slavery. White women, on the other hand, were understood as weak, childlike, and delicate in a way that both justified white male violence toward Black men under the guise of "protecting" white women and the white race and sharply contrasted the roles of enslaved women. Whereas Black women are stereotyped as masculine, white women are often represented in exaggerated opposition to masculinity.[75] Racialized gender roles therefore limit the roles appropriate for white women like Palin even as they render women of color all but completely inaudible on the national political stage. Comparing Palin's voice to that of a "teenage girl"[76] therefore overtly infantilizes her, a tactic long used to dismiss white women from electoral politics, as the dramatic raising of pitch in vocal impressions covertly marks her as childish and immature. Fey's exaggerated northern accent further foregrounds the former governor's whiteness, eliding the identity components of gender, race, and regionalism into a vocal persona unfit for office. Certainly, Palin may be unfit for office based on more logical reasoning. The danger here is in aligning white femininity, or a performance of traditionally understood femininity in general, with political ineptitude. The quick and wide shifts in pitch range similarly are more typical of a child, and so dramatic are Fey's pitch movements in her oft-quoted "Russia" line (figure 3.5), they would be somewhat unbelievable for a typical adult speaker. As a medium of delivering comedy in this sketch, then, Fey's voice is coded with a particular brand of humor that vocally infantilizes the white feminine political candidate.

FIGURE 3.5. "And I can see Russia from my house," Fey on *Saturday Night Live*.

In both of the previous examples, *SNL* writers and Fey drew Palin's dialogue from real interviews, creating the illusion that Fey's caricature is only slightly exaggerated. A *New York Times* blogger argued that Fey's line "I can see Russia from my house" "was not much altered from an actual statement that the real Ms. Palin made."[77] Commenting on a *Chicago Tribune* blog, TJW further noted, "Thing is, the script is pretty much written already! You didn't need comedy writers to write the line about 'I can see Russia from my house,'" implying that the line was drawn from real life.[78] Indeed, as I pointed out in the introduction to this chapter, Palin was widely credited with saying Fey's line about Russia, when in actuality the politician only remarked on the visibility of Russia from an island in Alaska. This was an oddly placed claim within the context of the interview, but it was nonetheless true.[79] In the Couric-Palin sketch, on the other hand, writers drew many of Fey's lines directly from the interview transcripts. In both cases, the similarities between Palin's actual utterances and Fey's *SNL* lines are crucial to the illusion of the comedian's accuracy. By closely aligning Fey's dialogue with Palin's interviews, *SNL* suggests that accuracy is at the heart of its impersonation sketches. The linguistic choices Fey made are, indeed, close to Palin's actual interview responses. My point here is that the similarity of language effectively overshadows the exaggeration of vocal identity to particularly racialized gendered ends.

The illusion of accuracy draws not only from the sketches' linguistic rhetoric but also from the visual references to Palin. As Fey recalls in her recent memoir, immediately following the McCain campaign's announcement of Palin's vice presidential run, the comedian's friends, family, and former *SNL* co-workers guessed that Fey would impersonate Palin. Fey initially resisted, noting that she "didn't do impressions,"[80] and yet online discussions increasingly commented on the two white women's similar appearances.[81] Discourses comparing Fey and Palin's appearances were reinforced by instances of mistaken identity; most notably, the French newspaper *Le Soleil* accidentally ran a picture of Fey alongside a story about Palin, a mistake that would reoccur on US America's *Fox News* three years later.[82] Fey and Palin were framed as nearly identical, then, in terms of both linguistic utterances and physical appearances, overshadowing the ways that the women's performances were different. Specifically, Palin's language and appearance were mapped onto Fey's body incredibly successfully, and this alignment drew the attention of fans and political pundits. Missing from the discussion was the exaggerated white femininity and infantilization added to the impersonated vocal identity through the sound of Fey's voice.

Hidden behind Fey's interpretation of Palin's vocal identity is a notably erroneous replication of the politician's vocal pitch. The exaggerated pitch formations in Fey's impersonation are noteworthy primarily because they are completely absent from the online commentary I found in the research for this chapter, even in a cultural context brimming with allusions to both Palin's voice and Fey's impersonation of the politician. Commenting on a *Jezebel* article about Fey's initial appearance as Palin, Sassette marveled at "how perfectly [Fey] had Sarah Palin's voice down."[83] A *Wall Street Journal* article on the same sketch incited commenters like Brian to observe "how closely Tina's voice is to Sarah's."[84] Professional political pundits, too, remarked on the "pitch-perfect" quality of Fey's impersonation.[85] This commentary illustrates the fact that Palin's voice, at least for *SNL* audiences, was never actually a culturally privileged voice; rather, Fey's impression of Palin stood in as a culturally privileged voice inextricably linked to Palin's body. The Palin we hear through Fey is a subjective interpretation posing as precise mimicry. Fey's impression is even more effective because it seems primarily to replicate Palin's accent, as evidenced by the many comments on dialect I discussed above. This approach obfuscates the racially gendered exaggeration of Palin's vocal identity, a claim evidenced by the lack of attention to vocal racialized gender in the comments I examined for this chapter. When linked to Fey's dialogue, which often positions Palin as uninformed and stupid, the comedian's vocal performance subtly offers white femininity as an argument for Palin's political ineptitude.

The cultural discourses surrounding Fey's impersonation of Palin, I have suggested here, lay in the accuracy of the accent, dialogue, and physical resemblance. Missing from the conversation is the importance of vocal identity in the way that Fey represented Palin on *SNL*. This representation vocalizes a northern US white femininity often assumed to be representative of both Alaska and white women in general. By deploying the white Alaskan dialect of the Anchorage area, Fey-lin's speech replicates the marginalization of Alaska Natives in mainstream representation. Whiteness is deployed as normative for Alaskans, despite the state's Native heritage. Whiteness, too, propels Fey's impression of Palin's femininity, rendering it weak and infantile. In this way, Fey's impression ran counter to progressive efforts, not only in its encouragement of sexist stereotypes but also in its furthering of a strategic whiteness for Palin. If, as previous literature on the show indicates, mimesis has been the nemesis of satire,[86] then the near replications in the impression would not be expected to contribute to the political rhetoric of the sketch; specifically, Fey's appearance, much of the dialogue, and the "Palin-esque accent" could be considered mere parody.[87] The remaining components of Fey's Palin impression foreground the rhetoric of white femininity including rapidly moving pitch patterns and a raised, infantilized average pitch. These components can be understood as part of the process Fey brought to her experience as an audience for Palin. Fey watched the politician, interpreted her persona, and reframed Palin for *SNL*'s audience.

THE INTIMACY OF FEY-LIN

The case of political impersonation offers an unusual perspective of vocal intimacy, reflecting not only the connection of speaking and hearing bodies but a chaining out of intimacies across Palin and Fey as both speakers and listeners as well as the audiences for their various vocal identities. As with other speech, the voice of the impersonator forges what Gunn has described as "the most intimate and 'private' of human feelings," in the form of an intimate union between speaker and listener.[88] Unlike other forms of vocal rhetoric, the impressionist draws from and manipulates the previously crafted relationship between impersonated politician and listener. Three vocally intimate relationships are present in any impersonation, then, for that impersonation to communicate effectively as an impersonated vocal identity: the relationship between impressionist and audience, the relationship between impersonated speaker and audience, and, as I discussed in the previous section, the relationship between impressionist and impersonated. In the case of Fey's Palin impersonation, the first of these relationships seems to have been quite strong; from John McCain's announcement that Palin would be his running mate, a growing chorus called for Fey to play Palin on *SNL*.[89] The second of these relationships was significantly weaker in the early days of Palin's candidacy. Soon after Palin's introduction, the *New York Times* observed, "everyone knows that Governor Palin looks like Tina Fey. In fact, for many people, it's just about all they know."[90] As I suggest in this section, this imbalance of relationships created a situation in which Palin's vocal identity was filtered through a strong sense of vocal intimacy between Fey and her audience.

When the McCain campaign introduced Palin as the vice presidential candidate on August 29, 2008, Fey had already developed a strong fan base. As head writer for *SNL*, Fey had anchored the show's popular "Weekend Update" segment from 2000 until 2006, when she left the show to star in her own NBC series, *30 Rock*. By 2008 Fey had written and appeared in the popular film *Mean Girls,* and only four months before Palin's announcement, *Baby Mama* hit theaters with Fey as costar. When Fey returned to *SNL* to play Palin, online reactions highlighted audiences' loyalty toward Fey, and, since the sketch placed the comedian in comparison with Palin, commenters were quick to note their preference for Fey. Alongside comments by fans like Diane S. declaring "Tina Fey 4 Prez,"[91] listeners/viewers joked about "kidnap[ping] Palin and substitut[ing] Tina Fey for her on the campaign trail."[92] Similarly, a *Jezebel* reader argued that Palin owed her nomination to Fey, commenting that "McCain picked Sarah Palin because she looks like Tina Fey."[93] Weighing in on a *Washington Wire* article, Gilli remarked, "[Palin] looks like Tina Fey—and THAT is why she is so popular. She looks like someone we know and love (Tina Fey). That got her foot in the door."[94] Under the pseudonym "SNL fan of yore," a *Chicago Sun Times* reader even called Fey's Palin impersonation "destiny fulfilled."[95] In short, Fey's Palin impersonation revealed much about commenters' previous relationships with Fey and demonstrated that most of Fey's commenting fans were not interested in supporting Palin.

The enormous popularity of *SNL*'s Fey-as-Palin sketches also meant that consumers of the impersonations forged a relationship of vocal intimacy with Palin through Fey's impression. In other words, the impersonation sketches, rather than Palin's actual media appearances, began to define and redefine the relationship between Palin and, at least, the *SNL* audience. Framed by comments that Palin "had been instantly pegged as a Tina-Fey look-alike"[96] and comic slips like "Tina Fey—I mean Sarah Palin,"[97] *Time* claimed that "when voters close their eyes now and envision Public Palin, likely as not they see Tina Fey."[98] This same process of replacing Palin with Fey's impression occurred in online article comment sections. E. Hussein, commenting on an article about Fey and Poehler's impression of Palin's Couric interview, remarked, "When I see Sarah Palin (actually speak) I always expect her to be just like Tina Fey is in this video."[99] Similarly, in response to an article discussing Fey's choice to return to *SNL* to play Palin, J. Michael argued, "Tina Fey did a better 'Sarah Palin' than Sarah Palin."[100] As videos continued to circulate the internet, Palin's identity was increasingly layered into Fey's impression, with one listener/viewer even (incorrectly) claiming that "on [one] part of the *SNL* interview, it wasn't Tina Fey speaking. They cut in audio from the actual Palin/Couric interview."[101] So closely was Palin's voice associated with Fey's impression that Palin's actual vocal identity began to dissolve into the parody.

Even as Palin's voice was being replaced by the sounds of Fey's performance of the politician's vocal identity, listeners claimed that the impression captured some essential core of Palin, reflecting the "hear[ing of] a body" at the heart of vocal intimacy.[102] Fey, they believed, had "obviously keyed in to the overall atmosphere of Palin's consciousness and self-awareness"[103] in order to "capture some of the actual heart of [the politician]."[104] Many of the comments circulating along with *SNL*'s parody videos were even more explicit about Fey's ability to, in *Chicago Sun Times* readers' words, "get to the essence"[105] of Palin and "[capture] the essence of Sarah, you betcha."[106] For vocal impressions, the use of descriptions like "essence" and "heart" is telling. If, as Don Ihde describes, the voice reveals the deep interior movements and pathologies of the body, then a replication of the voice layers not only sound but also the internal and external functions of organs, sinews, and saliva used to produce that voice.[107] Through this lens, the act of speaking and listening to an impersonated vocal identity becomes a deeply intimate physical and psychic transfer between impressionist, impersonated, and listener. As with all vocal intimacies, the simultaneous physiological movement between speaking and hearing bodies creates a communal connection shaped by the ideological contexts of sound and identity. Perhaps it is not surprising, then, that Palin reported watching Fey's impression with "the volume all the way down"[108] as a way of avoiding the intensely intimate reproduction of her own voice through Fey's body, or that some listeners noted being "kind of scared of Tina Fey now."[109] The transfer and renegotiation of spoken essence makes public an incredibly intimate exchange of corporeal sound.

Taken together, my analyses of the vocal identity and vocal intimacy of Fey's Palin impersonation situate an exaggeratedly white, feminized identity within the context of vocally intimate speaker–listener relationships. As I have argued here, the two most salient aspects of Fey's impression were the northern dialect and, much less obviously, the exaggeratedly white feminized childlike pitch patterns. In the first of these, whiteness is deployed strategically, naturalizing the colonization of Alaska Natives by white immigrants. In the second, whiteness overlays femininity, with whiteness providing leverage to run for office and femininity defusing the potential for power. Whiteness marked by femininity (as well as poverty, queerness, disability, and other axes of oppression) is still whiteness, but it is no match for the unmarked whiteness that dominates political discourse. Despite dramatic differences in Fey's and Palin's pitch patterns, audiences argued that Fey "captured the essence" of Palin.[110] It is certainly true that much of Palin's public persona relied on her recognizable accent. That dialect would play a role in audience interpretations of "the actual heart" of Palin may not be surprising. What is unsettling, though, is that alongside reports that McCain chose Palin largely on the basis of her sex,[111] *SNL*'s parody was not only calling attention to Palin's many media gaffes but also exaggeratedly feminizing the deeply physical aspects of her speech patterns. Through pitch characteristics hidden behind the exaggerated northern accent, the borrowed lines of dialogue, and the two women's physical resemblance, Fey's Palin impression invited an interpretation of the politician's qualifications based not only on her highly publicized media gaffes but also on the basis of her femininity.

THE MANY VOICES OF FAUX-BAMA

In striking contrast to Fey's hit impression of Palin, *SNL*'s Barack Obama sketches have struggled to gain footing with audiences. The show's initial Obama impression featured Fred Armisen, whose Japanese, Venezuelan, and white descent led makeup artists to darken his skin with the same honey-colored base they used when the actor portrayed Prince in previous seasons.[112] Despite claims that Armisen was donning Blackface to impersonate Obama and the impression's generally low popularity, he remained in the role until the show's summer break in 2012, sharing the role only when Dwayne "The Rock" Johnson appeared twice as "The Rock Obama." When the show returned the following September, newer cast member Jay Pharoah, who had honed his impression of Obama in his stand-up routine prior to joining the *SNL* cast, took on the presidential role. Throughout the transition between Armisen and Pharoah, as I discuss in this section, themes of race and mimetic accuracy peppered commentary about *SNL*'s Obama impressions. As Mary Beltrán notes, Armisen's impression was primarily critiqued for a perceived racial incongruity between the comedian and Obama.[113] These critiques were missing from discussion of Pharoah's and The Rock's performances. Furthermore, both Armisen's and Pharoah's impersonations were critiqued for being overly accurate.[114] Whereas Fey's Palin impression was lauded for its progressive social connotations, *SNL*'s Obamas have more often been criticized either as racially problematic performances or as mimetic nonsatire.

Whereas Fey's comic Palin impersonation was aided by the distinctive properties of the politician's dialect, Obama impersonators find little help in his decidedly presidential voice. In many ways, the president's voice exemplifies the culturally privileged voice, even though his skin color places him at a distinct cultural and political disadvantage in the political arena. As the "leader of the free world," the president of the United States is associated both with a great deal of authority and with white masculinity, traits culturally imagined to manifest in the voice.[115] Rindy C. Anderson and Casey A. Klofstad's experimental studies demonstrate that listeners across genders tend to attribute stronger leadership skills to people with lower voices.[116] In their study, participants were more likely to place a mock "vote" for candidates with lower voices, specifically attributing greater authority to men with lower voices.[117] Such bias is widely documented, as evidenced by a slew of online articles instructing women to speak with a lower voice as a way of projecting stronger leadership skills.[118]

Second, and relatedly, the particular type of authority associated with US American presidents and politicians is built on a foundation of masculinity. Not only has the US never elected a woman president, women, particularly women of color, are also dramatically underrepresented in all levels of electoral politics. The masculinity of US politics has further marked voices of prominent political figures through media representations; as an example, although Abraham Lincoln reportedly spoke with a "high keyed, unpleasant voice,"[119] he is regularly portrayed with the same type of rich baritone for which Obama is praised. Indeed, the frequent references to Obama's "baritone"[120] align the president's voice with the same musicality I discussed of Morgan Freeman in the previous chapter. Obama's voice, in other words, is pleasantly melodious as it reifies the masculine imagery of the historical presidency. The role of the presidency, in other words, can be understood as a masculinized form of authority.

In stark contrast to Palin's voice, Obama's vocal sound has been widely lauded as attractive and credible, often with a nod to the president's low, masculine pitch. David Bernstein describes Obama's "trademark baritone" as "deep in pitch, authoritative and reassuring in tone," and *Late Night with Jimmy Fallon* showcased the president's smooth, low voice when Obama appeared on the show to "slow-jam the news." Perhaps more importantly, during the 2008

Democratic primary race, Frank Browning even argued that "the very essence of Obama's voice—its tone, its timbre, its resonance—" gave the then candidate "an edge" over his opponent Hillary Clinton.[121] Barbara Apple Sullivan, too, speculates that Obama's "soaring and inspirational tone" on the 2008 campaign trail helped boost the candidate to victory.[122] In a country where forty-four men and zero women have served as president, the presidency has been imagined through masculine, low voices like Obama's much-lauded "deep and rounded and melodious . . . mellifluous baritone."[123] Indeed, much of the president's praise on the 2008 campaign trail pointed directly to the sonic components of his rhetorical style.

While my purpose in this chapter lies more with the vocal identities created by impersonators, Obama's voice itself reflects citationality in terms of both the context of its acquisition and his ascent to the highest office in the land. Obama's early childhood, in the aural context of a Kansan mother and a Kenyan father with a British accent, would serve him well in his later endeavors. In *Dreams from My Father*, the president recalls his father's voice "deep and sure, cajoling and laughing," and the way his "father's voice had nevertheless remained untainted, inspiring, rebuking, granting, or withholding approval."[124] The sense of depth and certainty registers in the president's voice, despite the fact that Obama spent little time with his father, learning about the man primarily through the stories others told.[125] More to the point, the intense diversity of vocal sounds and patterns, from Hawaii to Indonesia to Seattle, and articulated through a variety of languages and speech styles, meant that Obama learned early to adapt to various sonic situations. This sonic flexibility, H. Samy Alim and Geneva Smitherman argue, is key to his success as a speaker. As they write, "We don't speak only the language of our family or hometown. If we are sufficiently motivated and have a broad range of experiences, we pick up ways of speaking throughout our lifetime."[126] Central to this argument is the premise of experiential learning, in which Obama had the opportunity to hear and speak in various contexts, adopting the traits of the culturally privileged voice that helped him earn the presidency. Throughout his career as a politician, and even in his first speech at a rally while attending Occidental College, Obama has received feedback praising his voice for its depth of pitch.[127] This particular timbre, Alim and Smitherman argue, marks the politician as masculine, but more importantly as a speaker who can appease both Black and white audiences; by tapping into the "Black preacher" sound, Obama marks himself as Christian, staving off white fears of possible immigrant and Muslim status and appealing to Black Christian voters.[128] In this way, the initial shaping of Obama's vocal identity from childhood serves him through its adaptability later, allowing him to adjust to his audiences' likely ideological readings.

A distinctive and consistent component of Obama's vocal rhetorical style is illustrated by his exceptionally low pitch. In his "More Perfect Union" address, a 2008 campaign speech that has gained much attention from rhetorical scholars, Obama directly addresses racial tensions in America.[129] Polls conducted by the Pew Research Center note that 85 percent of US Americans heard at least a little about the speech, which came as a response to a growing scandal regarding racially charged comments by Obama's pastor Jeremiah Wright, and 51 percent actually watched the address on television or online. In the speech Obama presents his ideas sincerely and with authority, and, perhaps more importantly for this chapter, he speaks in a remarkably low range.[130] Indeed, Obama's range is similar to the pitches highlighted in the previous chapter's discussion of Morgan Freeman, suggesting that the "gravitas" that Freeman produces through his voice is similarly present in the president's very low spoken pitch patterns.[131] Specifically, as the excerpt in figure 3.6 demonstrates, the then candidate's voice rarely approaches the staff and often dips well below; Obama hovers around an A2 (the first pitch of the selection, which lies at the low end of adult men's average spoken pitch[132]) and often stretches to an F2, the bottom of the comfortable range for a trained bass singer.[133] This speech addresses such somber issues as slavery, contemporary racism, and the continued divisiveness of racial tension in US American media and politics, and Obama uses an especially low pitch range to communicate a sincere and sober tone.

FIGURE 3.6. "Launched America's improbable experiment," "More Perfect Union."

The depth of range in the "More Perfect Union" address was not an anomaly; in perhaps the most frequently heard sound bite for any political candidate, Obama's voice sank even lower. As dictated by the McCain-Feingold Act, television and radio campaign ads must include a statement of disclosure from the candidate. Phrases like Obama's "I'm Barack Obama, and I approve this message" are repeated frequently, running at the end of every ad. In fact, while the act does not require the message at the end of online ads, many of the then candidate's ads still featured the phrase, making it, arguably, the most ubiquitous sound bite in the Obama campaign. As I have argued of Fey, Palin, and, in the previous chapter, Morgan Freeman, such continuous repetition defines a speaker's voice by implying that the repeated sounds are "authentic" for the speaker. A campaign-disclosure sound bite therefore plays an important role in defining a candidate's voice and, by extension, the body that produces that speech. In Obama's disclosure phrase, the president's voice dropped to a D2, a note that sinks below the limits for standard men's ranges (figure 3.7). Such an extreme pitch range marks Obama as decidedly masculine, aligning him with the historical masculinity of the presidency.

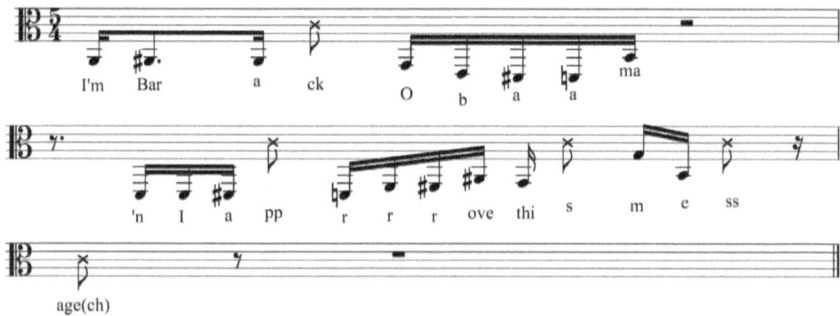

FIGURE 3.7. "I'm Barack Obama, and I approve this message," Obama campaign disclosure.

The ubiquity of Obama's highly masculine campaign-disclosure message makes it an important consideration in *SNL*'s vocal impersonations. Since the repetition and consistent pitch pattern of the recorded statement worked to define Obama's voice, divergence from the message's vocal sound is likely to be noticeable. This notability offers an opening for comedy, as with Fey's Palin impression and its exaggerated performance of feminized and infantilized pitch and pitch patterns, but Obama's already incredibly low voice made such a caricature largely impossible; to exaggerate the masculinity of the president's voice would have meant dropping the vocal pitch even lower, a feat that would prove impossible for a vast majority of people. While *SNL* featured Armisen as Obama in two mock campaign ads leading up to the 2008 presidential election, neither of the ads features the signature ad disclosure. Still, based on Armisen's other appearances as the president, Armisen's naturally higher voice clearly put him at a disadvantage in terms of impersonating Obama, as the comedian's impression of the baritone politician most often sat directly in the center of average human speech pitch as opposed to Obama's very low pitch range.

Additionally, as Beltrán points out, audiences disliked the misalignment between Armisen's visual whiteness and Obama's visual Blackness, a contrast that was also underscored vocally.[134] As figures 3.8 and 3.9 demonstrate, whereas the opening lines of Obama's 2010 State of the Union address were split primarily between the lower range of the staff and the notes below, for example, Armisen's impersonation remained more strictly in the center of the staff. Armisen's range, then, was not so different from Palin's average pitches, which had been superimposed with the exaggerated white femininity of "the high pitched voice of a teenage girl,"[135] as it fell squarely in the overlap between the average adult man's voice and the average adult woman's voice.[136] Additionally, despite the fact that the scarce research comparing the voices of Black men and white men shows no significant differences in pitch,[137] popular culture stereotypes Black men as having significantly lower voices.[138] As I briefly discussed in the previous chapter, this type of racial stereotyping may be an extension of the hypermasculinization and hypersexualization of Black men historically.[139] Regardless of the issue's roots, Armisen's androgynous vocal sound placed him at a distinct disadvantage when imitating Obama's extremely masculine, and therefore stereotypically Black male, vocal sound.

FIGURE 3.8. "Members of Congress," Obama in "State of the Union Address (2010)."

FIGURE 3.9. "Members of Congress," Armisen on *Saturday Night Live*.

In stark contrast to Armisen's androgynous vocal portrayal, Pharoah's portrayal of the president during his second campaign and term of office resonated at the low pitches typical of Obama's actual voice. Pharoah's voice naturally falls much lower than Armisen's, fulfilling the stereotypes of Black men I discussed earlier. When Pharoah appeared on *The Wendy Williams Show*, for example, his pitch ranged from the average androgynous pitch of E3 at its highest to the quite low range of G2. Just as Fey's and Armisen's voices were imprinted onto their impressions, Pharoah's typically low pitch was incorporated into his Obama impersonation; the important difference, of course, was that Pharoah's voice is well aligned with the president in terms of pitch. Armisen's Obama impression never included a campaign-ad disclosure message, making comparisons difficult. Pharoah's tenure as Obama, on the other hand, included a number of instances of this message. Pharoah's take on "I'm Barack Obama, and I approve this message" employs a slightly slower pacing than the president's disclosure message, but the men's pitch deliveries are very similar in pitch and tone, with Pharoah stretching almost as low as Obama himself (figures 3.10 and 3.11). Pharoah, in other words, replicated the cultural privilege of vocal masculinity in a way that Armisen did not.

FIGURE 3.10. "I'm Barack Obama, and I approve this message," Obama campaign disclosure.

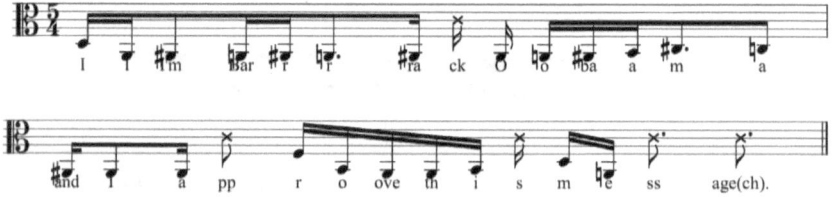

FIGURE 3.11. "I'm Barack Obama, and I approve this message," Pharoah on *Saturday Night Live*.

The problem of Armisen's higher-pitched Obama impression did not go unnoticed in online discourses, which highlighted the importance of Obama's masculine baritone. Responding to Pharoah's initial presidential performance and comparing it with Armisen's impression, *Salon*'s Alex Pareene noted that Armisen's "biggest problem was simply that his voice just isn't deep enough," a description that is accurate and that also speaks to the notable connection between vocal pitch, the presidency, and Obama's speech.[140] Likewise, commenting on a *Breitbart.com* article about Armisen's return as Obama in *SNL*'s fall 2012 season, NJRightwinger12 argued that Armisen "has his voice too high,"[141] and a *DemocraticUnderground.com* reader noted that Armisen's "Voice Is Too High."[142] At the same time, Pharoah's impression is often simultaneously criticized for its visual presentation and praised for its vocal accuracy. For example, lobbyist and campaign adviser Jamal Simmons argued, "Jay Pharoah got the voice best, but Armisen's physical impersonation was better."[143] On *datalounge.com*, a reader similarly called Pharoah "terrible physically, but he had the voice down,"[144] and Akimbo commented on the blog *Shadow and Act*, "He sounds like Obama, but makes Denzel faces."[145] Comments like these illustrate the importance of accurate vocal pitch for *SNL* listeners/viewers and, given the link between the presidency, masculinity, and authority with which I opened this section, offer an explanation richer than visual race for why Pharoah's impression was more successful than Armisen's.

While Pharoah's Obama impression incorporated the deep baritone masculinity often associated with the presidency in a way that Armisen's did not, discussions of the two impressionists often centered on issues of visual race. As I highlight in the next section, impressions like these illustrate the intersection between gender and race. The voiced connection between presidential performances and vocal gender I have discussed in this section is important in its propensity to recirculate and reinstate images of an exclusively masculine presidency, but Obama's marginalized racial identity complicates this issue in important and vocally salient ways.

THE PRESIDENTIAL RACE

The exaggeratedly low pitch patterns of Obama's speech and of Pharoah's impressions not only connect the men's voices with the historically masculine pitches of presidential speech, they also connect Obama's vocal identity to his racialized presidential persona. There are likely many reasons audiences were underwhelmed by Armisen's Obama impersonation, including visual race and dialogue content, but comparisons in pitch resonance offer one dimension of the explanation. If, as I have argued here, one salient aspect of the president's persona is his deep, rich speaking voice, a characteristic that stands in for both the Blackness and the presidential character of his performance as the first Black commander in chief, then the inaccuracy of that pitch in Armisen's impersonation creates an incongruity not only between Obama and Armisen's visual race but also between their aural race, as a product of social conditioning. This type of vocal dimension contributes additional layers of meaning to Beltrán's analysis of the intersection of visual race and online commentaries that centralized Armisen's makeup as the primary blockage in the comedian's communication.[146] As I suggest here, the rhetoric of very deep vocal tone, as an artifact of both Black masculinity and presidential ethos, is central to audiences' understanding of Obama's voice. Impressionists like Armisen who were unable to replicate this dimension, then, were less likely to be taken seriously than actors with deeper voices like Pharoah and Dwayne Johnson.

Audience preference for a lower-pitched Obama impressionist speaks not only to the president's gender but additionally to the gendering of Black masculinity as hypermasculinity. Patricia Hill Collins traces the rhetorical meaning of African American masculinity from slavery through the Jim Crow South and contemporary popular culture.[147] As she argues, Black masculinity has always been tied to hypersexualization and exaggerated heterosexuality, since framing Black men as subhuman sexual predators first functioned to justify African enslavement and later promoted terroristic acts like lynching; when Black men were and are understood through a lens of hypermasculine heterosexuality, all manners of violence can be justified as ways of "protecting the body of the white woman (and thus the white race) from penetration."[148] As I discussed in the previous chapter, this ongoing stereotype of Black men as sexually aggressive often is reshaped into an exaggerated Black corporeality and engrained into white understandings of the Black masculine voice through the increased presence of the body in speech. In Freeman's case, this involves an excess of breathiness in the actor's whispered vocal tone; a hypermasculine performance of Obama, on the other hand, must contain the overt authority I have described previously. In short, the most successful *SNL* Obama impressionists incorporated Black hypermasculinity through both their physical appearance and their replication of Obama's low pitch.

A blatant example of Black hypermasculinity in *SNL's* Obama impressions comes through the show's two "The Rock Obama" sketches. Most consumers preferred Pharoah to Armisen's Obama impersonation, but Dwayne "The

Rock" Johnson emerged as a crowd favorite among audiences. In these sketches, various politicians meet with Armisen's Obama in the Oval Office. As discussions get tense, the Obama impression takes on characteristics of "The Incredible Hulk," first growing angry, and then transforming into a larger, mutant version of the president played by Johnson. Johnson's "The Rock Obama" throws people through windows and smashes furniture, among other violent behaviors. Like Fey's, Johnson's fame precedes Obama's, so that fans of the former wrestler often understood Obama's voice through a framework of Johnson's. Certainly, "The Rock Obama's" angry and violent behavior is, in many ways, not comparable to impressions by Armisen and Pharoah. Still, audience response was strong, with multiple online polls and discussion boards comparing Obama's voice to Johnson's even before the wrestler appeared on *SNL*. Polls at YouChoose.net, Yahoo! Answers, and CityData.com all got enthusiastic affirmations from fans; some argued, in a way that mirrored discussions of Fey's Palin, that "Obama studied [Johnson's] promos in order to get into office,"[149] and that Obama's "success is not only due to his eloquent speaking but to the fact that he sounds exactly like Dwayne Johnson."[150] Johnson's impersonation was not intended to be mimetically accurate, but his Obama sketches did use The Rock's body to draw from essentialisms that exaggerate Black masculinity. Aligning with the vocal pitch that solidifies the president's hypermasculine vocal identity, Johnson's *SNL* sketches map the former wrestler's muscular physique and his deep, rich voice onto Obama's presidency, accentuating the corporeality often associated with Black masculinity, and resulting in a widely praised impersonation of the president.[151] Just as fans of Fey's Palin tended to layer the two women together, fans of Johnson's impersonation peppered the internet with votes for The Rock's political career. On *The Daily Mail*, for example, joan remarked, "Love the Rock, they should make him president!!"[152] Fan discussion board PopWatch.com, too, featured comments like Rebornknight's, "Can you smell what the POTUS is cooking?,"[153] a reference to The Rock's former tagline "Do you smell what The Rock is cooking?"

While Armisen's Obama was immediately criticized based on the perceived incongruity between the actor's Japanese-Venezuelan heritage and Obama's Black identity, Johnson's appearance as The Rock Obama went largely uncriticized. As Beltrán speculates, Johnson was "black enough" to play the first Black president.[154] Such a critique translates to the vocal dimension as well. As I discussed in the case of Fey's Palin impersonation, vocal impressions involve a layering of three vocally intimate relationships, and in this case, these relationships can be understood through a lens of hypermasculinity. First, the impressionist must form a relationship of vocal intimacy with the politician by hearing and interpreting the voice. Whereas Fey dramatically reshaped her vocal delivery to impersonate Palin, and whereas Armisen attempted to lower his voice, the vocally intimate layers of Pharoah, Johnson, and Obama were closely aligned. In other words, Pharoah's and Johnson's adaptations were minimal, given that their voices are similar in pitch to the president's vocal identity. Second, the audience must draw from their relationship with the impersonated to understand the messages from the impressionists. Here, as Beltrán observes and as I argued previously, race was a pivotal factor.[155] The lower and more narrowly pitched, and therefore constructed as more masculine, vocal identities of Pharoah and Johnson allowed their voices to be layered into audience understanding of Obama as the first Black president, and, unlike Armisen, their deep, rich tone referenced the presidential sound that many have come to expect from Obama's culturally privileged voice.

Notably, Fey's celebrity preceded her portrayal of Palin, whereas neither Armisen nor Pharoah were particularly noteworthy prior to their performances of Obama. Aside from several marginal roles in films like *Anchorman* and character voice-overs on Adult Swim cartoon series like *Squidbillies* and *Aqua Teen Hunger Force*, Armisen's only visible acting had been through *SNL*. Pharoah was an even more extreme case, having been plucked directly from his strictly live performance career as a stand-up comedian to join the *SNL* cast. In contrast, Obama was already gaining steam as a presidential nominee in the months leading up to Armisen's first impression of him, famously prompting the McCain campaign to run an ad accusing Obama of being more fit as a celebrity than as a leader.[156] Obama's already strong presence on the US political stage meant that Armisen's audiences had likely already developed a relationship with Obama's vocal identity; his voice was already a culturally privileged voice enjoying widespread circulation and common points of cultural reference. As that of one of two strong Democratic nominees for the 2008 presidential race and, later, as the president, Obama's voice was ubiquitous in 2008 and grew even more saturated through political ads, stump speeches, and news media sound bites. The comedians' voices, then, were reduced to proverbial needles in a vocal haystack, providing additional pieces of information about the president's vocal identity in an already saturated vocal environment.

The particular audience is key to both vocal identity and vocal intimacy. Vocal identity is not only dependent upon the body of the speaker as it develops within particular ideological contexts, it is also dependent upon how listeners/viewers interpret that voice. In a mediated culture, this interpretation is shaped by the ways that other visually identified speakers present vocal identities, but it is also shaped by the general context of listening. For *SNL* to maintain its audience, potential critiques of Obama were limited.

This is not to say Obama's policies were above reproach, but rather that *SNL* had good reason to assume heavy-handed criticisms of the president's policies and behaviors would not be well received by the audience. On the other hand, *SNL*'s largely Democrat-aligned audience might be expected to accept in good humor most criticisms of Palin. Yet, although a left-leaning audience could be expected to accept criticisms of GOP politicians, they might also be expected to be more sensitive to issues of identity, including gender and race. Given her conservative political stances, *SNL*'s audiences may have been more receptive to criticisms of Palin. That they accepted so fully a subtle critique of her white feminine vocal identity is telling. The voice is not biological or natural. It is socially constructed. So thoroughly has the voice been naturalized historically that most of us struggle to recognize when the social construction of a vocal identity is being deployed toward bigoted ends; perhaps this recognition is even difficult for the person deploying the vocal identity in this way.

Whereas the vocally intimate relationship between audiences and Fey's Palin seemed to emerge as a solid connection between Fey and listeners/viewers, the connection between speaker and listener in the case of Obama's impersonators was characterized by ambivalence. I suggest that this reaction was a result of the alignment between stereotypes of Black masculinity and the presidency; through the exaggerating of Palin's white femininity, the candidate became less desirable for political office, whereas Obama's masculinity, when exaggerated, only made him a stronger, more authoritative fit, especially against his feminine competitors. In Armisen's case, online commentary by both professional pundits and casual audiences pointed to the abstraction that makes vocal description so difficult, as audiences described the things the comedian did well but struggled to identify the element missing from *SNL*'s original Obama impersonation. One *Satired* blogger remarked that "Armisen has Obama's halting cadence . . . but little else,"[157] and a commenter on *All Things Obama* noted that the comedian "didn't sound like [Obama] . . . couldn't even get the right intonations, or his rythmic [sic] parlance."[158] Still others believed that the problem lay elsewhere; an anonymous blogger on *All Things Obama* opined that Armisen "did sound very similar to Obama,"[159] and Mrs. Shermender, a commenter on *Pink Is the New Blog*, called the comedian "dead on with the way he talks."[160] Amid this ambivalence the consensus was clear: audiences did not like Armisen's impression, often for vague or ambiguous reasons that pointed to something missing "in the very essence of Obama's voice."[161] A major difference between Fey's Palin and *SNL*'s Obama impressions lay in a kind of representational loyalty. Audiences' understanding of Palin seemed to shift based on Fey's performances, incorporating the higher-pitched speech into their memory of Palin, but listeners/viewers held fast to their concept of Obama.

The context of the presidency may make the concept of vocal "essence" less probable for impressions of Obama than for performances of Palin's voice. As I argued earlier, the presidential voice broadly defined has historically tended toward a masculine character, generally communicating through low pitch and deep resonance. If the essence of Palin in Fey's impression was a gendered exaggeration of her white femininity, then the essence of Obama's voice is likely to be the form of exaggerated masculinity evidenced in his low, deep resonance. Fey's Palin, then, gains much of its comedic heft from incongruity between her vocal identity and the vocal identity of the nation's (second) highest office. Conversely, the masculinized essence of Obama's voice, even when exaggerated by *SNL*'s performers, only makes his vocal identity more suitable for the presidency. Since in this case the salient element of the impression, Obama's deep, rich voice, is a naturalized, invisible norm of the US American political system, its manipulation is unlikely to communicate either humor or a satirical message.

CONCLUSION

Televised political impersonations are powerful not only for their ability to precisely replicate vocal identities and vocal intimacies, but rather for their power to subtly shift identities based on ideological contexts. Mimesis is a form of vocal performance that places impersonator and impersonated in a cyclical relationship: the impersonator must interpret and reperform the impersonated, and audience understandings of the impersonated are shaped by the impersonator. Rather than being oppositional to satirical performances, then, precise or seemingly precise imitation creates a form of political commentary that foregrounds the identity categories of candidates like Palin and Obama, since these categories emerge in the cyclical process of reading and imitation.

As a dimension of identity, the voice plays an important part in communicating the types of roles appropriate for particular voices. In this chapter's case studies, gender and race emerged as important dimensions in satirical commentary that, perhaps inadvertently, reinforced the types of voices suitable for presidential speech. In both Palin's and Obama's vocal impressions, exaggeratedly racialized gendered performances of vocal pitch in *SNL*'s impressions mapped racialized gendered stereotypes onto their bodies. For Obama, this exaggeratedly masculine impersonation did little to harm his image among the left-leaning audiences of *SNL*, but in Palin's case, Fey's impression cast her in the white feminine stereotypes of weakness, delicacy, and emotional instability, associating these traits with her political ineptitude and reasserting the colonized linkage between Alaska and whiteness that effectively erases Alaska Natives from representation. Indeed, *SNL*'s impressionists of both Palin and Obama demonstrated the ways that racialized and gendered vocal patterns generally, and pitch movement specifically, constrain the contexts in which particular voices are taken seriously. Given the heavily masculinized office of the US president, this meant that Fey's exaggeratedly white feminine Palin impression infantilized the politician, making a subtle commentary on Palin's intelligence and maturity not only through the sketches' text but also through the sound of Fey's vocal delivery. Conversely, satire of Obama politically strengthened textual links between masculinity and the presidency, adding an additional set of low voices to the repertoire of presidential politics on television. Through the precise mimesis of Fey, Pharoah, and Johnson, the satirical points of *SNL*'s sketches were enhanced as the impressionists added a layer of satirical vocal identity to the delivery of the show's political humor.

As an extension of vocal identity, the intimate nature of the speaker and listener relationship in these cases intensified the gendered and racialized dimensions of the impersonated voices. Based on their interpretations of political personae and numerous media and cultural artifacts, *SNL*'s impressionists cobbled together vocal impressions that channeled gendered and racialized layers of presidential history, which were consequently integrated into the information available to audiences during the election cycle. Because these vocally intimate relationships are layered, drawing from at least three different relational connections, the complexity of vocal intimacy obfuscated the gendered satire in these cases. Fey's Palin, for example, seems rooted in dialect, an interpretation that mimics the reactions of many online commenters, and, as a result, the white feminized element of pitch is made even less visible. In a context that frames presidential voices as masculine, lower pitch resonance is further obfuscated by its naturalization. Unlike Palin, whose femininity is nonnormative in a vice presidential race, the gender of Obama's vocal identity is hidden by its unremarkable nature in this particular context. In this case, as in many media contexts, the match between context, identity, and sound is key to governing the level of intimacy facilitated in the listener/viewer. The relationship between speaker and audience in the case of Obama and his impersonators is characterized by the familiarity of his already culturally privileged voice. In both cases, then, the relationships of vocal intimacy serve the sounds of vocal identity.

CHAPTER 4

Whitevoice 2.0

Online Speech and Comedians of Color

THE INTIMATE SHARING of the comments section beneath a YouTube video of Richard Pryor's stand-up routine comparing Black women and white women is reminiscent of a multiuser scrapbook. Alpinorico2 recalls "drinking beer with [his] brothers black & white & brown, 1981 in the airborne infantry, listening to Pryor."[1] Just a few lines below, differentandalike remembers that his "late cousin Todd and I would sit by the basement door while the adults were laughing hysterically. I miss those moments."[2] David Beverley recollects, "Growing up, one of the best things about being a 'latchkey kid' was, I was at home alone w/ a record player and every Richard Pryor album, I know his routines verbatim."[3] Within its public online viewing space, Pryor's video is not an isolated example of this sort of public, collective remembering; similar comments are common across YouTube videos for many Black and Latino stand-up comedians including George Lopez and Eddie Murphy, and more contemporary comics like Dave Chappelle and Gabriel Iglesias.[4] These audience comments illustrate how stand-up comedy leverages vocal intimacy to drive home its messages, asking listeners/viewers to build relationships with comics through their voices and centralizing familiar comedic vocal identities.

YouTube comments discussing stand-up comics like Pryor point to the role of vocal intimacy in the comedy situation: a lone speaker with a microphone, directly and conversationally addressing a club full of listeners. This familiarity establishes a particularly personal vocal intimacy both through the genre's conversational feel and through many audiences' fan loyalty to particular comics. Folklore historian Ian Brodie calls stand-up comedy "performed autobiography," noting, "over a comedian's career some form of persona is established . . . [and] returning audience members bring a foreknowledge of this persona to subsequent performances, and a framework for how to interpret a specific performance is already established."[5] Loyal fans listen and re-listen to particular comics' vocal identities, forming long-term relationships of vocal intimacy through the voiced storytelling of the stand-up genre. Furthermore, stand-up bits are built on shared assumptions between audiences and comics, as speakers reveal personal details of their lives and upbringings that are, in many cases, assumed to be experiences shared with the audience. Moreover, the means of sharing these intimate stories, standing alone on a stage with a microphone, both necessitates the conversational style of directly addressing the audience and allows the comedian to employ a relaxed, natural form of vocal rhetoric.[6] In other words, the very genre of stand-up comedy employs elements of the experience of listening to a friend share personal, humorous stories.

For comedians of color, these personal stories become more than a way of building intimacy for the purpose of financial gain; for many Black and Latino performers, stand-up routines offer a way of sharing marginalized stories that might otherwise be missing from white mainstream culture. As comedians aurally articulate intimate details of comedians' and listeners' personal experiences, they do so through their consistent vocal identities, and, in the case of comedians of color like Pryor, these vocal identities link particular histories to particular racial and gendered situations. Stand-up comedy, a contemporary mode of storytelling, uses comedy to share and circulate cultural truths that might otherwise be buried in pressures of assimilation. For critical media scholar Bambi Haggins, comedy plays a particularly important role in Black history since "the function of humor and the therapeutic value of the accompanying laughter, inside safe, communal black spaces—whether Granny's front porch or center stage at the Apollo—spoke to specific black experiences."[7] Stand-up comedy, then, not only offers a means of establishing intimacy between speaker and audience, building a community of people with shared experiences of oppression and domination, but also acts as a way of remembering, defining, and reimagining racialized identities.

Comedians of color have also used comedy as a way of challenging the rhetoric of whiteness through performances. Pryor, for example, performed numerous bits including impressions of white people, allowing the comedian to imagine and embody what it might mean to perform whiteness in the deeply tumultuous racial environment of 1960s and 1970s America. Following Pryor's lead, numerous Black and Latino comedians developed their own approaches for performing whiteness as part of their routine. Importantly, these performances were not aimed at passing in the public sphere or assimilating into white culture; instead, these comedians used whiteness impressions, or as I call them here, *whitevoice,* as a way of resisting white supremacy and rearticulating the meanings of racial segregation and hierarchy. In other words, they were aimed at challenging stubborn and naturalized links between particular vocal identities and particular material circumstances that cast Black and Latinx US Americans as violent, lazy, and deserving of structural poverty and discrimination. Whereas the US history of speech training and vocal hierarchy would traditionally demand an assimilated vocal identity, stand-up comedy has been a place where a markedly Othered vocal identity could be reclaimed, in part by holding up a whitevoice identity for ridicule. Through generations of comedians of color, including Pryor, Eddie Murphy, Chris Rock, George Lopez, and Dave Chappelle, these whitevoice impressions have been performed, circulated through media, and recirculated through sites like YouTube.

Even while stand-up comedy has provided spaces of resistance for Black and Latino comedians to share counterhegemonic stories of marginalization and oppression, it has simultaneously functioned as a hostile space for women within and outside those racial groups. Indeed, stand-up comedy, and much of comedy in general, has historically been a masculine performance space. In her groundbreaking study of Black women's representation on television, Beretta Smith-Shomade argues that genres like situation and sketch comedy have either projected stereotypes of white women onto representations of Black women characters or ignored Black women completely.[8] Likewise, referring to Whoopi Goldberg as "an entertainment anomaly," Haggins notes that women of color have rarely told the stories of marginalization in the way that Black men stand-up comics have, despite their stereotyped presence in these narratives.[9] This is not to argue that women of color have never occupied a position on the stand-up comedy stage; Goldberg, Wanda Sykes, Margaret Cho, and others disprove such a claim. Instead, I mean to question not only the racial performances but the ways that gender and sexuality cut across the rhetorics of stand-up comedians of color who employ whitevoice as a comedic vocal identity, most of whom are men.

This chapter examines the whitevoice impressions of thirteen stand-up comedians of color as they circulate through YouTube. By examining these vocal impressions in conversation with one another, I argue that these comedians approach the issue of whiteness from three vocal-identity positions. First, these comedians use the issue of privilege to frame their impressions of whiteness by initially discussing situations of white privilege and then altering their vocal identities to physiologically define what privilege might sound like. Here, comedians of color distance their normative vocal identities from whiteness by reversing elements of their typical vocal identities, including African American English (AAE), in their whitevoice vocal identity. In doing so, they highlight the constructedness of voices and, as an extension of this critique, render audible the ideological rhetorics camouflaged within culturally privileged voices. Second, comedians highlight the physical process of speaking to resist stereotypes about Black and Latinx hypercorporeality by reframing whiteness as both exaggeratedly physical and comically silly, linking their vocal identities with their physical bodies. In other words, they physically "try on" the vocal identity and physical demeanor of their white characters through embodiment. Finally, and ambivalently, these two approaches to constructing a whitevoice vocal identity result in a gendered production of whiteness that addresses and pushes back against the white threatening body. By drawing together issues of white supremacy and hyperfeminized vocal pitch patterns, these comedians use the vocal intimacy they establish with their listening audience to both highlight issues of violence against marginalized populations and assuage those fears for their audience. Through the combined enactments of vocal identity and intimacy, comedians of color communicate with both their immediate audiences, often visible through the camera's viewpoint, and their extended audiences on YouTube. Their rhetoric of whitevoice in these spaces facilitates a forum for Black and Latino men whose voices are familiar to their audiences even if they are not culturally privileged on a larger scale. At the same time, it does so through a nonintersectional analysis of oppression that limits its resistant potential for feminine and queer audiences and performers.

Since I am considering the politics of comedians of color in conversation with one another, I begin this chapter by situating stand-up comedy in the context of cultural resistance. I then expand this work by considering how online video circulation impacts the project of stand-up comedy, particularly in terms of structural and institutional power, as a way of accounting for stand-up in a digital environment.

STANDING UP: COMEDY AS RESISTANCE

Particularly for stand-up comics in the twentieth and twenty-first centuries, humor has been an effective method of resistance, as it has allowed comedians of color to discuss issues of racial politics and marginalized experience with a broad and sympathetic audience. Haggins describes this type of performance as "using the microphone as a weapon," noting that Black stand-up comics like Eddie Murphy, Chris Rock, and Dave Chappelle have used comedy as a way of challenging "myriad social and political maladies, including issues of race, and [speaking] to multiple articulations of blackness."[10] For Latino stand-up comics, too, stand-up comedy has offered a way of exploring racial difference as a site for identity building, and, as Guillermo Avila-Saavedra notes, a means of "establishing Latino narratives as legitimate US social and cultural discourses."[11] The conversations begun and continued on the stand-up stage offer an ambivalent and contested space for exploring issues of racial politics. As Michael Eric Dyson argues, comics explore the contemporary racial climate in terms of lived experiences, allowing them to "stress its positive features and acknowledge its detrimental characteristics."[12] This type of performance, in turn, invites audiences to ponder, celebrate, and critique their own lived cultural experiences. In this section, I trace the roots of stand-up comedy's relationship to US racial politics from the mid-twentieth century to contemporary comic stylings.

The use of comedy to highlight oppressive social conditions did not begin with media or formal public performance, but the tradition of bringing resistance to the stand-up stage can be traced back to at least the mid-twentieth century. Later known for his role on *Sanford and Son*, Redd Foxx actively resisted the tendency for white audiences to define his comic contributions through the popular sitcom.[13] Instead, Foxx emphasized his revolutionary work on the Chitlin' Circuit, the collection of venues that welcomed Black performers and audiences during pre–civil rights era segregation.[14] In settings like the Apollo, Foxx was well received, but, as Christine Acham writes, white audiences and owners expected the comic to censor his act.[15] Acham points out that Foxx adapted the stylistic influence of performers like Moms Mabley and Pigmeat Markham, but his act shattered norms by incorporating not only sexual references but also discussions of racial violence and protest. Foxx was so thoroughly associated with discussions of anti-Black racism that *Sanford and Son* was even located in Watts, the site of the massive 1965 uprising against white supremacist violence. The fact that Foxx was both openly resistant to white structural violence and successful in mainstream media cleared a path for those who would follow. Certainly the comedian's career did not solve issues of racial discrimination and violence, but it did allow for generations of similarly resistant stand-up comics to highlight the structural oppression of Black, Latinx, and other communities of color.

Other comedians soon joined Foxx in the struggles and successes of resistance comedy.[16] These performers faced an unfriendly cultural climate to make "that comic middle passage" as an early community of popular Black stand-up.[17] As Black men who came of age in the pre–civil rights era, these comics, including Dick Gregory and Flip Wilson, were as groundbreaking in their presence on mainstream television as in their content. As Haggins notes, these men "brought Negro-ness—and then blackness—into American living rooms," often in a way that drew out commonalities between Black and white cultural experiences.[18] Wilson, for example, pushed the difficulties of his childhood upbringing to the side, despite youth experiences marked by poverty, fatherlessness, and the pre–civil rights era foster care system. Gregory, on the other hand, used a clean-cut, soft-spoken delivery style to make important messages about the Civil Rights Movement more palatable for white audiences. For example, Gregory forwent the traditional talk-show plugs for upcoming tours or concert appearances, instead using his time on *The Steve Allen Show* "to reflect on why legislation (the Civil Rights Act) could not eradicate racial inequality."[19] Despite these comics' important messages of resistance, either through their presence on the previously white landscape of television or through quiet calls for social justice, the social climate of the 1960s meant that these messages were characterized by a quiet, subtle delivery.

Richard Pryor was a contemporary of comedians like Wilson, but his approach to comedy, particularly in the late 1960s and 1970s, pushed the limits of the genre to an unapologetic brashness. Pryor's early performances had much in common with Wilson, with Pryor even serving as a writer and occasional guest star on *The Flip Wilson Show*. However, in the late 1960s Pryor took a hiatus from comedy to study with Malcolm X and other Black intellectuals at Berkeley. Following this cultural re-education, Pryor's comedy was "earthy, profane, and true, rooted not only in the lived experiences of those he had observed during his Berkeley exile but also those who peopled the sketchy spaces of the Peoria, Illinois brothel run by his family . . . as well as numerous encounters with a distinctly Midwestern brand of racism."[20] Most notably, Pryor's humorous retelling of his experiences was designed to shock; as Pryor's biographers note, the comedian reclaimed the n-word "as an empowering term of endearment and spoke with startling candor about things many people at the time were uncomfortable admitting even to themselves."[21] By bringing issues of racism to the fore of US American media culture, and by using bold, brash language to differentiate privileged white experiences from those of African Americans in the civil rights era, Pryor defined stand-up comedy as an important instrument for racial resistance.

Pryor's legacy as a Black stand-up performer influenced nearly every Black comedian who followed him, but none were as forward about this lineage as Eddie Murphy.[22] Set against a backdrop of Reagan-era policies that pushed ideologies of individual agency above social responsibility, Murphy's comedy was constrained by the comedian's desire to become a successful crossover star with a film and television career in mainstream US media.[23] The result, racial historian Donald Bogle points out, was that Murphy's persona nodded toward issues of systemic racism without engaging with the historical issues that supported Reagan-era attacks on ideas like affirmative action and welfare as a safety net for the Black poor.[24] Perhaps Murphy's subversive humor was hidden beneath a layer of white accessibility. Whatever the reason, the comedian's rhetorical style and substance were certainly a tempered version of Pryor's brash resistance.[25] Thus, although Murphy tried to "position himself as a sort of heir apparent to Pryor," his performance of Black stand-up was based on a type of neoliberal assimilation that was ambivalent at best.[26]

Following Murphy's lead as a Black stand-up comic with film and television crossover appeal, a generation of Black and Latino comedians emerged in the late 1980s and 1990s, primed to comment not only through their stand-up routines but also through television roles. Comics like Chris Rock, George Lopez, Jamie Foxx, Carlos Mencia, and Dave Chappelle entered the comedy scene during the 1990s, when networks like Fox were capitalizing on the politics of representational diversity. As Dyson notes, this climate encouraged a brand of comedy that engaged with social politics by positioning comedy as a space of discursive resistance.[27] This context allowed racial discussions to grapple with internal contradictions, with comics like Rock making visible a "kind of relentless self-investigation," and Chappelle drawing from "a sort of dual credibility" that blended "black hip-hop intelligentsia and the skater/slacker/stoner ethos of suburban life."[28] Latino comics like Lopez similarly foregrounded issues like immigration through a lens that both acknowledged the racial judgments at the heart of social attacks on Latinx US Americans and appealed to mainstream white audiences through attempts at assimilation. Following the legacy of other television and film crossover comedians including Gregory, Wilson, Pryor, Cosby, and Murphy, these comics juxtaposed their racial standpoints against the softened perspective necessary for lasting crossover appeal. Late 1980s and 1990s sitcoms like *The George Lopez Show*, *Chappelle's Show*, *Mind of Mencia*, and *In Living Color* are representational evidence of this negotiation.

The stand-up comics following the crossover generation were charged with creating a different type of multimedia appeal. With the advent of social media, stand-up comics gained visibility not only from television and film but increasingly from an online presence through YouTube excerpts of their acts spread through Facebook, Twitter, and Google+. Whereas crossover has typically meant performing as a character in a sitcom or a comedy movie, contemporary stand-up comedians also traverse formats, translating their live comedy shows to online video platforms. Videos like these, which are often circulated without the consent of the performer, were the subject of Chris Rock's ire when he told *The Daily Show* host Jon Stewart that YouTube made it difficult for him to craft and workshop new material because his acts immediately land on YouTube, whether or not they are ready for a mass audience.[29] At the same time, contemporary popular press literature on starting a stand-up career often urges potential comics to watch stand-up on YouTube to learn from previous generations of comedians and to post videos of comedy club performances on the social networking site in hopes of gaining "viral" circulation.[30] In contrast to the television and film crossover appeal necessary for 1980s and 1990s comics to gain footing in the media industry, comedians like Aries Spears, Kevin Hart, Russell Peters, Gabriel Iglesias, and Hannibal Burress have had to focus on online crossover appeal.

Given stand-up comedy's history of challenging and resisting cultural messages of white supremacy, the steadily increasing necessity for crossover performances is problematic. Specifically, as I discussed in the previous chapter, television has not been historically friendly to overtly political messages, and, as I discuss in the following section, social media can be a toothless platform for structural political change.[31] This online context is an important consideration in the study of contemporary antiracist stand-up comedy, since YouTube is a common platform for viewing these comedians' messages about racial resistance. Historical stand-up performances often circulate via YouTube's platform in contemporary US culture, with videos featuring comedians like Pryor, Rock, Chappelle, and Lopez gaining thousands of views, even, in Pryor's case, years after the comic's death.

YOUTUBE AND RHETORICS OF RESISTANCE

Like many social media platforms, the YouTube context offers users both video content and comment sections as spaces for circulating discourses of resistance. Flying in the face of YouTube's invitation to "broadcast yourself" is the fact that the bulk of YouTube's content represents video created by the media industry.[32] However, even within the constraints of the Google-owned site, users often enact rhetorical resistance through the practice of resharing counterhegemonic content that previously circulated through platforms like television and film. Drawing from Kent Ono and John Sloop's conceptualization of vernacular rhetoric, Guo and Lee assert that a specific YouTube vernacular must consider users' enactments of "pastiche" by repurposing "fragments or 'scraps' from hegemonic discourse to construct subjectivities," in this case, uploading bits of institutional media that have been cut or "mashed up" by the uploading user.[33] This is particularly common among social movement formations on YouTube, with users circulating informational resources developed by mainstream media producers.[34] For many users, YouTube is "more like TiVo than like Facebook," as YouTube users most often search for content created by traditional media sources.[35] It is possible to imagine that these institutional searches favor hegemonic media messages, but these searches also include progressive or resistant media content. The idea that YouTube users use the site to seek out institutional messages, then, does not foreclose the possibility of using the site for progressive purposes, since institutionally circulated messages can be framed for resistant purposes by individual uploaders.

Whether YouTube users are enacting resistance through user-generated content or through repurposed fragments of institutionally created media, YouTube serves as a site for creating and maintaining a sense of community and communal identity. YouTube's potential for creating collective social identity lies in the availability of videos across geographic space. The individual practice of watching a video, particularly a funny one, offers a space of identification between listener/viewer, uploader, and others who use comments to publicly decode the video's content; the context makes room for users to feel "in on the joke." Individuals isolated across space and time, then, gain a sense of community by participating in the shared decoding practices within the YouTube platform. For pre-existing communities, too, humorous videos allow users to circulate inside jokes throughout friend groups, building intimacy through laughter. As a community shares various videos along its networked connections, users within those communities are exposed to curated, shared content, which has the potential to further bond the community through shared messages. When these communities bond around messages of resistance, this communal function is particularly politically salient.

Humor not only plays an important role in building online communities and in circulating intimacy within offline communities but also contributes to the successes and failures of particular media clips on the site, taking on a disciplinary role in YouTube resistance. Skeptical of YouTube's potential for facilitating communal resistance, Aaron Hess notes that YouTube users tend to approach the platform as a "medium for entertainment and play rather than deliberation and resistance."[36] A great deal of political information and deliberative content exists on the medium, but YouTube users primarily turn to the medium as an entertaining distraction rather than for a political education; hence the unofficial mantra of the site, "LOL or leave."[37] The most potent political messages on YouTube, then, are those that adeptly use comedy to advance a political position, thereby bypassing the disciplinary mechanism of comedy by absorbing it into their political message.

Messages of resistance on YouTube that fail to garner significant communal support become less relevant within search results and therefore more difficult to uncover. This process works alongside the threat of copyright violation to function as a comic gatekeeper along two disciplinary mechanisms. First, YouTube's feedback system, which allows listeners/viewers to offer "thumbs up" or "thumbs down" ratings for a particular video, feeds into the site's system of referral. This process casts users as "wire editors" who determine which videos are recommended to other users and which rarely surface.[38] Second, YouTube's comment function allows users to discipline one another through short messages below the video content. These comments reproduce broader social disciplinary mechanisms, often judging videos against normative notions of identity performance including gender and race. In other words, comment sections can be spaces in which nonnormative content is often policed through aggressive or dismissive comments to uploaders and other commenting users. Crucially, these forms of disciplinary action are unlikely to impact videos that are not sought out in the first place. Therefore, videos that circulate under the radar of mainstream YouTube users may go unnoticed and, consequently, undisciplined, allowing community-specific messages of resistance to survive the site's filtering processes.

In many cases, comment sections on YouTube videos offer important insight into the polysemic quality of messages circulated on the site, whether those messages are intended as humorous, political, or both, resisting the notion that YouTube comments are entirely or even primarily disciplinary. The ambivalent nature of YouTube's comment sections poses challenges for fully understanding the site's facilitation of online community.[39] For videos that emphasize racialized communities, Elaine Chun argues, comment sections can create spaces in which listener/viewers can "experience an interpretive multiplicity across its disparate audience."[40] In other words, commenters leave traces of their decoding processes, thereby modeling hegemonic, negotiated, or resistant viewing positions.[41] YouTube comment areas can thus be understood as spaces of performative production and consumption. In these spaces, agreement and disagreement are on display, demonstrating dissent within YouTube's institutional space.

As a location for circulating various cultural and social rhetorics, YouTube is politically ambivalent, requiring a great deal of negotiation from users with messages of resistance. On one hand, it offers a potential space to facilitate conversations necessary for deliberative democracy. On the other, it always contains the threat of reproducing and recirculating the same types of disciplinary mechanisms at work in other institutionalized and hegemonic communicative practices. For messages of resistance to survive, then, uploaders and commenters must collaboratively navigate limitations of discipline. One of the most successful strategies of negotiating this situation is through comedy. Previous research has shown YouTube's greatest potential to be in the area of political humor.[42] Indeed, the power of Black and Latinx stand-up comedy on YouTube is likely due to the site's privileging of humor as a mechanism of resistance.

In the following sections, I explain how Black and Latino stand-up comedians on YouTube use voice to carve out distinct conceptions of whiteness, categorizing whitevoice as a complex and ambivalent combination of privileged, silly, threatening, and, above all, funny.[43] I discuss each of these issues in turn, paying particular attention to the many similarities that emerged across the somewhat diverse body of texts. First, I argue that whiteness is framed as privilege through a combination of explicit identification of privilege alongside an implicit performance of formal vocal training as a component of whitevoice. Second, I examine how the white speaking body is constructed as vernacularly and physically silly, as comedians position the bodily and vocal movements of their white characters in opposition to the comedian's "cool" demeanor. Third, I examine the use of these strategies to address a fear of whiteness (and white fear) in communities of color, as comedians deconstruct the threat of white violence by regendering whiteness as feminine. I conclude by examining these performances as resistance to and reaffirmation of particular combinations of stereotypes, and, perhaps more importantly, participatory spaces for communally shaping the rhetoric of race and gender through the institutional mode of YouTube vernacular.

VOICING PRIVILEGE

Incorporating whitevoice into stand-up comics' routines questions white privilege covertly, through situational jokes rather than through direct accusation or argument. Occasionally, privilege is named directly, as in Kevin Hart's "Rich White Dude Laugh" or Chappelle's white banker, both specifically described as wealthy. More often the privileged nature of the white character is enthymematic. When Richard Pryor compares how white and Black families eat, for example, he observes that white families eat quietly and politely compared with the Black family who lick plates and bowls clean, exclaiming "there's meat in there" and chiding the children for "throw[ing] shit away [because they've] been eating with their white friends." Implying that white families are privileged enough to waste food, Pryor asks audiences to fill in the gaps in his argument by drawing a line of economic disparity between white and Black families.

Comics also designed their white characters to demonstrate privilege by discussing their priorities. When Steve Harvey's white person loses his job, he asks, "What about the children's college fund?" When the Black character is fired, on the other hand, his only concern is for the paycheck he is owed for that week's work. Here, white characters are marked as saving money, while Black characters focus on one paycheck at a time. Further marking privilege and difference, Harvey's Black worker expects to be fired. Even white teens in these sketches demonstrate privilege, as Aries Spears's white friend, aghast when Spears's mother demands that they clean up, exclaims, "She can't do that, man . . . She's violating your right to privacy." Spears's white character, like the other comics' white people, expects a level of entitlement foreign to the comics and their Black characters. Indeed, in these cases, Pryor, Harvey, and Spears react to the white characters with shock and disbelief, marking privilege as foreign and puzzling.

These jokes leverage vocal intimacy for their humor. As Brodie and others have noted, stand-up comedy is a genre of intimacy in which a performer speaks directly to the audience, replicating the communal process of sharing personal and familiar stories.[44] If the white characters' privilege is marked as unfamiliar, then it is unfamiliar not only to the comic who performs the role of disbelief but also to the audience who empathizes with, or at least understands, a context in which privilege is marked as separate from the comic's friends and family. To be "in on the joke," the audience must recognize how distant this type of white privilege is from the comedian of color. These white-voice impressions, then, reverse the typical use of vocal intimacy; rather than creating connection, comics use this particular performance of vocal identity to manufacture a lack of intimacy with white characters.

The performance of privilege extends beyond the language and situations these comics describe. As Greg Goodale notes, speech education has historically encouraged crisp consonant sounds in trained speakers.[45] Such "standardized" training functionally declares the sounds of whiteness "a non-accent."[46] Carlos Mencia demonstrates the link between whiteness and this type of speech education through his performance of whitevoice laughter. His line, "That was a good one," draws on previous media codes of wealth from excessively rich characters in movies like *Titanic* and stiffly refined butlers like the iconic Jeeves character. Like these prep-school-trained men, Mencia's white character laughs in a way that is coded as wealthy, as Mencia moves only his bottom lip and jaw, maintaining obvious visual control in a way that seems refined and highly

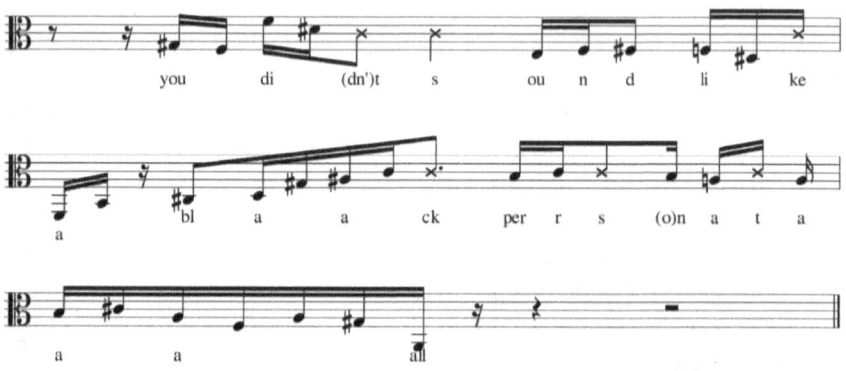

FIGURE 4.1. "You didn't sound like a Black person at all," Jay Walker.

trained in etiquette, and the phrase emphasizes an exaggeratedly crisp "t" at the end of "that" as well as clearly enunciated consonants throughout.

Pryor's character, too, uses exaggeratedly crisp diction, enunciating each consonant in the highly formal phrase "Are we having sexual intercourse this evening, darling?" Gabriel Iglesias's white woman asks, "Who's been on television?" drawing out the "z," "t," and "j" sounds (in "Who's" and "television," respectively). Jay Walker's white person, diagrammed in figure 4.1, even overtly comments on the association between whiteness and "proper English," noting, with exaggeratedly pronounced "s," "k," and "bl" sounds, "you didn't sound like a Black person [on the phone] at all." In these cases, the comic value of a whitevoice vocal identity comes in the form of disassociation. For Walker's bit, in particular, the joke of the routine is that his voice does not sound "Black"; instead, it simply sounds educated, proper, and well trained in clear speech diction, traits that Dyson notes are often considered oppositional to a Black masculine "cool" vocal identity.[47] Through the overly enunciated consonants in their whitevoice impressions, Pryor and Iglesias denaturalize the association with vocal diction and whiteness. Their exaggeratedly crisp enunciation exceeds the type of diction used by most speakers, even those on television and radio. However, since crisp diction corresponds with Dolar's "accent . . . declared a non-accent," its racial association is typically hidden.[48] By calling into question the naturalized association between proper speech and whiteness, then, these comics performatively challenge the ideological concept of a racial vocal identity.

These comics' communication of white privilege through vocal identity emphasizes difference between the comedians and their white characters, a move that sometimes emerges through specific regional accents rather than the subtler forms of privileged enunciation. When Mencia discusses white people's penchant for stalking and touching wild animals, he introduces the character as a generic white person, but uses Steve Irwin's (best known as Animal Planet's "The Crocodile Hunter") thick Australian accent. Likewise, Russell Peters's white person is actually a Canadian, Dave Chappelle's police officer speaks in a Boston dialect, and Gabriel Iglesias's white person declares his Scandinavian heritage. These accents stand in stark contrast to the accents the comics use in their typical stage personae. Mencia exaggerates the Mexican accent he uses in performances just before and after moving into his white character, and Chappelle increases his signature a-nasal quality prior to performing whitevoice to mark the differences between him and his white characters. In other words, these vocal identities do not simply read as white or privileged; they also read as different.

The difference that comedians communicate through exaggerated regional accents is also mirrored in the minutiae of their speech patterns. With Black comics, in particular, white characters are marked by the absence of African American English (AAE) dialect patterns that are exaggerated in the comics' standard performance personae; specifically, white characters exaggerate the long "ee" sound at the end of diphthong vowels and the "r" sound at the end of words, formations typically omitted in AAE.[49] First, white characters tend to use clearly demarcated vowels in diphthong formations like the "ah-ee" sound in the word "I." In the diagram in figure 4.2, for example, Chappelle's character, Chip, tells police, "I didn't know I couldn't [drag race]." In this excerpt, Chip gives equal weight to the "ee" sound as the "ah" sound, making Chappelle appear to "chew" on the sound as he pronounces it. This type of pronunciation is remarkable since, in the AAE dialect the comic typically uses, the "ee" sound would either be dramatically shortened or missing altogether.[50] Similar examples occur, too, when Harvey's white character says "for crying out loud" and when Pryor's character says "alright," since in both examples, the "I" sounds contain a dramatically elongated "ee" sound (figure 4.3).

FIGURE 4.2. "I didn't know I couldn't do that," Dave Chappelle.

FIGURE 4.3. "Alright cut the sh[it]," Richard Pryor.

Second, the "er" sound, which pulls the tongue to the back of the mouth in words ending with an "er" or an "or," is typically absent from AAE dialect but is foregrounded in many comics' whitevoice vocal identities.[51] The dialect pattern in Eddie Murphy's typical stage persona does not include the hard "er" sound at the end of words, as he instead softens the sound to a soft "uh" known as a schwa. When his white character, on the other hand, asks, "Why [are] those niggers in here," the "er" sound at the end of "nigger" lasts three times as long as any other consonant in the phrase. Chappelle, too, marks the difference between his AAE dialect and his white characters' speech patterns. When the white character addresses the police, he draws out the end of the word "officer," stretching the syllable across five discrete pitch movements and more than one-third of a second. Notably, the elongation of the "er" sound seems particularly affected, given that this sound is rarely a stressed syllable. Instead, the emphasis on the "r" sound must be performed as a way of differentiating the unvoiced "r" in AAE from the hypervoiced "r" in exaggerated impressions of the generic white person.

Given the importance of vocal intimacy to the formation of vocal identity, these comics' rejection of white privilege and reversal of AAE is important. Cultural disciplinary practices shape voices based on which kinds of sounds are culturally privileged and which kinds of sounds are culturally disciplined. As Mary Bucholtz and Qiuana Lopez note, the AAE dialect is often reduced to its most stereotypical form in mainstream media as a way of fetishizing Black characters, Othering Black culture, and dichotomizing Blackness and whiteness, a move that erases oppression by Latinx, Indigenous, and Asian Americans.[52] By exaggerating and stereotyping whitevoice vocal identities, these Black and Latino comics challenge the notion of whiteness as "normal" and contest whitevoice's position as "an accent that has been declared a non-accent."[53] Moreover, since these comics assert the linkage between whitevoice and white privilege by using their Black and brown bodies to perform whitevoice vocal identities, their impressions highlight the constructed nature of race. For audiences of AAE, immigrant, and other vernacular speech patterns, then, these whitevoice performances fly in the face of ideologies that dismiss and disparage AAE and immigrant accents, instead reframing vernacular speech patterns as one type of constructed vocal identity among many. Given that people of color more often achieve culturally privileged voices either through a "match" between the stereotyped visual body and the exaggerated dialect, or by performing whitevoice in an unmarked and naturalized way, these performances of whitevoice openly resist cultural privileging, instead choosing to invite vocal intimacy with their particular, often racially marginalized, audiences.

"COOL" BODIES, "COOL" VERNACULARS

In these impressions, white vocal identities are communicated not only through allusions to privilege but also through exaggerated differences in linguistic communication patterns. Specifically, through the use of "cool" vernacular phrasing and particular practices of naming, white characters are framed as both different and out of touch. Nicole Fleetwood argues that the concept of "coolness" has developed through performances of Black masculinity that draw from "racialized and masculine difference and diaphanous 'outlawness.'"[54] In other words, Dyson adds, the performance of "cool" is positioned as oppositional to rule-following practices that follow from "formal education and erudition."[55] Such performances translate to the use of language and sound, too. "Coolness" can be contrasted with white "nerd" culture to observe that communities marked by coolness often incorporate slang and other nonstandard English terms, differing from "nerd" culture, which tends to foreground "superstandard," or exaggeratedly correct English forms.[56] Formal English is not usually performed with the same kind of verbal exactness with which it is written; instead, English speakers shorten the word "them" to "mm" or "going to" to "gonna" in daily speech. Since, like Fleetwood, Bucholtz links the "coolness" of rule-breaking practices like slang with Black cultural patterns often appropriated by white US American teenagers, she argues that superstandard English represents a performance of exaggerated whiteness that is labeled as "nerdy" in mainstream culture.[57]

The comedians in this chapter marked whiteness as "nerdy" through the linguistic mechanisms of superstandard English, drawing punchlines from the contrast of the comedians' "cool" vocal identities and the whitevoice impression's "nerdy" English. During a dinner conversation, for example, Pryor's white character describes the food as smelling "scrumptious." This choice of word emphasizes linguistic exactness, contrasting words like "good" that more effortlessly integrate into casual spoken English. By choosing such a precise and unusual word, Pryor distances the white character's vocal identity from the slang he generally uses in performing his "cool" persona. Simultaneously, this odd word choice breaks the continuity of vocal intimacy, in which listeners/viewers are encouraged to settle into a storytelling scenario with Pryor via his typical vocal identity. Chappelle's white character, too, uses the odd phrase "close your butt cheeks" as a way of telling Chappelle to relax. This phrasing, in which white vocal identities resist the rule-breaking connotations of using a curse word, in this case substituting *butt* for the slang term *ass*, is reminiscent of previous generations of stand-up comedians like Jamie Foxx, Harvey, and Pryor. These comedians each use a string of misconstrued curse words to represent whiteness. Foxx's white person calls his Black peers "sons of bastards . . . those mother penises." When Harvey's white person is fired from his job, he responds with "for Pete's sake." Pryor's angry white person, too, exclaims, "cut the fucking crapola" and "come on, pecker head." In each of these cases, the comedians, who generally incorporate curse words into their acts, demonstrate a white vocal identity through a rigid adherence to the "rules" of linguistic decency. By failing to perform the "'outlawness'" of cool Black masculinity, these whitevoice identities are presented as nerds.[58]

The white vocal identities constructed by these stand-up comics often have the name equivalents of superstandard English, emphasizing the rigid and repetitive rule-following of bourgeois culture as it is typically associated with whiteness. The use of these very standard names marks white characters as generic and monolithic, allowing these comics to reverse stereotypes that paint all Black or Latinx people as Other, often through stereotyped discussions of "Black names" like "Jamelle, LaShonda, . . . [and] LaShaniqua" or "Latina/o names" like "José," which have been shown to contribute to racist, discriminatory hiring practices.[59] These comics resist the Othering practices mapped onto stereotypical Black and Latinx names by ridiculing "normal" names through implication. Eddie Griffin, for example, uses a number of "white" names including "Steve," "Jim," "Phil," and "Bob," the last of which is also present in both Aries Spears's and Harvey's routines. Additionally, Harvey positions "Bob" as friends with "Tom" and "Becky," but names his Black characters "Willie Turner" and "Willimena."

In the Latino comics' cases, so oblivious are these white characters that they are not even able to understand the names of people of color in the sketch. George Lopez's white character mispronounces the name "Soccoro" to sound like an amalgam of "soccer" and "oh," converting the Spanish name into an Anglicized combination of English words. Racist rhetorics often use a rubric of "speaking English" to justify violence and aggression toward immigrant communities, particularly those from Central and South America. These Latino comics, then, deploy whitevoice vocal identities to turn the tables on white supremacy, instead demonstrating white characters as unable to phonetically and linguistically meet expectations. Gabriel Iglesias's white person, as well, mispronounces the Spanish word *flaco*, which Iglesias has written on his name tag. Iglesias' whitevoice vocal identity includes a pronunciation of the word with a long "a" sound and a pronunciation of the "ck" sound that pushes air forward in a more typically English pronunciation rather than the Spanish pronunciation that moves to the back of the mouth in a way more similar to the English "g" sound. In each of these cases, part of the routine's comedy comes from audience knowledge of racialized naming practices. The use of these generic names as white, and the exaggeratedly mispronounced Latinx names and nicknames, contributes to the comics' jokes only if the audience accepts the premise that white names are boring and that white people are culturally ignorant.

This type of joke implicitly positions the audience and the speaker in agreement about the racialization of sounds as they relate to naming practices. Names like Willie and Socorro not only speak to stereotypes about naming practices linguistically; they also specifically showcase particular pronunciation associated with racialized dialects. Steve Harvey's "Willie," for example, allows him to play up the liquid vocalization of the "l" sound, a standard trait in AAE.[60] As Lisa Green's authoritative text notes, a marked feature of AAE dialect is the fluidity of the "l" sound, which, when followed by a vowel sound at the end of a word, softens that vowel sound. Harvey's pronunciation of the name, indeed, ends in a softened "i" sound (as in "pill") rather than an elongated "ee" sound (as in "tree").[61] "Willie," then, is racialized not only through stereotypes about which types of names belong to Black characters but also through Harvey's vocal identity, including pronunciation in a racialized dialect. Likewise, Lopez's Latino character, Socorro, foregrounds an "r" sound within the word, which would be trilled in Spanish or Chicano English.[62] Just as "Willie" was racialized by its AAE pronunciation, "Socorro" is racialized through Lopez's vocal identity, including the structure of the name's pronunciation. At the same time, the subtle differences in pronunciation of these names are not immediately legible to listeners with different dialects, a point illustrated by Lopez's white character's mispronunciation of "Socorro." Even as the comics use whitevoice vocal identity to discourage intimacy with whiteness, then, they simultaneously use these names to invite vocal intimacy by embedding the familiarity of dialect communities in their characters. Vocal intimacy, then, reinforces an in-group connection between audience and speaker by limiting the accessibility of the jokes within particular dialect communities, rather than aiming for the larger audience of culturally privileged voices.

Vocal-identity differences are also emphasized by comics through the use of nonlinguistic vocalizations, as a number of comedians incorporate unusual or elongated vocal sounds into their whitevoice identities. These nonlinguistic sounds frame whiteness as "nerdy" and out of touch by referencing the stoic self-control implicit in performances of masculinity. As Mark Anthony Neal notes, contemporary Black masculinity is dependent upon the performance of hypermasculinity and heterosexuality.[63] This performance relies on avoiding any trace of queer sexuality, often projected as excess in bodily movements and speech.[64] Put another way, heterosexual hypermasculinity only works when bodily excesses are restrained and controlled. This type of queer excess is present in whitevoice identities through uncontrolled extralinguistic vocal expressions. In an example that crosses into the discussion of strange ways of cursing, Russell Peters uses imitation to argue that white people "sound like donkeys" when swearing. Moving from a higher pitch to a lower pitch, much like a donkey's "ee-aw" bray, Peters mimics white people saying "fuck off" and "bullshit" before moving into full-fledged donkey sounds (figure 4.4). In Peters's impression, whitevoice vocal identities reject the notion of physical restraint and control to such an extreme degree that the performance ceases its masculinity and instead takes on the form of animalistic excess.

FIGURE 4.4. "Fuck off," Russell Peters.

Nonlinguistic sounds are not only reserved for the paralanguage of particular vocal identities; they also appear in the presence of bodily excess through strange uses of the vocal body. Both Chappelle and Hart incorporate audible smacks and clicks into their whitevoice impressions, with Chappelle's character using three lip smacks after discussing "vegetables" and Hart's white person building up for a particularly bad "joke" about staplers with an "ahm," a click of the tongue, and an elongated "ss" sound in the word "so." Another of Chappelle's white vocal identities incorporates a nearly half-second-long "ff" sound in the midst of a half-second's worth of an "oh" syllable as he leads up to speaking with police officers (figure 4.5), and Eddie Griffin's white person peppers his greeting with several audible "hh" sounds. Gunn calls utterances like these "uncontrolled speech," arguing that "controlled, measured speech is masculine and betokens a mastery of the passions. Uncontrolled speech is feminine and represents the anarchy of the body."[65] By sonically regendering their white male vocal identities, these comedians effectively queer whiteness. In contrast to their own masculine performances, the whitevoice performance of linguistic excess allows the comedians to become a proverbial "straight man," in terms of both comedy roles and sexuality, and they position the white character as a queer foil to their heterosexual masculinity.

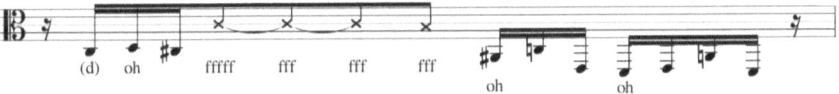

FIGURE 4.5. "Oh, oh, oh," Dave Chappelle.

The emphasis of whitevoice on particular enunciative sounds links back to the vocal identity issues of white privilege I discussed earlier. White privilege is associated with vocal training, either formally or informally, through access to education designed to build crisp consonants and clearly articulated diphthongs. Performed in an earnest and naturalized way, this type of speech is often a component of a culturally privileged voice. Instead, here this performance is taken to extreme lengths as a way of distancing "superstandard" vocal identity from the cool vernacular space occupied by the comics. Whereas whitevoice privilege relies on particular forms of articulation to demonstrate its training and fitness for advantages like employment and education, in Black and Latino stand-up comedy, such performances mark white vocal identity as alien and unable to adapt to the appropriate surroundings.[66] The emphasis on "coolness," in this case, additionally emphasizes the mechanics of vocal intimacy. Critical cultural vocalics asserts that vocal intimacy structures vocal identity through the media's framing of which experiences of intimacy are desirable and which are not. In this case, normative media notions that advance what is here articulated as whitevoice diction are overturned. In the context of these stand-up performances, markers of whitevoice are taken to their extremes to demonstrate the ridiculousness that can result from vocal-identity components like consonant overarticulation. In short, these performances use the markers desirable within white culturally privileged voices and, through their "cool" persona, mark whitevoice as an undesirable, unwelcomed, foreign sound.

The foreignness reflected by extralinguistic vocal sounds also emerges in white characters' strange physical movements, a feature that, like vernacular and naming practices, reverses white stereotypes about Black physicality by framing Black movements as normative and white movements as odd. When Hart's "rich white guy" "laughs," for example, Hart is nearly silent, emphasizing the jerking movement of his head from side to side and his exaggeratedly wide smile, and this head movement is mirrored in Peters's character, who, as the comedian describes him, "looks like [he's] part bobblehead when [he's] saying stuff to you." The jerking movement of white characters' heads takes on a disciplinary bent as both Pryor's and Chappelle's characters move their heads to indicate that the Black person has cut in line in front of them, in Pryor's case, or that Chappelle's attempt to scare the white person was inappropriate. Stereotypes of people of color often attempt to reduce Black women and men to their bodies, using an emphasis on corporeality to undercut Black movements for intellectual and economic equality.[67] These comics reverse such representations by attaching exaggerated physical movements to their white characters where it is limited in the stand-up comics' typical stage personae.

The contested ground in conversations of racialized physical movement often unfolds through discussions of refinement and hierarchy, areas that are challenged through white impressions that uplift Black vernacular while mocking generic whiteness. In Eddie Murphy's "White People Can't Dance" video, for example, Murphy's Black characters have visited a white club to mock the white characters' dance move, a single repeated step that later became known as "The Carlton" when Alfonso Ribeiro repeatedly performed it on *The Fresh Prince of Bel-Air*. This progression links the dance not simply with whiteness but with an out-of-touch, "nerdy," upper-class vocal rhetoric. Indeed, in *The Fresh Prince of Bel-Air*, Ribeiro's dancing is used to position his character Carlton as a nerd foil to Will Smith's coolness, pointing to the role of class in demarking levels of privilege and oppression within and between racial groups. Often accompanied by Tom Jones's "It's Not Unusual," a song marked by the singer's whiteness within *The Fresh Prince's* typically hip-hop soundtrack, the Carlton dance was generally met with looks of disdain and judgment by Will Smith as a way to illustrate Smith's superior sexual and masculine prowess. In Murphy's performance of the dance, too, the comedian demonstrates the move's ties to nerd culture by making an exaggeratedly happy face to break an important rule of Black masculine cool: stoicism.[68] In this way, whiteness is marked as oppositional to the "cool" persona that Murphy projects throughout the rest of his act as he uses the physical performance of his body to emphasize the resistant whitevoice vocal identity.

The comic strategy of aligning exaggerated physicality with whiteness and class privilege extends beyond visually physical movements to incorporate corporeal affectation in vocal production. Just as comics use shifting vernacular to emphasize difference between their typical vocal identities and their white characters, they also use a dramatic shift in vocal "grain" to differentiate their established vocal identities from whitevoice.[69] Since stand-up shows involve a near-constant verbal performance, audiences become accustomed to the grain of a comedian's typical vocal identity. Comics like Chappelle and Pryor, who normally speak with a flattened soft palate and slightly closed-off nasal passages, present their listeners with a sharp, cutting vocal identity, whereas Murphy and Harvey tend to speak with a deeply resonant tone produced by opening the nasal passages as if to yawn. To emphasize the level of internalized difference from their conceptions of whiteness, then, these comics reverse their typical speech formations, with Chappelle and Pryor using a much more open head space for their white characters' vocal identities and Murphy and Harvey flattening their palates and blocking off air from resonating in the sinus cavity to create a nasal sound.

In performing whiteness, then, these comedians rearrange the normative positioning of their vocal organs. If, as Barthes asserts, the movements of the vocal body foster attachment between speaker and listener, the dramatic rearranging of vocal movement in these comics' performances of whiteness creates a fissure or dissociation where intimacy had previously been formed.[70] In simpler terms, such a shift is jarring. These comics can be understood as forming a vocally intimate relationship with the audience before introducing a new and unexpectedly different vocal identity into the mix. Where a Black or Latinx identity had been socially constructed as Other, this new (white) vocal identity now intrudes as the outsider. Strategically, each of these comics has developed a vocal identity of "coolness," marking themselves—and Black or Latinx heritage—as hip, laid-back, and contemporary within their typical vocal identities. By distancing their bodily performances of dance and speech from their whitevoice characters, then, these comics distance their contemporary appeal from whiteness, reframing whitevoice as an intentionally discarded vocal identity.

WHITENESS AND THE GENDER OF FEAR

In the clips I analyzed, comedians of color often explicitly discussed issues of racism and violent expressions of white supremacy, a commentary that came either through a discussion of white behaviors or through the performance of whiteness itself. First, many comedians used their stand-up routines to address issues of white-supremacist violence and fear in Black and Latinx communities. Framing a scene in which his white friend speaks to police, Chappelle notes that fear of white police brutality is "a big part of our culture," and Foxx responds to a white comment about violence in the Black community by saying, "Damn, what [white people] did to Rodney [King] was kinda violent too, right?" Three different comics also describe situations in which white people kill or attack them: Murphy would be "killed" by an Italian who "got . . . so amped up" from watching *Rocky*; Chappelle could be killed by police who cover up their crime by "sprinkl[ing] some crack on him"; and Griffin mimes being tackled by authorities when he tries to "run through the airport" like O.J. Simpson. In each of these instances, comedians use the context of a white vocal identity to bring to light the legacy of physical violence driven by white supremacy.

Second, comedians incorporated particularly threatening racial slurs into their whitevoice impressions. When Murphy's white character sees a group of Black men at a primarily white dance club, for example, the character asks, in a whitevoice vocal identity, "Why are those niggers in here?" One of Chappelle's white characters orders him to "get away from my cart, nigger," and Mencia's white person responds to Mexican immigrants by saying, "Why don't you niggers go back to where you came from?" Rock even includes a bit in which he jokes that white people can only use the word *nigger* during a very particular (and unlikely) circumstance, but eventually Rock's white character exclaims, "catch that nigger." In these cases of whitevoice performance, comedians used their white vocal identities to embody a particular, threatening form of whiteness through an elongated "er" sound. On one hand, this performance denotes what can be understood as a poor white Southern US American speaker, an identity stereotypically, if perhaps unfairly, associated with racism and violence.[71] Simultaneously, the strong pronunciation differentiates the AAE term *nigga* from the white-supremacist slur *nigger*. Not only did these stand-up routines highlight a form of white-supremacist violence that has historically resulted in evils like lynching, but the whitevoice impressions did so by actually embodying the white threatening body through their purposeful inclusion of and regionally affected performance of the "er" sound. Through this tiny syllable, these comedians use an embodiment tactic that echoes that of the *Saturday Night Live* impersonators I discussed in the previous chapter. Like Tina Fey in her interpretation of Palin's interview text, these comedians map a foreign body onto their own vocal organs, replicating the disturbing violent imagery associated with this particularly violent racial slur.

By mapping the white threatening body onto their own bodies, Black and Latino comedians took on the role of puppet master, and they used this role to soften the threatening whitevoice by feminizing it. Although some typically higher-voiced comedians like Pryor and Chappelle lowered the pitch of their voice to perform whiteness, nine of thirteen comics raised their vocal pitch into feminized ranges.[72] More notably, many of the comedians used a widely and quickly fluctuating pitch range, similar to the patterns that Fey used in her impersonation of Palin, to map femininity onto their white vocal identities. For example, whereas Spears's vocal pitch moves very little in introducing his white friend, the friend's vocal identity immediately shoots up and down more than a full octave in the first second, a pattern that repeats in his second phrase. In this case, Spears's friend is considering talking back to Spears's mother, and the comedian's whitevoice pitch range emphasizes the friend's relative weakness in comparison to the family matriarch (figure 4.6).

FIGURE 4.6. "[D]ude, what the fuck? She can't do that, man. This is your space," Aries Spears.

Foxx also characterizes his white audience member, called out for being the sole white person in the front few rows, as feminine, moving his pitch not only a good deal higher than Foxx's normal pitch but also more quickly up and down the scale, demonstrating an affected but transparent toughness in his phrase "Yea, I came to the front. What's up? So what?" Fearing Black uprisings in 1990s Washington, DC, Chappelle's white family is afraid to travel to DC from Virginia, and the father's pitch moves dramatically when he notes that it is "not yet" safe to leave Virginia. And, finally, Murphy's white people slide up and down the staff when, after watching *Rocky*, they gullibly exclaim "Hey! This is real!" In these examples and others, comedians used a feminized pitch range to soften the threat of violent white supremacy that they illustrate earlier in their acts. In doing so, they demonstrate that, although these white characters used threatening language, they were actually hierarchically subordinate to the comedians because of their feminine status. Thus, the whitevoice character might attempt to physically threaten the comic, audience members of color, and members of the Black and Latinx communities, but comedians' pitch patterns demonstrate that these threatening vocal identities are actually weak, vulnerable, and, in essence, feminine.

Employing feminized speech patterns to disarm threatening white bodies offers a coping mechanism that simultaneously displaces issues of gender hierarchy. On one hand, these comedians offered spaces to raise issues of fear and pain that historically and contemporarily shape the rhetoric of Black and Latinx identity in US American culture. By drawing these issues to the fore, these comedians give voice to what Deborah Walker King calls "the culture of black pain" while using comedy and laughter to provide emotional release.[73] At the same time, the linkage between femininity, weakness, and silliness reinscribes hierarchies of gender and sexuality even as it attempts to dismantle racial inequalities. Spears's character above, for example, positions the Black matriarch as a threat to his own whiteness within the discursive space of stand-up comedy, one of the most persistently antifemme spaces in popular culture. Commenting on the comparisons often drawn between Whoopi Goldberg and Eddie Murphy in the 1980s, Haggins writes that, within the stand-up context, "the audaciousness of the male's content is viewed differently from that of a female's—with greater license being granted to the former in terms of being as 'nasty as you want to be.'"[74] What is rightly seen as revolutionary resistance by Black and Latino male comics is frequently inaccessible for women of all races. This is particularly clear in the instance of whitevoice performances, which use feminization to render whiteness laughably innocuous. In these performances, it is not only the whiteness but also femininity that transform white violence from threat to punchline. To perform these whitevoice impressions as a woman stand-up comedian, then, would be to present your own gendered identity, the racialized femininity that remains a stubborn block to career success in the comic realm, as the butt of the joke. Comics like Goldberg, Wanda Sykes, Monica Palacios, and Margaret Cho have all performed jokes in resistance to white supremacy. They perform them effectively and from their own standpoint rather than with the voice and body of caricatured femininity.

Not only does the feminization of whiteness in these acts use sexism to advocate for antiracism, already a double bind for women of color in audience and industry; it also furthers stand-up comedy's persistent homophobia. When these Black and Latino men perform feminized whiteness, they not only perform women; they also perform queerness. Sexuality, like other axes of identity, is not biologically linked to particular vocal-identity patterns. Still, listeners often understand conflicting visual and vocal gender performances as representative of queerness: men who speak with stereotypically feminized vocal speech patterns, and women with lower, narrower pitch ranges, are often heard as gay.[75] In performing femininity as oppositional to their stoic, masculine "cool" personae, these comics disarm their whitevoice characters not only by attributing feminine characteristics to them but also, simultaneously, by depicting them as queer. This vocal disparagement of both femininity and queerness functions in much the same way as racial triangulation; latching on to some accepted norms of cultural domination, in this case sexism and homophobia, appears to offer a way of moving subgroups such as straight men of color up the ladder of privilege. However, as Claire Jean Kim points out, this type of horizontal violence cements the power of those at the top of the intersectionally oppressive hierarchy.[76] Rather than a form of sustainable, communal resistance, such performances of feminized degradation maintain previous relations of violence like those the whitevoice impressions seek to dismantle in the first place.

If the process of vocal intimacy works with disciplinary mechanisms to frame particular speech patterns as more desirable than others, then these comedians' attempts to uplift Black and Latinx vocal identities are undercut by the political project of disparaging speech forms associated with femininity and, when performed by an apparently male comic, queerness. In other words, they uplift their own voices as culturally privileged voices at the expense of their queer and women-of-color peers. Illustrating this through absentia, this chapter does not include any women stand-up comedians because none were returned by my YouTube search.[77] Such an issue is likely a combined result of YouTube's aggregate "thumbs up" and "thumbs down" system reflecting YouTube users' disinterest in women comedians across races, a tendency for

Black women comedians not to engage in performances of white vocal identities, and the fact that women are often not welcomed in the comedy arena generally.

BUILDING INTIMACY

The manipulation of vocal identity central to these comics' performance of gendered whitevoice drives participatory vocal intimacy through YouTube's comment space. Stand-up comedy is a particularly intimate genre, built on the assumption of shared experiences between speaker and audience. This type of intimacy is documented in the comment areas of the YouTube videos I examined. As may be expected in comments from fans who have sought out and watched videos of their favorite comedians, comments often praise the comics generally. Alonzo Lockhart and Billie Brunson call Kevin Hart the "best comedian ever" and note "lol love him," respectively.[78] Ravi Parekh calls Gabriel Iglesias "such a good impressionist," and Clinton Cota comments, "I love Dave Chappelle. Great comedian."[79] More than simply speaking to general fandom and admiration, these listeners'/viewers' comments illustrate the way that the sounds of comedy impressions invite intimacy by allowing audiences to hear themselves in the comedy performances. As I explore in this section, nods to vocal intimacy are woven through fan responses in the YouTube comment sections of the comedy clips I analyzed in this chapter.

Stand-up comedy plays on a timeless strategy of storytelling as a way to build vocal intimacy between speaker and audience. Through the comedians' aural narratives, listeners/viewers are invited to hear their own histories in the comedians' jokes, both through the familiar sounds of their friends and family members and through the sounds of stories that ring true for audiences who share backgrounds similar to those of the comedians' characters. First, YouTube commenters recognized themselves and their family and friends in the clips they viewed. Referencing Iglesias's bit about being drunk at his high school reunion, Skerdy remarked, "WHAT THE FUCK?! Is he trying to make an impression of me when drunk, and if so, how does he knows [sic] me?! Something is fishy here . . ."[80] Similarly, responding to Aries Spears's comparison of African Americans and Black Africans, Ladu AU laughed, "his African voice sounds just like my dad . . . lol."[81] In these comments, it is not only intimacy or familiarity that is referenced but specifically the sound of the vocal identity. In a comment about Carlos Mencia's white characters who wave at cars when they drive by before trying to figure out who is driving through their neighborhood, anniemomi17 commented, "Oh my gosh that's me. Haha."⁸² These comments situate impressions as the connecting tissue between these clips' humor and the vocal intimacy solicited by the stand-up genre. For these commenters, the comedy emerged, at least in part, from the familiarity of the comic's vocal sound and physical performance. Vocal intimacy here is formed not only through the connection between voice and ear but also through the repeated experience of hearing a similar voice in the audience's past experience.

Second, the relationship of vocal intimacy in these stand-up comics' routines is also supported by discussion of shared experiences explained through shared vernacular. Responding to Chappelle's association between Black children and "grape drink," for example, Firstblk notes, "This is funnier if you grew up in the hood in the 70s and 80s. In the hood most [households] never bought grape juice because it was too expensive, so they brought grape drink and a 10 cent pack of kool aid."⁸³ Here, the commenter offers a shared experience of poverty as a conduit for the video's humor and, importantly, does so by referencing the slang term *hood* and reiterating the vernacular label *grape drink*. Similarly, joining in Jamie Foxx's mockery of whiteness, DrAbstracked remarked, "Well im white n I remember da 90s most ppl I grew up around dat was white did curse.funny n couldnt dance for shit [sic]."⁸⁴ Taking the previous commenter's vernacular a step further, DrAbstracked uses phonetic spelling in his comment, replacing the "th" sound with a "d" sound, as is common in AAE forms.⁸⁵ Although written and not spoken, this commenter offers a map for trying on a vocal identity imagined to occupy the same experiential space as the comics' vocal identities. These voices are tied together by the shared performance space of the YouTube platform. By aligning humor, shared experience, and vernacular, these commenters assert their relationships with the comedians, identifying speaker and listener through both experiential commonality and sounds that identify the speaker's vocal identity with the listener's performance of written language.

This pattern of identifying with comedians' stories through shared vernacular occurred across the videos I studied. In a comment left on a different Chappelle video exploring differential treatment of Black and white citizens by police, CHEF ASHER addresses commenters who call Chappelle racist by exclaiming, "WHAT THE PROBLEM IS!. . YOU EITHER LAUGH OR CRY OR PICK UP A GUN, when treated this way. . as you can see we chose to laugh!"⁸⁶ As Green points out, this phrasing of "what the problem is" is, like the replacement of "th" with "d," a common marker of AAE.⁸⁷ Commenters on George Lopez's video about how Latinx mothers discipline their children similarly drew expressions of shared experience with shared vocal identities. Castle Coatl recalled his mother saying "that shit to me. I was crying listening to him," and r0413900 similarly remarked, "Wow memories my mom used to do that every time I did something bad in public. I got my ass whopped when we got home. Lol xD."[88] Phrasing like "said that shit to me" and "ass whopped" allows these commenters to enact their vernacular similarity with the comedians even as they express the ways that their upbringing aligns them with the comedians. As a performance of vocal intimacy, this alignment indicates how particular material circumstances shape the voice. A shared understanding of what a particular experience sounds like facilitates vocal intimacy by making a particular vocal identity seem commonsense and normative.

As these commenters spoke to their relationships with the comedians, they reported intimacy with the comedians rather than their whitevoice vocal identities, even in cases of white commenters like DrAbstracked. Indeed, the intimacy formed between audiences and comedians overwhelmingly preceded the commenters' interactions with the YouTube clip. Jason Fontaine shared, "I still have the original vhs somewhere . . . Both Delirious and Raw were a blast," and Heather Toll noted having seen the same Chappelle routine "so many times I've lost count. Still makes me crack up!"[89] Annette Jenkins similarly remembers watching Aries Spears on television, noting, "I loved him and Debra Wilson on MADTV," the comedian's sketch comedy series in the mid-1990s.[90] This ongoing fandom often stretched even further back. DALE7XCHAMP recollects seeing Eddie Murphy "do RAW at the Philadelphia Spectrum," dating their speaker–listener relationship back to 1987, and, like the comments I highlighted in the introduction to this chapter, many users fondly remembered early Black comedians like Richard Pryor.[91] These commenters illustrate the component of familiarity central to stand-up comedy's enactment of intimacy, a component that, in whitevoice vocal identities, is crucial to separating the in-group comedians from the Othered white characters.

The relationships of intimacy these fans had for their comedians extend beyond simply allowing them to interpret the comedians' whitevoice impressions, encouraging a community of understanding between speakers, listeners/viewers, and other members of marginalized groups. Commenters most often express these feelings of intimacy by referencing family members or friends in their comments. Beyond the several references to commenters' mothers, fathers, and friends, many YouTube users remembered listening to these comedians in a supportive communal environment.[92] Alongside the deeply intimate memories with which I opened this chapter, Greg Michaels recalls that after meeting Eddie Murphy thirty-two years before, "I went to school the next day told all my friends and no one believed me," Matt Ruth recollects watching Dave Chappelle "on CABLE back in 2000 when it came out," and Karen Ramos remembered "watching [Gabriel Iglesias's] CD's ever since I was little."[93] These comedians' voices are deeply woven into audience members' memories. These relationships emerge as a form of community that helps support the kinds of counterhegemonic missions that Haggins describes as a primary goal of stand-up for comedians of color.[94]

Through historical and contemporary references to the parallel experiences between these stand-up comics and their own lives, YouTube commenters demonstrated the powerful transgressive potential of whitevoice comedy for these male comedians of color. These comedians' use of stand-up's aural, public storytelling encourages relationships between speaker and listener that speak to the racially progressive intimacy that emerged through fans vehemently defending the character of the comedians in the videos. In the comments section for Dave Chappelle's "white People" video, for example, audience members speak to the comedian's socially progressive storytelling. TruthfullyRude, for example, wrote, "It's very clear [Chappelle] loves everybody and that he's a character driven by critical thinking and common sense . . . he's just an awesome guy," and Zanny Boy noted, "Dave Chappelle would be ashamed to see all this racist talk going on."[95] These comments and others demonstrate fans' sensitivity to the mission of racially transgressive stand-up and illustrate the intense intimacy that fans bring to viewings of these comics' whitevoice impressions. For comedians like Eddie Murphy, whose previous work pushed racial boundaries, fans bemoaned, "miss real Eddie. happy he's made his Disney money but i yearn for the return of real Eddie."[96] Finally, speaking to the trust that fans had for these comedians' progressive goals, marliatou Diallov wrote, "JAMIE FOXX IS OPENING HIS HEART TO ALL AMERICANS NO MATTERS [sic] THEIR COLOR AND RACES," and Peanut Butter and Jelly argued, "Richard Pryor's jokes come from his experiences . . . He turns the negatives into a positive."[97] These commenters' advocacy for the comics in the videos speaks to the ongoing closeness in the relationship between speaker and listener and supports Haggins's assertion that stand-up allows comics to "use the microphone as a weapon," veiling their criticisms in a format that encourages community and a sense of openness, at least for heterosexual male audiences.[98]

CONCLUSION

Stand-up comedy offers spaces for exploring marginalized identities through a contemporary form of public storytelling. This chapter demonstrates the additional ways that the voice, particularly as a performance of whitevoice, contributes to and at times conflicts with this political project. The comedians I studied used a whitevoice vocal identity to contest the naturalized privilege of whiteness. By enacting whitevoice as a foil for nonwhite performances of heterosexual hypermasculinity, these comics targeted issues of privilege and fear while framing vocal identities like AAE as culturally privileged and whitevoice as culturally devalued, nerdy, and pejoratively emasculated. Although this approach allowed comedians to both bring marginalized stories to the public eye and uplift Black and Latinx voices, it did so by feminizing whiteness, reinforcing sexist and homophobic ideologies, and reasserting hypermasculine ideals that limit the emotional expression of all men, especially men of color.[99]

The identity politics centralized in these comedians' performances were further encouraged by the YouTube platform through which they circulated. I suggest that the process of vocal intimacy occurred across two axes. First, the YouTube platform brought viewers'/listeners' historical experiences with the already intimate stand-up genre into a contemporary media environment. As YouTube commenters shared memories and stories about their experiences with these stand-up comics, they reinscribed feelings of intimacy with the comics as though they were sharing stories about old friends. In this way, the intimacy comedians create through their "performed autobiography" is mirrored by the performance of audience autobiography, and this dialogue becomes a documented part of the YouTube listening/viewing experience for future listeners/viewers, who often respond by sharing their own experiences of intimacy.[100] Vocal intimacy uses audiences' previous experiences of comic fandom as a foundation for current speaker–listener interaction. As I have argued throughout this chapter, the effectiveness of whitevoice as a punchline is dependent upon the audience's association and vocal intimacy with the comic rather than the white character. Such an association is reinscribed through the YouTube channel, allowing online viewers to connect transhistorically and across space.

Second, these comics rely heavily on listener/viewer understanding of dialects and slang commonly associated with Black and Latinx communities as well as the listeners' knowledge of the comics' standard vocal rhetorical form. In order to be "in on the joke," listeners must be aware of the comic's standard speech style to differentiate their normative vocal rhetoric from whitevoice vocal rhetoric. In this way, the vocally intimate relationship between speaker and listener builds the political project of challenging white normativity by creating a comfortable relationship between speaker and listener and then disrupting the vocal intimacy of that exchange through a sudden shift to whitevoice. In short, the comics frame their own voices as culturally privileged, at least in the performance space of the live audience. This type of framing strengthens the political project of Black and Latino stand-up comedians, since it takes what Dolar calls "an accent that has been declared a non-accent" and foregrounds its constructedness.[101] In this way, the cultural value of white-voice, assumed in a white-supremacist society to be the ideal speech sound, does not structure intimacy; instead, in this case, intimacy between Black and Latino comedy speakers and listeners structures the value of identity. These stand-up comics reverse the normative pattern of vocal identity and vocal intimacy by using familiarity and comfort as a counterhegemonic tool.

CONCLUSION

A Call to Listen

IN THIS BOOK'S case studies, I have demonstrated how feminist and critical race theory might be applied to rhetorically understanding the voice. This project is necessarily interdisciplinary in its theoretical and methodological grounding and intersectional in its understanding of systemic oppression and privilege. As a critical perspective on vocal sound, critical cultural vocalics pushes back against assumptions that voices are biologically sexed or naturally racialized to assert that the sounds of our speech are socially constructed. In other words, they are developed through a cyclical process of speaking and listening that is linked to other, more established systems of privilege and oppression including white supremacy and sexism. Critical cultural vocalics can be understood through two interrelated concepts: vocal intimacy and vocal identity.

First, vocal intimacy describes the interconnected physiological processes simultaneously at work in the bodies of speakers and listeners. Here, I build on Cavarero's assertion that the voice always points to a physical, live person: "It communicates the presence of an existent in flesh and bone; it signals a throat, a particular body."[1] This perspective echoes Barthes's concept of "the grain of the voice," an aural manifestation of Cavarero's speaking body, as movements in the speaker's mouth, chest, gut, and masses of spit and sinew throughout the speaker's body allow sound to be produced as a mechanism of rhetoric.[2] The grain allows a listener to "hear a body . . . as though a single skin lined the inner flesh of the performer and the music he [sic] sings."[3] Through the interior processes of listening, the speaker's "inner flesh" moves inside the listener, connecting the two in the process of speaking and hearing. The voice, then, must be understood as an active, aural body connected to other aural bodies through the intimate process of speaking and listening.

Between speaker and listener is a socially constructed decoding process. Cultural codes condition listeners and speakers to understand particular voices in particular ways through disciplinary mechanisms. Humor, for example, works as a disciplinary mechanism to train listeners to understand which types of voices are desirable and which are not. Early radio programming used the sounds of laughter to mark particular voices with an air of ridiculousness, and often these voices were simultaneously marked as emerging from nonwhite or immigrant bodies.[4] Early sound films continued this tradition, attaching silly, exaggerated voices to immigrants and other characters of color. Through media, then, the ethnically marked body was constructed as undesirable, at least in part through the ethnically marked voice, an effect that was compounded by its intersection with gender, sexuality, class, education, region, and other axes of oppression and privilege. Voices that emerge with the mark of undesirability are further characterized as unintelligent and otherwise unfit for public discourse, and these vocal stereotypes circulate broadly through media.[5]

Second, we translate our experiences as listeners into a particular performance of speech, or, as I have termed it here, "vocal identity." Ideologies of the voice are often built not from the literal body of the performer but from the cultural context that allows that performer's body to be interpreted. From the earliest sound-film synchronizations, cinematic conventions matched visually stereotyped Black bodies with vocally stereotypical traits like thick southern accents and softened or dropped consonants.[6] This audiovisual stereotyping concealed its ideological roots by implying that the mediated bodies and voices were naturally connected to one another, or—as is often assumed in our culture—that these voices were biologically predetermined. Additionally, the body speaks within particular material circumstances, which shape both the body and, by extension, the voice. Since the body is the voice's instrument, factors that shape the body also shape the voice.

Critical cultural vocalics begins from the assumption that the voice is an ideologically shaped extension of the body. As such, it is molded by the external forces of material and social pressure. As vocal intimacy solidifies the transmission of vocal identity, vocal identity simultaneously contextualizes and frames the process of vocal intimacy. Cyclically joined, these two co-constitutive processes function in tandem to define which types of voices are culturally privileged and which must be systematically disciplined. Judith Butler suggests that the body is shaped by material gendering processes.[7] Critical cultural vocalics argues that, similarly, material processes shape and reshape the voice. The resulting vocal sound is neither natural nor biologically predetermined but is instead socially constructed in terms of both production and reception. As a result, particular voices are marked as culturally privileged, based on widespread media circulation and consequent cultural familiarity. Since culturally privileged voices are not always attached to culturally privileged bodies, the study of voice allows scholars to better understand how particular bodies are expected to sound to the public ear writ large. Decoding this connection requires attention both to the types of sounds spoken by particular speakers and to the ways that those sounds elicit particular reactions from their audiences.

This book began as a way of concretizing a critical approach to studying the voice as a sonic component of rhetoric. By exploring the four case studies offered here, I demonstrated a series of theoretical tenets that together comprise critical cultural vocalics. In this section, I explore the implications of both theory and method in turn, emphasizing how vocal identity and vocal intimacy come together in the culturally privileged voice as one interlocking whole. The critical cultural vocalics I propose in this book includes four primary tenets: (1) voices are complex, (2) voices interact with media formats, (3) repetition structures vocal rhetoric, and (4) the voice is always ideological in terms of both identity and intimacy. I discuss each of these in turn.

The ubiquity of vocal sound in media and culture lends to the voice a degree of invisibility; since voices are everywhere and present in nearly every media artifact, they can blend into the fabric of our culture. It is easy to take the voice as a natural product of the body. As a primary tenet of critical cultural vocalics, however, I emphasize that vocal identities are incredibly ideologically complex and, therefore, must be taken seriously in critical analyses of cultural production and consumption. As my case studies demonstrated, the complexity of the voice demands an intersectional approach as well. The comedians of color that I studied, for example, advanced a transgressive vocal performance that unmasked the invisibility of whiteness in the voice, but at the same time, these comedians replicated oppressive hierarchies of gender and sexuality. Adele's performance of vocal racial passing shares aspects of these comedians' performance of transgressive vocal identities, but the meanings of Black women's blues sounds reflect complex circumstances of pain and resistance that may be glossed over by simply labeling Adele a vocal appropriator. Tina Fey's impression of Sarah Palin aimed to highlight the politician's shortcomings, but Fey's voice further entrenched the kinds of misogynist assumptions that block women of all races from being taken seriously in public sphere discourses. The propensity for the voice to function as a hidden ideological argument emerged repeatedly through this book's case studies, emphasizing the importance of taking the voice seriously as a technology of both marginalization and resistance. Each of these culturally privileged voices emanates from and embodies various complex contours of oppression and privilege; common to all is the consistent interaction of historical ideological rhetorics of identity. These culturally privileged voices therefore demonstrate how vocal identity often contains socially embedded messages about which speakers are fit for particular public arenas and which are not.

Moreover, media's increasing dominance in our lives plays an important role in the circulation of vocal identities, positioning itself as a primary gatekeeper for which voices are culturally privileged and as a defining mechanism in how these culturally privileged voices circulate. This tenet emerged in my analysis of Morgan Freeman through the specific ways that formats like direct address and voice-over encourage vocally intimate relationships. Furthermore, the actor's career demonstrated how particularly structured intimate relationships replicated hierarchical racial subordination. In Freeman's case, then, media's particular mechanisms circulated his voice in a way that undercuts his potential to be a truly progressive Black figure in his roles as president and God. On the other hand, YouTube's format allowed a collage of voices from comedians of color to push back against the same kinds of racial subjugation that I found in Freeman's performances. Rather than reinforcing the dominance of white supremacy represented in Freeman's deferent characterizations, these comedians foregrounded and challenged whiteness, a project that was supported by the propensity of YouTube's comment sections to document and describe vocally intimate relationships between these comics and their fans. The ambivalent nature of media's relationship with the voice is further emphasized by *Saturday Night Live*'s political impressions. Since television had already made Fey famous, her impression of Palin was viewed through a lens of the comedienne's popularity, whereas Obama's popularity controlled the direction of vocal intimacy with listeners/viewers of Armisen's, Johnson's, and Pharoah's impressions of the president. As these four case studies demonstrate, vocal intimacy relies heavily on the particular format of the media in question, marking technology as a key component in studies of the voice in culture. The concept of the culturally privileged voice is dependent upon media, as it requires that some voices are more broadly circulated than others. Taken together, these case studies mark the differences and similarities in distribution mechanisms from radio to film to digitally uploaded audio/visual artifacts.

As a partial explanation for the media's importance in vocal study, these case studies together demonstrate the importance of repetition in establishing culturally privileged voices. My discussion of *Saturday Night Live* illustrated the ways that the normative masculinity of presidential speech pushes feminine voices from the realm of the presidency. Here, general repetition of a particular type of vocal identity influences the types of voices that listeners are open to inviting into a vocally intimate relationship. This relationship between vocal identity and vocal intimacy is key to understanding the elevation of culturally privileged voices. For example, Morgan Freeman's vocal repetition demonstrates the propensity of the actor's vocal consistency to entrench his vocal identity as submissive. Why did Adele "sound Black" to so many listeners? In part because the vocal identity she performed has been attached to Black women's bodies, repeatedly, for the past century. Similarly, the stand-up comedians I studied performed transgressive whitevoice supported, at least in part, by their audience's familiarity with their normative stand-up performance voice. In each of these cases, repetition laid the groundwork for strong vocally intimate relationships. From this intimacy, vocal identity could be reinforced or manipulated to ideological ends. It stands to reason, then, that repetitive patterns of vocal sound serve as an underlying artifact important to the understanding of race and gender in the voice and the ways that these and other axes of identity combine in culturally privileged voices.

This type of repetition is also crucial since the voice can reinforce or challenge larger cultural notions of identity. Culturally privileged voices very often reinforce at least some traditional ideologies of identity and of how these identities are understood to sound. When considered as a culturally privileged voice, Morgan Freeman's speech demonstrates how history is layered into individual voices. For Freeman, the oppressive environment of the Jim Crow South emerged as a consistent dimension of the actor's vocal sound that replicated hierarchical racial power relationships. Although the actor's casting in subordinate roles also played a role in this dynamic, his voice continually and invisibly reinforced a context of white supremacy. Similarly, Armisen's vocally androgynous impression of Obama fell flat with *Saturday Night Live* audiences, when more traditionally masculine impressions by Pharoah and Johnson were more warmly received, again demonstrating the voice's potential to work with visual cues to maintain status quo ideas about the gender of the presidency. This book's stand-up comedy performances, too, similarly reinforced notions of femininity as weakness and impotence even as they demonstrated the potential for voices to transgress normative identity notions. As a bearer of cultural assumptions about identities, the voice is thus always ideological, either reinforcing cultural rhetorics about race, gender, and other attributes of intersectional identity or challenging those same symbols. Like other aspects of identity performance, vocal identity is never ideologically neutral.

Finally, just as vocal identity signifies particular identity characteristics, vocal intimacy, too, is always ideological. The familiar relationship between voice and ear always has the potential to recreate inequalities between speaker and listener. The vocal identity that Adele appropriated from Black women blues singers also allowed her to create an intense connection between singer and listener. The presence of the body in the music served both identity and the profitable component of vocal intimacy developed by Black women blues singers since the early twentieth century. In Freeman's case, speaker–listener vocal intimacy is directly shaped by the contours of a deferent, subordinate vocal identity. For *Saturday Night Live,* Fey's vocal intimacy with Palin contributed to a troublingly feminized vocal impression which, consequently, shaped the experiences of vocal intimacy between Palin and her listeners. In stand-up comedy, too, vocal intimacy demonstrates its potential for reproducing inequalities. Even as comedians pushed back against the dominance of whitevoice as "an accent that has been declared a non-accent," they simultaneously reproduced the types of gendered hierarchies that have maintained women's marginalization on the stand-up stage.[8] The relationship between listener and speaker, then, must be considered an essential component in the power dynamics marked within culturally privileged voices.

In addition to the tenets of this book's theoretical grounding, I used these case studies to explore the more practical procedures involved in studying the voice as a sonic artifact of oppression and privilege. One important intervention I demonstrated in this book is the use of Audacity to code and transcribe the spoken voice. Audacity allowed me to home in on the smallest units of vocal sound within my artifacts and then compare the resulting musical annotations with other vocal utterances from the same and different speakers. While visual transcription of voices has been used in sociophonetics, the highly specialized charts used to communicate findings are challenging and often contain a good deal of digital noise. Programs like PRAAT, for example, produce a series of dots and lines tracing the pitch movement of a voice over time. An important difference between this style of transcription and the musical annotation I proposed in this book is the utility of the transcription process in tracing the precise movement of individual words and sounds. In my analysis of comedians' whitevoice impressions, for example, I was able to identify the comedians' use of drawn-out, nonlinguistic sounds because the program allowed me to listen individually to each unit of the utterance. Furthermore, the musical notation system I used here allowed me to draw interdisciplinary conclusions about the transcriptions. In my analysis of Morgan

Freeman, the actor's voice emerged in the musical form of an ostinato. Such a description would be hidden by the line-graph format produced by sociophonetic studies of PRAAT. By employing the particular approach I used in this book, I have demonstrated the precision and adaptability of musical notation for the study of the spoken voice.

By using Audacity, I was also able to identify tiny movements in phonetic patterns within my larger media samples, and this attention to the phonetic component of vocal identity is a second intervention in terms of method. Attention to the phonetic pronunciations of the speakers in my case studies allowed me to identify historical and regional trends in speech patterns, and these vocal characteristics facilitated historical contextualization of particular ideological identities. My analysis of whiteness in stand-up comedy offers an example of this, as the African American and Chicano English dialects played an important role in defining both vocal identity and vocal intimacy; both the comedians and their commenters relied on racially associated dialect patterns to communicate their racial and cultural affiliations. Much of the body of literature on phonetic distinctions lies outside of rhetoric. Still, enough previous research regarding cultural phonetics has been gathered by sociophonetics to facilitate this type of examination within the discipline. As I have illustrated throughout this book, attention to phonetics is necessary to fully explore the contours of vocal identity.

Finally, I began this book by approaching the voice from the theoretical branches of vocal intimacy and vocal identity. These dimensions proved to be particularly helpful in breaking down the methodological challenges that emerge in the study of something as abstract as vocal sound. By breaking down each artifact in terms of vocal identity and vocal intimacy, this study has demonstrated these theoretical dimensions as a useful way of approaching the voice. For future studies of the voice, I suggest that thinking in terms of identity and intimacy, terms I have defined and applied throughout this book, offers a useful way of concretizing the components of voice as a cultural mechanism.

Taken together, this study's theoretical and methodological suggestions offer a direction for moving forward with analyses of voices in media and culture. I believe this direction is promising for future research, some ideas for which I suggest below.

LISTENING FORWARD

As an understudied and particularly abstract component of communication, the voice poses a challenge for rhetorical analysis. This book brings together and concretizes many of the central theoretical perspectives of vocal study, drawing from rhetorical and media scholars who have embraced the role of the voice. Still, more work is necessary to fully integrate the spoken voice into rhetorical and media studies.[9] My purpose in this project was not to shift critical attention away from visual and language-based media forms but rather to urge additional focus on the voice as a medium of expression. In the tradition of media and rhetorical studies, I chose to approach this topic through a series of case studies. Although this approach allowed me to thoroughly parse out the nuances present in the particular voices I examined, it necessarily limited the project's scope. I chose case studies strategically to represent varied identities and media contexts, but this book is not intended to generalize to larger populations. The observations and analysis in this book should not be understood as advancing claims about identity groups in general, but rather as focusing only on particular speakers whose identities and histories are shaped by intersectional oppressions and privileges and are therefore unique. I have provided four case studies here along with a theoretical perspective and method for approaching this type of scholarship, but I urge others at the intersection of rhetoric, media, identity, and sound studies to join in developing a broader range of cases from which to draw. My goal in this book was to represent a number of media contexts and genres, but even more variety can be useful to fully exploring this area of our discipline.

As we incorporate more vocal sound into our analyses, we should also expand our approaches to understanding mediated vocal power. Since this book was an exploratory study into the role of the voice in defining identity categories, I approached my chosen case studies using rhetorical analysis, but other methods could be helpful in understanding the role of the voice in communicating identity and intimacy. In particular, I used online commentary to examine audience readings of popular voices. Compared with an interview protocol, rhetorical analysis of online commentary limited the depth and thoroughness of the audience data that I was able to collect. Notably, only listeners/viewers who actively comment in online spaces were available for my study, and I was not able to ask follow-up questions or direct the discussion to better answer my research questions. On the other hand, this approach allowed me to gather the perspectives of listeners/viewers more efficiently, thereby facilitating a larger variety of case studies.[10] From my interdisciplinary perspective, the audience studies tradition, reflected in exciting developments from scholars of participatory critical rhetoric and rhetorical field methods, offers an additional outlet for understanding not only how the voice reads as a text, but also the ways that it travels from producer to consumer.[11]

Online commentary provided useful insight here in understanding how vocal intimacy bonds audiences to speakers, but online commentary is necessarily limited to the minority of listeners who share their thoughts on the internet. Methods offered by reception studies and rhetorical field methods, including interviewing and ethnography, would provide a wealth of additional information not only on the ways that people hear voices, but also on the ways that we describe those voices. Through interviewing and ethnography, researchers can also more clearly shape the kinds of audience data they receive, since online data collection does not allow for follow-up questions or carefully considered interview protocols. Additionally, the technological possibilities afforded by Audacity as an analysis and editing tool present a range of options for quantitative inquiry into the role of the voice in shaping cultural understandings of identity. To extend my research on presidential candidates, for example, Audacity could be used to isolate and adjust the pitch of presidential campaign addresses, and these manipulated audio tracks could provide interesting conditions for an experimental design that explores audience preference for particular voices in political contexts. Overall, I urge rhetorical scholars, particularly those studying at disciplinary and identity-based intersections, to take up study of the voice from a variety of methods beyond traditional textual analysis.

Not only should we expand beyond traditional rhetorical analysis as an approach; we should also stretch our focus to include neglected forms of media messages, specifically radio and animation. Radio accounts for a large portion of the media that US Americans encounter, and yet it remains a marginal topic in the media studies landscape. Likewise, animation has received little attention from media scholars. While both areas could provide interesting case studies for examining the role of voice in media identities, the lack of visually recorded bodies in radio and animation placed them beyond the scope of my study. The format of radio, with a rich but somewhat siloed tradition in media studies and very little scholarship in the rhetoric tradition, offers an additional context for vocal analysis. As an older form of media technology, radio still represents a basic source of information and entertainment in contemporary culture. Through both local and national programming, radio is a format of distribution for spoken voices through news, political and social commentary, sports programming, and the banter that characterizes many music-based shows. In addition to the film, television, and online formats represented in this book, vocal research should explore the unique position of radio in the transmission of the voice.

Finally, by using musical notation systems to transcribe the spoken voice, I have worked in this book to open up the possibility of interdisciplinary collaborations with ethnomusicologists to examine how spoken voices borrow cultural cues from particular musical formats. Freeman's spoken musical ostinato represents a small foray into this type of analysis, but the possibilities for better understanding the spoken voice through musical notations is much broader and more expansive than one small example can demonstrate. Philip Tagg argues that spoken voices may influence cultural developments in music, pointing specifically to the "Scotch snap," a rhythmic pattern in music that he believes could have derived from the melody of the Scottish accent.[12] I support Tagg's call in this area and urge more research of how sound influences in the opposite direction, specifically in terms of the influence of contemporary music on dialects and speech patterns in popular culture. By drawing from cultural theories of music, rhetoric and media scholarship will be better poised to communicate the value of sonic literacy to students and those outside the academy; linking the spoken voice to music could allow scholars to exploit the cultural love of popular music in service of important messages about more equitable and open listening.

HEARING REPRESENTATION

This book was completed in the midst of a national conversation about representation. In this era of Black Lives Matter, #ConcernedStudent1950, the Women's March on Washington, and many other moments in which ordinary people stood in the rich tradition of protest, it has grown even clearer how deeply media is entangled with structural inequality, marginalization, and violence. The hashtag #IfTheyGunnedMeDown, for example, highlighted the ways that corporate news media coverage often "treats white suspects and killers better than Black victims."[13] Following Michael Brown's murder at the hands of white police officer Darren Wilson, many media outlets circulated images of Brown not "in a graduation picture or in a sports team" but wearing an athletic tank top, sporting what some read as an overly stoic or aggressive expression, and holding his hand to make a sign with his fingers.[14] Conversely, the white Aurora theater shooter who killed twelve people was depicted in formal portraits, smiling and wearing a suit and tie.[15] Outcry from antiracist groups pointed out the white supremacy that structures conventions of portraying Black victims as deserving of their own deaths, and eventually many media outlets switched their stock image of Brown to his graduation photo. Similarly, in 2015 Laverne Cox called on the fashion media to "join with [her] in showing the world that trans is beautiful in terms of how we cover trans stories and diverse stories in general," a charge taken up on social media with the #TransIsBeautiful hashtag that has continued to uplift transgender self-representation years later.[16] Cox and others demonstrated the ways that transgender people, particularly those of color, are often Othered by media outlets in ways that perpetuate violence and discrimination against the trans community, and she used the politics of representation to push for change. With each new movement to protest oppression and uplift the marginalized, images circulate around the web, marking identities and highlighting power imbalances.

Representations matter, not only because they offer evidence of history through their engagement with stereotypical and conventional depictions of marginalized groups but also because they shape the ways that people within and beyond those groups understand marginalized identities. Representation structures access to resources, the relationships we form with one another, disproportionate experiences of violence, and other crucial aspects of daily lived experience. From this perspective, the #OscarsSoWhite hashtag and boycott marked an important intervention into a major media industry's limited representation, potentially bolstering a wave of Black cast films from major studios the following years. In this context of the critical and box-office successes of Black films like *Moonlight, Hidden Figures,* and *Black Panther,* representation of Asian, Native, Latinx, and other racial groups remains weak. This is the context in which Warner Brothers' 2018 romantic comedy *Crazy Rich Asians* emerged. As director Jon M. Chu wrote, "The fact that [Asians and Asian Americans] had never shared a communal experience of joy, laughter and emotions at the movies like this has been an injustice. But now we have. And there's no going back."[17] Chu's tweet, along with myriad other social media posts and think pieces, demonstrates the intense "power in *seeing* faces like [your own] on screen," particularly given that the film is the first major Hollywood studio film in twenty-five years to feature an entirely Asian or Asian American cast.[18]

However, representation is not only visual, and we must attune to the power of sonic representations to frame identities and encourage intimacies just as visual representations do. Even as Chu celebrates his film as a moment when Asian Americans "saw each other," *Crazy Rich Asians* offers a rich diversity of voices that deserve attention and analysis. Minority representation is not only important for those within the group but, as I have argued in this book, also a key factor in guiding interactions between groups. Encouragingly, the vocal identities highlighted in *Crazy Rich Asians,* along with the vocal intimacy experienced by many audiences, were the subject of a number of online commentaries surrounding the film. Often this criticism focused on accents, an important aspect of Asian and Asian American representation since, as

Ono and Pham note, exaggerated accents that mark Asian characters as both markedly foreign and laughably ridiculous have been normative in Hollywood since the beginning of Asian and Asian American representation.[19] As Ishani Nath's think piece on *Crazy Rich Asians* astutely explains,

> The problem with accent roles isn't the accents themselves—plenty of characters in *Crazy Rich Asians* have accents, but no one has the exaggerated or generic "Asian" accent that has historically been played for laughs in Hollywood . . . These portrayals are the difference between portraying people of colour as the lesser "other," and authentic representation—which is what we're now seeing in films like *Crazy Rich Asians*.[20]

The variety of Asian accents in the film, including the "British accent," technically called "received pronunciations," of the Oxford-educated Singaporean American Nick Young (Henry Golding) and the US American accent of Rachel Chu (Constance Wu), speaks to the film's attention to representational detail; rather than emphasizing the "foreignness" historically used to exclude Asian Americans from the full rights of US citizenship, the film instead portrays the characters as people whose accents mark their fleshed-out, complex histories and experiences.

Even as commentary on *Crazy Rich Asians* engages with character accents, perhaps the most noticeable component of vocal identity, much remains to be said of the film's voices. Although the Asian accents in the film are voiced in good faith, breaking the mold of a history of Hollywood mockery, the romantic comedy does little to break down barriers of gender and sexuality. How might a critical cultural vocalic analysis reveal the range and movement of pitches that characterize the film's many heterosexual characters as different from, or similar to, its openly gay character? If, as I suggest, hyperfeminized performances are often used to caricature gay men characters, how can Nico Santos's performance of Oliver T'sien's queerness be understood? After all, this is a character marked by queer masculinity and Asian masculinity, two axes of masculine identity often dismissed through performances of hyperfeminization both similar to and different from those performed in Tina Fey's impression of Sarah Palin. Furthermore, in a film that highlights discourses about the intersection of class with East Asian and Chinese American identity, what are the political implications when, as Fei Lu points out, "low income Asians as well as other people of color" are seen but not heard?[21] Might these mirror the ways that Morgan Freeman's voice is tuned out in service to his white costars, or might they differ from those mechanisms of vocalization in important ways? Goh Peik Lin's (Awkwafina) "blaccent," slang for AAE, was critiqued by some in the blog-o-sphere as a dialect, but how does Awkwafina's overall vocal performance contain other elements of identity beyond this apparent use of Blackvoice?[22] Is the marked, racialized masculinity of the comedians of color discussed in this book mapped onto rapper and actor Awkwafina's vocal body? These questions raise the point that, although it is heartening to see the voices in *Crazy Rich Asians* discussed in terms of accents, such commentary does not go far enough.

This conversation neglects both the deeper meanings of vocal identity and the consideration of how vocal intimacy shapes reception of representations like those in *Crazy Rich Asians*. Perhaps these meanings are not the goal of the online commentary cited here, but it should be the goal of critical rhetorical and media scholars. If voices, like language-based and visual representations, guide how we interact with one another, then they also shape the mechanisms of structural oppression. We need, then, much more exploration of emerging voices, such as those of Asians and Asian Americans whose representation in media ranged from absent to mocking, as well as those who have been made silent. How have Latinx voices been represented in an era with increasingly cruel policies tearing families apart at the southern border of the United States?[23] What of Native voices at a moment when Native people face the greatest likelihood per capita of being killed by police?[24] Vocal identity and vocal intimacy shape not only our deeply held meaning of self and others but also the circulation and reception of voices in our everyday interactions. Therefore, an attention to voice is not simply tangential to the struggle for justice; it is integral to that work. The call to listen is a call for more research. It is also a call to interrogate the role of the voice as bodies travel or are restricted, as relationships are formed or denied, and, finally, as some cries for justice are heard while others are ignored.

APPENDIX

Using Audacity and MuseScore for Critical Cultural Vocalic Analysis

AUDACITY[1] is an open-source program that allows users to record, edit, and analyze audio files in a user-friendly, visually based format. In this appendix, I detail the steps involved in Audacity's "plot spectrum" analysis, focusing specifically on the collection of pitch/frequency and rate data. I then demonstrate how I use MuseScore[2] to chart this data onto a musical staff. To make this process more concrete, I draw an example from my previous analysis of Hillary Clinton's Benghazi address, which I compared with Rush Limbaugh's imitation of Clinton.[3]

STEP 1: LOAD AND SELECT A SOUND TO ANALYZE

If the file is already in .WAV or .mp3 format, it can be loaded directly into the program. Most audiovisual media are not in this format and must be converted for the program. Audacity facilitates this through its "record" function. To transfer the Clinton testimony from YouTube to Audacity, I clicked the Record button in the top-left corner of Audacity's home screen, then played the YouTube video of the testimony. When the clip finished playing, I stopped the Audacity recorder, and the program mapped the sounds from YouTube into a waveform in the program's workspace. As the screenshot in figure A.1 demonstrates, silence is represented by a thin line, while speech bursts appear as wider bubbles. The example in the figure is the Audacity waveform of Clinton saying "What difference at this point does it make," which I selected because I was interested in comparing Clinton's delivery with Rush Limbaugh's mockery of this phrase.

Audacity allows users to select particular speech bursts and listen only to that isolated selection. Analyses of pitch engage primarily with voiced sounds (which include all vowels and voiced consonants usually including "m," "n," "v," and "b"). Voiceless sounds (like "p," "t," and "s") do not engage the vocal cords and therefore are not understood as having pitch. The distinction between voiced and voiceless consonants can be easily heard by listening to which parts of the voice are being engaged in the syllable; voiced consonants incorporate vibrations in the vocal cords, whereas voiceless consonants are formed with the lips, teeth, and tongue only. This distinction is easily demonstrated by placing your fingers lightly on the front of your throat and speaking a particular consonant; if you feel vibration in your voice box, the consonant is voiced.

I selected the voiced sound I wanted to analyze, refining my selection until I could no longer hear pitch movement within the highlighted portion. Pressing the space bar to start and stop the selection, I listened to the sounds and watched the waveform until I had isolated a single pitch. In the example in figure A.1, I wanted to document the movement of Clinton's pitch throughout the utterance. I therefore isolated each voiced sound, beginning with the first word, "what." As the screenshot below demonstrates, I highlighted the waveform bubble that visually represents this sound. Her utterance of "what" was brief (approximately 0.08 seconds), and she did not change pitch within that

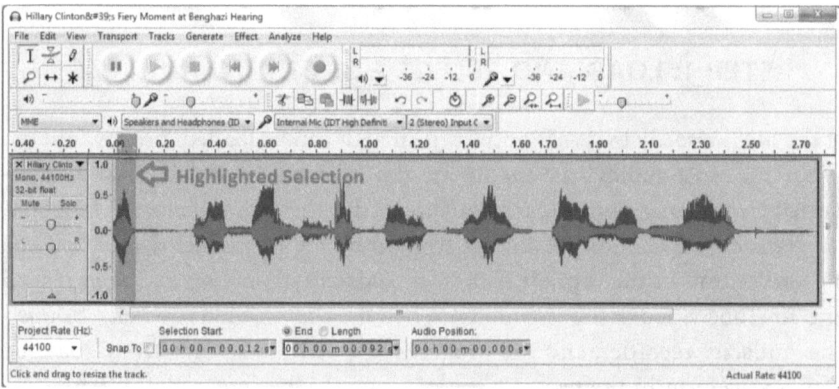

FIGURE A.1. Step 1: Load and select a sound to analyze.

sound. I have indicated the highlighted section with an arrow and annotation in the example image.

STEP 2: READ AND NOTE FREQUENCY AND PITCH INFORMATION

With the selection highlighted, I pulled down the Analyze menu from the toolbar and selected "Plot spectrum . . ." In this example case, I chose Analyze while keeping Clinton's "what" utterance highlighted, giving me a visual representation of that sound's pitch (see figure A.2). The Frequency Analysis window appears as several jagged peaks, each of which represents a frequency present in the voice (including the fundamental frequency, the voice's overtones, and any background noise). The vertical axis represents decibel level, or loudness, and the horizontal axis represents frequency from lowest pitch (on the left) to highest pitch (on the right). The lowest-pitched (furthest-left) major peak is the fundamental frequency, or the pitch perceived by the ear when Clinton spoke this word. When the cursor is held over this peak, the reading at the bottom of the screen notes the Hertz frequency (374 Hz) and the corresponding pitch (F#4). I noted this pitch along with the syllable ("what") for later transcription.

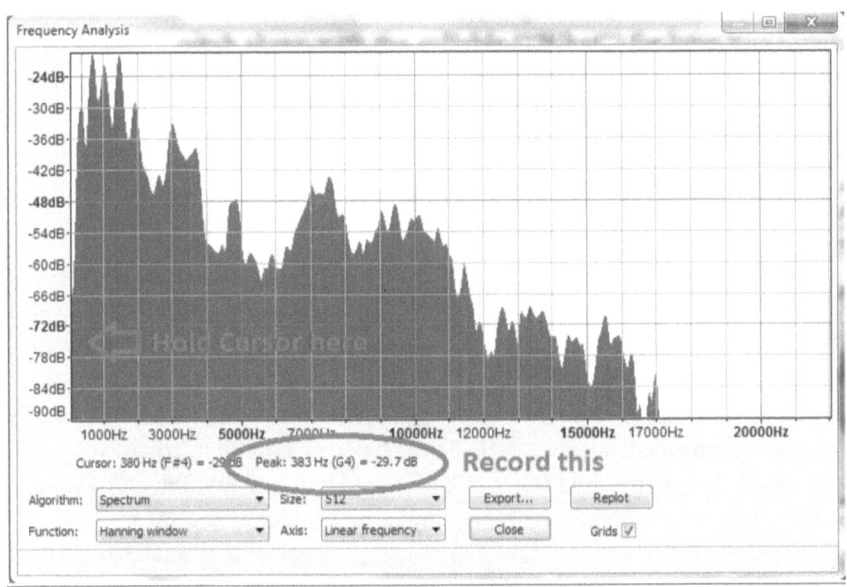

FIGURE A.2. Step 2: Read and note frequency and pitch information.

STEP 3: READ AND NOTE RATE INFORMATION

Along with the pitch and syllable for the "what" utterance, I wanted to note the length of the sound as a way of documenting rate of speech. To do this, I closed the Frequency Analysis window and made a note of the selection start and end points, displayed at the bottom of Audacity's screen, for later use in examining and transcribing the rate. In this case, I added "start—0.012" and "end—0.092" to my notes, pulling those numbers from the bottom of Audacity's screen, which I have circled in the screenshot in figure A.3. This means that Clinton's word "what" began 0.012 seconds into the sample recording and ended 0.092 seconds into the sample recording. Therefore, her utterance of "what" lasted 0.08 seconds.

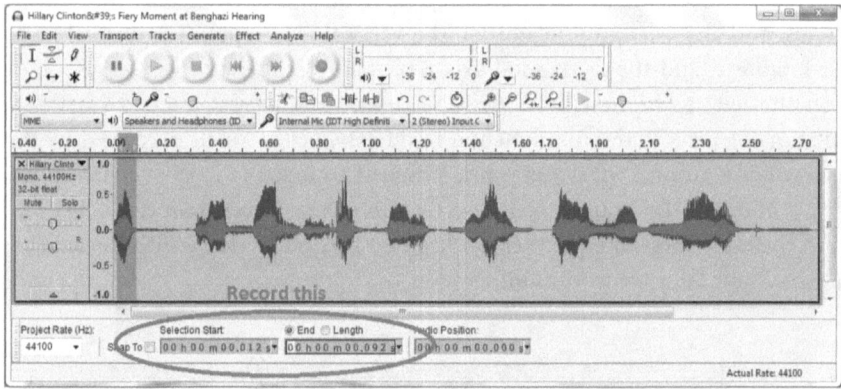

FIGURE A.3. Step 3: Read and note rate information.

STEP 4: REPEAT FOR FULL SELECTION

At this point, I had noted one sound from the string of sounds comprising Clinton's utterance "What difference at this point does it make?" Since I was interested in documenting the whole sentence, I then repeated the process for each sound. I found it easiest to compile this documentation in a chart (figure A.4), making notes about frequency/pitch and rate for each sound in the selection alongside Clinton's words. I then had a grid of pitch/frequency, start/stop point, and words. The distance between the highest and lowest frequency is the pitch range. I also noted any pauses and voiceless sounds ("f" and "s," in this case) since, in this case, Clinton drew out those pitchless sounds in her speech. While this information did not change my pitch transcription, it impacted my transcription of rate.

What	300 Hz	D4	0–.012
	374 Hz	F#4	–.092
silence			–.340
di-	344 Hz	F#4	–.450
ff			–.550
ren(ce)	393 Hz	G4	–.568
	328 Hz	E4	–.650
ss			–.850

FIGURE A.4. Step 4. Repeat for full selection.

STEP 5: TRANSFER NOTES TO STAFF

While this grid is useful in some ways, it can be difficult to process at a glance and even more difficult to use in comparisons with other speakers. Therefore, I transferred the information about Clinton's voice into traditional musical annotation, just as I did in this book. The data from the chart must be manually transferred into a notation program. A number of programs are available for this process, and in my experience, they all produce nearly identical results. Because it is a freeware program (unlike Finale and Sibelius, the leading programs in the music industry), I prefer to use MuseScore. It is difficult to discern which programs are used most often in translating spoken voices to musical scores, since the finished result of entering data into Finale would look identical to the same data entered into MuseScore, Sibelius, or any number of other programs. Importantly, the notation program employed for this task only processes and digitizes the data the user enters similar to the way Microsoft Word translates a user's words into a computerized file.

The process of entering the previously charted data into the notation program begins with finding the lowest common denominator. In the example of Clinton's address, I chose 0.1 seconds as the baseline because the numbers in the rate column often seemed to move by increments of approximately 0.1 seconds ("*silence*" from 0.34 to 0.45; "dif" from 0.45 to 0.55; and so on). I assigned this 0.1-second increment a note value of an eighth note (♪). A sound twice as long as this baseline (0.2 seconds) would then be assigned a quarter note (♩), which has a value twice as long as an eighth note. Because a sound less than 0.1 seconds long is very brief, I assigned these shorter notes the value of a grace note (𝄾), which denotes a very brief flourish. MuseScore, like other notation programs, standardizes the horizontal spacing of each note relative to its length, so while an understanding of musical notation is helpful in reading the transcription, it is not necessary to visually compare rates, as the following example illustrates.

My choice to assign ♪ the value of 0.1 seconds is arbitrary and offers meaning only relative to the other sounds in the study. This relativity can be imagined both horizontally and vertically. First, by consistently assigning a particular increment of time to a particular note value, the horizontal line of the spoken text is spaced out relative to time's passage. In the transcription of Clinton's speech in figure A.5, for example, the words at the end of the phrase occur more quickly than the words at the beginning of the phrase, as demonstrated by the relative spacing of the notes and words.

FIGURE A.5. Step 4: Transfer notes to staff.
Originally printed in "Toward a Genosonic Lens: Linking the Anatomy of a 'Screech' to Language and Body," Amanda Nell Edgar. *Velvet Light Trap* 74 (Fall 2014). The University of Texas Press, copyright 2014.

Second, by maintaining this consistency across multiple speakers' sounds, I can compare utterances from different moments in time based on a standardized rate. The transcription in figure A.6, for instance, directly compares Limbaugh's imitation of Clinton's phrase through consistently mapped units of time. Here, Clinton's "what" and the silence that followed lasted the same amount of time as Limbaugh's "what diff-rence," as illustrated by a comparison of the two lines. These comparisons, both horizontally across a single speaker and vertically between multiple speakers, are facilitated not by a hard and fast rule of ♪ = 0.1 seconds but by maintaining that arbitrary standard baseline throughout the transcriptions to be compared.

Using the baseline note values (♪ = 0.1 seconds) and the data I collected about the frequencies/pitches of the speakers, I mapped the utterances onto a musical staff. Musical staves can be understood as a form of chart, where the vertical axis represents pitch (higher points on the staff represent higher pitches) and the horizontal axis represents rate (denser notes indicates more condensed speech patterns). Just as figure A.6 illustrates comparisons in rate, comparing changes in vertical movement of pitch demonstrates similarities and differences in pitch patterns between and within speakers' utterances. Just as my transcription of rate maintained a standard notation baseline, the pro-

FIGURE A.6. Step 5: Repeat and compare.
Originally printed in "Toward a Genosonic Lens: Linking the Anatomy of a 'Screech' to Language and Body," Amanda Nell Edgar. *Velvet Light Trap* 74 (Fall 2014). The University of Texas Press, copyright 2014.

cess of mapping pitches onto a staff standardizes pitches between speakers. In this extended example, Clinton's and Limbaugh's pitch patterns overlapped a great deal. Clinton's first word "what" is actually lower on the staff (just below the top line) than Limbaugh's (above the top line), indicating that Limbaugh's voice was, in this instance, higher than Clinton's.

Note that this transcription only facilitates analysis. To offer an abbreviated account of the study from which this example is drawn, Limbaugh's pitch pattern is much wider than Clinton's (Limbaugh's first pitch is a bit higher than Clinton's first pitch, and in fact it is higher than Clinton's pitch ever reaches).[4] Furthermore, while Clinton's rate is measured and steady, Limbaugh completes the phrase (which he shortens by three words, "at this point") in approximately half the space Clinton uses. Limbaugh uses patterns of exaggeratedly wide range and fast, frantic rate to foreground Clinton's racialized gender, playing on stereotypes that associate women with uncontrollable emotional outbursts, a point that I argued through traditional textual analysis that used the finished transcription as a way of grounding my claims about both speakers' sounds.

Transcribing the voices in my study with Audacity and MuseScore offers a way of visualizing even the briefest fragment of sound, allowing me to closely and systematically examine voices that are otherwise ephemeral and constantly moving. As part of my larger analysis of textual and contextual elements surrounding the voice, this process offered an understanding of which types of vocal traits are attached to particular racial and gendered identities.

NOTES

NOTES TO INTRODUCTION

1. Casillas, *Sounds of Belonging*.
2. Cavarero, *For More Than One Voice*, 182.
3. Sterne, *The Audible Past*, 344.
4. Watts, *Hearing the Hurt*, 16.
5. Bucholtz and Lopez, "Performing Blackness, Forming Whiteness," 681.
6. Bucholtz, "Race and the Re-embodied Voice," 259.
7. Ono and Pham, *Asian Americans and the Media*, 46; Davé, *Indian Accents*.
8. Edgar, "Toward a Genosonic Lens."
9. Casillas, Ferrada, and Hinojos, "The Accent on *Modern Family*."
10. Smith, *Vocal Tracks*.
11. Douglas, *Listening In*.
12. Dolar, *A Voice and Nothing More*, 60; italics original.
13. Barthes, *Image, Music, Text*.
14. Butler, *Gender Trouble*.
15. Butler, *Gender Trouble*.
16. Goodale, *Sonic Persuasion*, 92.
17. Marks, *Touch*.
18. Marks, *Touch*; Watts, "'Voice' and 'Voicelessness' in Rhetorical Studies"; Gunn, "Mourning Speech," 102.
19. Stoever, *The Sonic Color Line*; Casillas, *Sounds of Belonging*; Cavarero, *For More Than One Voice*.
20. Barthes, *Image, Music, Text*.
21. Ibid., 181, 181–82; I use "sic" here to indicate that Barthes's observations are true for singers and speakers across genders. In the context of the original quote, Barthes is referring to Russian cantors who, at the time of his writing, were exclusively male. His use of "his" is therefore not incorrect, but I mean to note that "his" is an inappropriate adjective to refer to the population of speakers and singers more generally.
22. Ibid., 181.
23. Ibid., 188.
24. Nancy, *Listening*.
25. Suisman, *Selling Sounds*, 14.
26. Stilwell, "Sound and Empathy."

27. Ong, *Orality and Literacy*, 70; Cavarero, *For More Than One Voice*, 177.
28. Gunn, "Mourning Speech," 102.
29. Ihde, *Listening and Voice*, 195.
30. Douglas, *Listening In*.
31. Smith, *Vocal Tracks*, 3.
32. Chion, *Audio-Vision*, 126.
33. Lawrence, "Staring the Camera Down."
34. Davé, *Indian Accents*.
35. Ibid.; Ono and Pham make a similar argument regarding yellowface performances in media in *Asian Americans and the Media*.
36. Stoever, *The Sonic Color Line*.
37. Butler, *Bodies That Matter*.
38. Gorbman, "Aesthetics and Rhetoric," 23.
39. Ono and Pham, *Asian Americans and the Media*.
40. Taylor, "'Speaking Shadows.'"
41. Barnier, "The Sound of the First French Television Advertisements."
42. Attali, *Noise*.
43. Berland, "Locating Listening."
44. Suisman, *Selling Sounds*, 13.
45. Schafer, *The Soundscape*, 67.
46. Attali, *Noise*.
47. Hilmes, "Desired and Feared," 20.
48. Carson, "The Gender of Sound."
49. Dolar, *A Voice and Nothing More*, 20.
50. Goodale, *Sonic Persuasion*, 94.
51. Stoever, *The Sonic Color Line*.
52. Goodale, *Sonic Persuasion*, 94.
53. Maurice, "Cinema at Its Source," 49.
54. Lawrence, *Echo and Narcissus*.
55. hooks, *Talking Back*, 15.
56. Dolar, *A Voice and Nothing More*, 20.
57. Douglas, *Listening In*, 105.
58. Smith, *Vocal Tracks*.
59. Taylor, "Speaking Shadows."
60. Ono and Pham, *Asian Americans and the Media*.
61. Kim, "The Racial Triangulation of Asian Americans," 107.
62. Smyth, Jacobs, and Rogers, "Male Voices and Perceived Sexual Orientation."
63. Benshoff, *Monsters in the Closet*, 87.
64. Loviglio, "Sound Effects."
65. For a discussion of television sound's scholarly neglect, see Hilmes, "Foregrounding Sound."
66. Gunn, "On Speech and Public Release"; Watts, "'Voice' and 'Voicelessness'"; Goodale, *Sonic Persuasion*; Eckstein, "Sound Arguments."
67. Hilmes, "Is There a Field"; Douglas, *Listening In*; Loviglio, "Sound Effects."
68. Hill Collins and Bilge, *Intersectionality*, 2.
69. Calafell in Squires et al., "What Is This 'Post-' in Postracial, Postfeminist . . .'"
70. Understanding the sometimes fraught histories of feminist and gender studies in terms of race, sexuality, ability, and other axes of oppression and identity, I understand feminism as necessarily intersectional. Therefore, I eschew the recently popular descriptor "intersectional feminism," often measured against "white feminism," in favor of simply framing feminist work as intersectional. Work that does not consider intersectionality is not actually feminist, in my view.

71. Goodale, *Sonic Persuasion*, 12
72. Hall, "Introduction," 15.
73. Edgar, "Toward a Genosonic Lens."
74. McConnell-Ginet, "Intonation in a Man's World," 542.
75. Milroy and Gordon, *Sociolinguistics*.
76. Sound scholars have used this program for several years with reliable results, as demonstrated by myriad peer-reviewed articles that employ Audacity, which can be downloaded free from http://audacity.sourceforge.net/. See, for example, Bernhardt and Stemberger, "Translation to Practice"; Brinca, Batista, Tavares, Gonçalves, and Moreno, "Use of Cepstral Analyses for Differentiating Normal from Dysphonic Voices"; Ridgway, Carder, Jeffries, and Todd, "Spontaneous Human Speech Mimicry by a Cetacean."
77. Gunn, "On Speech and Public Release," 188.
78. Smith, *Vocal Tracks*; Goodale, *Sonic Persuasion*.
79. Berland, "Locating Listening," 343.
80. For an example of the latter, see Goodale's "The Sonorous Envelope and Political Deliberation."
81. Dolar, *A Voice and Nothing More*, 20.

NOTES TO CHAPTER 1

1. Rentboy, February 15, 2012, "Poll: Do You Think Adele Sounds Black?" *ATRL Classic*, http://classic.atrl.net/forums/showthread.php?t=186003.
2. Nina Needle, February 24, 2012, "Is Adele Part Black because She Sounds Like It.?" *Yahoo! Answers*, https://answers.yahoo.com/question/index?qid=20120224152253AAvUs59.
3. "Beyoncé, Adele, Chris Brown Up for NAACP Image Awards."
4. Weiss, "The Magnetic Fields' Stephin Merritt on Why Adele Fans Are Racist, and Other Topics."
5. Stoever, *The Sonic Color Line*.
6. DeChaine, "Bordering the Civic Imaginary."
7. Ibid., 51.
8. Brackett, "The Politics and Practice of 'Crossover.'"
9. Ono and Pham, *Asian Americans and the Media*, 58.
10. Richards, "The-Dream."
11. Irby, "Grammy Performances Range from Authentic to Absurd."
12. Port, "Adele's Grammy Performance."
13. Bizmichael, Twitter, March 2, 2012, 11:04 AM https://twitter.com/bizmichael/status/175627726357667840.
14. Kainer, "Vocal Racial Crossover."
15. See Davé, *Indian Accents*, for a discussion of "brown voice"; I have not seen the term *yellowvoice* in the literature but draw from Ono and Pham's (*Asian Americans and the Media*) discussion of the accents associated with yellowface throughout this book.
16. Adelt, *Blues Music in the Sixties*, 3.
17. Davis, *Blues Legacies and Black Feminism*, xii.
18. Hilmes, *Radio Voices*, xix
19. Stoever, *The Sonic Color Line*.
20. Marking the starting points of these industries is debatable, as defining industry beginnings depends on industry definitions. The formal split between hillbilly and race genres and the release of the first feature-length sound film are moments key to this analysis, and they occurred within a few years of one another. The former is marked by the first

hillbilly record, featuring Fiddlin' John Carson and released by Okeh Records in 1923, and the latter is marked by *The Jazz Singer*, featuring Al Jolson in occasional blackface and released by Warner Brothers in 1927.
21. Stoever, *The Sonic Color Line*; Beltrán, *Latina/o Stars in U. S. Eyes*.
22. Stras, "White Face, Black Voice," 209; Stoever, *The Sonic Color Line*, 30.
23. Maurice, "'Cinema at Its Source,'" 33.
24. Ibid., 62.
25. Hartman and Griffin, "Are You as Colored as That Negro?" 369.
26. Davis, *Blues Legacies and Black Feminism*.
27. Stoever, *The Sonic Color Line*, 247.
28. Adelt, *Blues Music in the Sixties*.
29. Ibid., 67.
30. Brackett, "The Politics and Practice of 'Crossover.'"
31. Adorno, *The Jargon of Authenticity*; Fast, "Calling Ellen Willis"; Jackson, *Real Black*; Judy, "On the Question of Nigga Authenticity."
32. Banet-Weiser, *Authentic™*.
33. Jackson, *Real Black*.
34. Ono and Pham, *Asian Americans and the Media*.
35. Ibid.
36. Stoever, *The Sonic Color Line*.
37. Ibid.
38. Lott, *Love and Theft*, 3.
39. Tate, *Everything but the Burden*, 4.
40. Lott, *Love and Theft*; Ono and Pham make a similar argument about yellowface performance in media in *Asian Americans and the Media*.
41. Kibler, *Rank Ladies*.
42. Kainer, "Vocal Racial Crossover," 74.
43. Davis, *Blues Legacies and Black Feminism*.
44. Ibid., 11.
45. King, *African Americans and the Culture of Pain*.
46. Barthes, *Image, Music, Text*.
47. Ibid.
48. Butler, "Taking It Seriously."
49. Ibid.
50. Gioia, *The History of Jazz*.
51. Daley, "'Why Do Whites Sing Black?'"
52. Jackson, *Real Black*.
53. Attali, *Noise*.
54. Ono, "Borders That Travel," 30–31.
55. DeChaine, "Bordering the Civic Imaginary," 51.
56. Fast, "Calling Ellen Willis."
57. Jackson, *Real Black*.
58. Lucaites, "Afterword: Border Optics," 227.
59. Jackson, *Real Black*.
60. Kainer, "Vocal Racial Crossover," 13.
61. Ibid., 27.
62. Butler, *Bodies That Matter*.
63. Ibid.
64. Butte, Yu Zhang, Song, and Jiang, "Perturbation and Nonlinear Dynamic Analysis of Different Singing Styles."
65. King, *African Americans and the Culture of Pain*, 46.

66. Ja'ManaTyler (@hi_imPRETTY_), Twitter, March 31, 2012, 1:44 PM, https://twitter.com/hi__imPRETTY__/status/186161980028096513.
67. Valise (@llcoolkay), Twitter, March 30, 2012, 9:48 AM, https://twitter.com/_llcoolkay/status/185740393281896448.
68. Kainer, "Vocal Racial Crossover."
69. Ibid.
70. Jaslow, "Meet Adele's Vocal Cord Surgeon."
71. Stoever, *The Sonic Color Line*, 30.
72. I have chosen not to anonymize comments for two reasons. First, by including all the information available, I aim to help clarify the type of source from which I drew each comment, an issue that becomes even more complex in later chapters as I integrate industry and nonindustry sources into my argument. Second, I have included this information as a way of demonstrating transparency in my research.
73. Alejandro Reyes, three years ago [accessed September 24, 2018], comment on Texhnician, "Adele Performing Someone Like You | BRIT Awards 2011," YouTube, February 15, 2011, 5:50, https://www.youtube.com/watch?v=qemWRToNYJY&lc=UgiRu-ddxQj6JngCoAEC.
74. Kavka, *Reality Television, Affect and Intimacy*.
75. Miss Cinabon roll, 11 months ago [accessed May 24, 2018], comment on Texhnician, "Adele Performing Someone Like You | BRIT Awards 2011."
76. Barthes, *Image, Music, Text*, 181.
77. Ibid.
78. Ibid.
79. Ibid.
80. Jackson, *Real Black*.
81. Dyer, *Heavenly Bodies*.
82. Kainer, "Vocal Racial Crossover," 27.
83. Barthes, *Image, Music, Text*, 188.
84. King, *African Americans and the Culture of Pain*.
85. Dyer, *Heavenly Bodies*, 187.
86. AWx51, October 8, 2012, comment on geomandre, "Adele—Someone Like You," https://web.archive.org/web/20121127165504/http://www.youtube.com/watch?v=jCya1yiFFP4.
87. Breelion55, October 8, 2012, comment on Adele, "Adele—Turning Tables (Live at the Royal Albert Hall)," http://www.youtube.com/watch?v=bsFCO8-0CEQ&feature=share&list=UUomP_epzeKzvBX156r6pm1Q.
88. YouTube has since removed the "Top Comments" function. In 2012 when these comments were recorded, the top comments appeared in a separate area above the main comment thread.
89. The Anti.Socialite, (@Jaidus_), February 12, 2012, 7:14 PM, Twitter, https://twitter.com/Jaidus_/status/168895723797102592.
90. JUMP$HOT BELO, (@JumpShotBelo), January 23, 2012, 1:54 PM, Twitter, https://twitter.com/JumpShotBelo/status/161567561299931136.
91. _jbirdfly, February 12, 2012, 7:12 PM, Twitter, https://twitter.com/_jbirdfly/status/168895223517282304.
92. Dyer, *Heavenly Bodies*, 14.
93. Spielberg, "Magnetic Fields' Stephin Merritt."
94. This quote has been attributed to Adele on numerous social media sites, including a variety of images that include the quote. I was not able to identify an original source or to confirm whether Adele actually said this or not. My point here is that the quote spread as though it were truth, whether or not it actually was.
95. Oliver, *Witnessing*, 159.

174 • NOTES TO CHAPTER 2

96. Rasheed Copeland (@dresssock), March 24, 2012, 2:14 PM, Twitter, https://twitter.com/dresssock/status/183663200036851712.
97. Davis, *Blues Legacies and Black Feminism*, xvii.
98. samiid443, March 31, 2012, 2:13 PM, Twitter, https://twitter.com/samiid443/status/186199533309542400.
99. Dyer, *White*.
100. Mohanty, "Drawing the Color Line."
101. Dyer, *White*, 136.
102. Ibid.
103. Ibid.
104. Ibid.
105. Davies, "All Rock and Roll Is Homosocial"; Fast, "Calling Ellen Willis"; Modleski, "Femininity as Mas(s)querade."
106. Fast, "Calling Ellen Willis."
107. LotusFlowerPower, January 16, 2013, comment on Texhnician, "Adele Performing Someone Like You | BRIT Awards 2011."
108. The Chratheostic Pwner of Megadeth Fanboys, November 19, 2014, comment on Texhnician, "Adele Performing Someone Like You | BRIT Awards 2011."
109. neek_lovex33, March 25, 2012, 8:25 AM, Twitter, https://twitter.com/neek_lovex33/status/183937661881417728.
110. mollylittletits, February 24, 2012, 2:19 PM, Twitter, https://twitter.com/mollylittletits/status/173170261456207872.
111. rafterman_, March 26, 2012, 9:28 PM, Twitter, https://twitter.com/rafterman_/status/184497037805502466.
112. brettikus, February 12, 2012, 8:25 PM, Twitter, https://twitter.com/brettikus/status/168913595055357954.
113. Zac Jackson (@AkronJackson), February 12, 2012, 5:54 PM, Twitter, https://twitter.com/AkronJackson/status/168875714605613057.
114. darkelem3nts, February 12, 2012, 3:27 PM, Twitter, https://twitter.com/darkelem3nts/status/168838591722684416.
115. HausOfRutland, February 12, 2012, 3:31 PM, Twitter, https://twitter.com/HausOfRutland/status/168839587718901760
116. Lott, *Love and Theft*.
117. aarongluzman, 6 years ago [accessed May 24, 2018], comment on The Music 411, "Grammys: Adele's First Performance since Her Throat Op. WOW!" https://www.youtube.com/watch?v=-G_MSQJNcLw.
118. Barthes, *Image, Music, Text*, 181.

NOTES TO CHAPTER 2

1. Frank, "True Facts about Morgan Freeman."
2. Ibid.
3. See also Mars, December 12, 2011, "Is Morgan Freeman Really God?" *Yahoo! Answers*. https://uk.answers.yahoo.com/question/index?qid=20111212092735AA3H6Jk; Meskimen, "Morgan Freeman Narrates Your Life"; Shado85, "What If Morgan Freeman Really Is God?"
4. Quoted in Peters, "Morgan Magic"; Gates, *In Search of Our Roots*, 59.
5. Quoted in Peters, "Morgan Magic."
6. Variety Staff, "Commanding Respect Even Sight Unseen." This article does not argue that Freeman is the most trusted man in America. Rather, it insinuates that Freeman is

trusted enough to take over for "Walter Cronkite, once called the most trusted man in America" (p. A12).
7. Gates, *In Search of Our Roots*.
8. Breathwaite, "Morgan Freeman," 38.
9. Gates, *In Search of Our Roots*, 58; Milchan, quoted in Gates, *America*; Freeman, "CNN Tonight."
10. Eberwein, "Clint Eastwood and Morgan Freeman"; Tracy, *Morgan Freeman*, xiii.
11. Sklar and Modleski, "A Split Decision" 8; Variety Staff, "Commanding Respect Even Sight Unseen."
12. "Morgan Freeman," *Urban Dictionary*; Frank, "True Facts about Morgan Freeman."
13. O'Sullivan, "Representations of Prison in Nineties Hollywood Cinema," 326; Gates, "Always a Partner in Crime."
14. O'Sullivan, "Representations of Prison in Nineties Hollywood Cinema," 325.
15. Chivers, *The Silvering Screen*, 114.
16. Modleski, "Clint Eastwood and Male Weepies," 143.
17. Boyle, Millington, and Vertinsky, "Representing the Female Pugilist," 108.
18. Gates, "Always a Partner in Crime," 28.
19. Ibid.
20. Ibid., 28.
21. Macek, "Places of Horror," 93.
22. Gallafent, "Violence, Actions and Words in *Million Dollar Baby*," 50.
23. Quoted in Eberwein, "Clint Eastwood and Morgan Freeman."
24. Hughey, "Cinethetic Racism," 544.
25. Liberato and Foster, "Representations and Remembrance," 376.
26. McGraw, "*Driving Miss Daisy*," 44.
27. Glenn and Cunningham, "The Power of Black Magic," 137.
28. hooks, *Art on My Mind*; Jones, Cox, and Navarro-Rivera, *The 2013 American Values Survey*.
29. Gates, *In Search of Our Roots*, 58.
30. Herndan, "The Police Psychologist on the Silver Screen," 33.
31. Liberato and Foster, "Representations and Remembrance," 376.
32. Williams, "In the Ring with Mildred Pierce," 167.
33. Ibid.
34. Ladino, "For the Love of Nature," 54.
35. Gertz, "How I Spent My Summer Vacation"; Eberwein, "Clint Eastwood and Morgan Freeman," 41.
36. Ladino, "For the Love of Nature," 66, 86.
37. THR Staff, "Morgan Freeman Narrates New Gay Marriage Ad (Video)."
38. Ibid.
39. Quoted in Barkley, *Who's Afraid of a Large Black Man?*; Couch, "Harrison Ford, Morgan Freeman Top Survey of Fictional Presidents."
40. Orgeret, "Mediated Culture and the Well-informed Global Citizen," 53.
41. Bugliani, "The Ideal and the Real," 470.
42. Cucca, "Biopics as Postmodern Mythmaking."
43. LaSalle, "Review: '*Invictus*' Narrows Its Viewpoint."
44. Asim, *What Obama Means*, 90.
45. Glenn and Cunningham, "The Power of Black Magic," 144.
46. Kinsley, "Barack Obama and the Voice of God."
47. Holden, "Film Review; God's Power as an Ego Trip for an Id."
48. Gates, *In Search of Our Roots*, 58; Glenn and Cunningham, "The Power of Black Magic."
49. Williams, "In the Ring with Mildred Pierce," 177, 178.

50. Stephen, "'At Last the Family Is Together,'" 117; Wexler, "Onward, Christian Penguins," 275.
51. Quoted in Kinsley, "Barack Obama and the Voice of God."
52. Timm, "But Morgan Freeman Is So Perfect," 57.
53. Gray, *Cultural Moves*, 115.
54. Variety Staff, "Commanding Respect Even Sight Unseen."
55. Shands, *Some Peculiarities of Speech in Mississippi*, 4.
56. Quoted in Gates, *In Search of Our Roots*, 65.
57. Goodale, *Sonic Persuasion*.
58. Litwack, *Trouble in Mind*, 307.
59. Fordham and Ogbu, "Black Students' School Success."
60. Barton and dal Vera, *Voice*.
61. Wolfram, "African American Englishes," 330.
62. Thomas, "Phonological and Phonetic Characteristics of African American Vernacular English."
63. Ibid.
64. Litwack, *Trouble in Mind*, 307.
65. Harold and DeLuca, "Behold the Corpse."
66. Goldsby, "The High and Low Tech of It," 249.
67. Holden, "Film Review; God's Power as an Ego Trip for an Id."
68. Barthes, *Image, Music, Text*.
69. Altman, "Television/Sound," 43.
70. In Barkley, *Who's Afraid of a Large Black Man?*
71. Barthes, *Image, Music, Text*, 296.
72. The mixed audible breathing sounds of Freeman and the boxers range from A_2 (or about 110 Hz) to C_3 (or about 130 Hz). Freeman's monologue hovers between an A_2 and an E_3, resonating in a nearly completely overlapping series of pitches.
73. Barthes, *Image, Music, Text*, 188.
74. Zumthor, *Oral Poetry*.
75. This type of notation indicates the pitch and the octave. In a notation of "A_4," for example, the "A" indicates the pitch and the "4" indicates that this is the "A" in the fourth octave. Higher numbers indicate higher-pitched octaves. In tenor clef, the type of staff I have used to diagram voices in this project, the center line is a C_4. The pitches below the center line begin with B_3 and go down, while the pitches above the center line begin with D_4 and go up.
76. Randall, *The Harvard Dictionary of Music*.
77. Watts, *Hearing the Hurt*.
78. Kavka, *Reality Television, Affect and Intimacy*, 42.
79. Berland, "Locating Listening," 343.
80. Chion, *Audio/Vision*.
81. Although *Amistad* is based on a true story, Freeman's character, Joadson, seems to be an amalgamation of "Robert Purvis and James Forten, wealthy mulatto sailmakers of Philadelphia" (Wyatt-Brown, "*Amistad*," 1175) or of many Black abolitionists of the time (Stoddard and Marcus, "The Burden of Historical Representation"). Whatever the case, people like Joadson existed and were involved in cases like *Amistad*; as Frederick Dalzell ("Review: Dreamworking *Amistad*") notes, "if Joadson is fictional, the African-American community he stands for was very real—and vitally engaged in the Amistad case" (131).
82. Kavka, *Reality Television*.
83. Ibid.
84. Since the decibel readings for particular segments coded through Audacity vary depending upon the volume settings in the program itself, I have noted a percentage comparison rather than the specific decibels. In my Audacity reading of this segment, Freeman's

voice registered at an average of −31.7 db. Three distinct string voices were present at −26.0 db, −25.4 db, and −24.3 db. Bear in mind that decibel readings are recorded from −82 ("negative 82") to zero, so that numbers closer to zero are louder.

85. Kalinak, *Settling the Score*, 94.
86. Stilwell, "Sound and Empathy."
87. Kavka, *Reality Television*.
88. Bugliani, "The Ideal and the Real."
89. See for example, Dlanga, "Invictus."
90. Branford, "English in South Africa."
91. While a production study to explore Freeman's use of the interjection "son" is beyond the scope of this research, I speculate that the addition of *son* at the end of phrases is something Freeman does off-script, given his frequent use of the word across a variety of films, characters, and genres.
92. While aging can and does impact the vocal organs in the same ways that it affects the body as a whole, the effects of this process tend to be less pronounced for professional speakers and singers, given that both vocal training and regular use limit the detrimental impacts of aging on the voice.
93. Barthes, *Image, Music, Text*.
94. Doane, "The Voice in the Cinema," 42.
95. Ibid., 42.
96. See, for example, Silverman, *The Acoustic Mirror*, and Lawrence, *Echo and Narcissus*.
97. Doane, "The Voice in the Cinema," 42.
98. missycottman, comment on "Morgan Freeman Wall." *FanPop*, http://www.fanpop.com/clubs/morgan-freeman/wall.
99. Sutton, Vee, November 5, 2014, comment on Morgan Freeman Official Facebook Profile Picture, November 5, 2014, https://www.facebook.com/MorganFreeman/photos/a.120835441332449.29252.120791238003536/723759091040078/?type=1&comment_id=723764531039534&offset=0&total_comments=8241.
100. Son, April, "Morgan Freeman Being Inspirational Will Get You Through Another Week," *Slate.com*, September 15, 2014, https://slate.com/culture/2014/09/morgan-freeman-inspirational-sayings-collected-wisdom-of-the-actor-with-the-great-voice-video.html.
101. Caughey, *Imaginary Social Worlds*.
102. Hughey, "Cinethetic Racism."
103. Blackman, *Immaterial Bodies*.
104. Emperor Bell, July 31, 2014, "ITT: We read everything in Morgan Freeman's voice," Forum, *Bungie.net*, https://www.bungie.net/sv/Forums/Post/67162949?sort=0&page=0.
105. There is no way of knowing whether this plea was posted by Freeman himself or by a user under the name of "Morgan Freeman."
106. Munroe, "Fremanic Paracusia."
107. Litwack, *Trouble in Mind*, xii.
108. bitteranagram, May 24, 2018, 9:02 AM, Twitter, https://twitter.com/bitteranagram/status/999682053661777924?lang=en.
109. See, for example, Newcombe, "Morgan Freeman."
110. Variety Staff, "Commanding Respect Even Sight Unseen."
111. "How Do We Stop Racism?"
112. Freeman, "Interview with Morgan Freeman."
113. ItsThePolicies, October 8, 2011, comment on "Morgan Freeman Wall." *FanPop*, http://www.fanpop.com/clubs/morgan-freeman/forum/post/153932/title/not-color-thing-policy-thing.
114. bebeep53, comment on "Morgan Freeman Wall." *FanPop*, http://www.fanpop.com/clubs/morgan-freeman/wall
115. Timm, "But Morgan Freeman Is So Perfect," 57.

NOTES TO CHAPTER 3

1. In an interview with Charlie Gibson, Palin shared, somewhat inexplicably, that parts of Russia are visible from parts of Alaska. The point about Russia's visibility from an Alaskan island is unrelated to Palin's foreign policy experience or knowledge. Yet, it is true that part of Russia, an island called Big Diomede, is visible from part of Alaska, an island called Little Diomede. This makes sense, given that only the Bering Strait separates Alaskan land from Russian land, but Fey's performance of the exaggerated line makes even the true status of international visibility seem ridiculous. At any rate, Palin did *not* say she could see Russia from her house, which is my point here.
2. Wilstein, "Rep. Louie Gohmert Quotes Sarah Palin and Tina Fey on House Floor."
3. Gray, "Throwing Out the Welcome Mat"; Jones, "With All Due Respect"; Smith, *The Presidents We Imagine*.
4. Hutcheon, *A Theory of Parody*, 33.
5. Jones, "With All Due Respect."
6. Smith, *Vocal Tracks*.
7. Jones, "Politics and the Brand," 80.
8. Gray, "Throwing Out the Welcome Mat," 4.
9. Kurtz, "The *SNL* Effect"; Abel and Barthel, "Appropriation of Mainstream News."
10. Jones, *Entertaining Politics*.
11. Ibid., 10.
12. Certainly I am not arguing that the only difference between the two politicians is their vocal tone. This chapter is in no way meant to argue a comparison of Palin and Obama. Rather, I am arguing that the vocal attributes of the two politicians, layered over with their impressionists' performances of their voices, enhanced their alignment or misalignment with the traditional identities of presidential politics.
13. Test, *Satire*, 42.
14. Gray, "Throwing Out the Welcome Mat."
15. Hilmes, "The Evolution of Saturday Night."
16. Matviko, "Television Satire and the Presidency," 334.
17. Gray, "Throwing Out the Welcome Mat," 21.
18. Matviko, "Television Satire and the Presidency."
19. Hilmes, "The Evolution of Saturday Night," 31.
20. Hill and Weingrad, *Saturday Night*.
21. Jenkins, "Rowan and Martin's Laugh-In."
22. As Day and Thompson point out, *Laugh-In* did not invent the "Weekend Update" format. Similar "fake news" segments were featured on *That Was the Week That Was* and Canada's adaptation of *TW3*, *This Hour Has Seven Days*.
23. Day and Thompson, "Live from New York, It's the Fake News!" 172.
24. Marx, Sienkiewicz, and Becker, "Introduction," 2–3.
25. Whalley, *"Saturday Night Live," Hollywood Comedy, and American Culture*.
26. Hill and Weingrad, *Saturday Night*.
27. Shales, "Zingers on Saturday Night," A19.
28. Kurtzleben, "Forget Diversity."
29. Johnson, "From Cultural Iconoclast to Cultural Icon."
30. Abel and Barthel, "Appropriation of Mainstream News."
31. Jones ("With All Due Respect") notes that Vaughn Meader had impersonated John F. Kennedy on his comedy album, *The First Family*, and on *The Ed Sullivan Show*, but that the president's assassination put a dramatic end to Meader's impersonation career.
32. Smith, *The Presidents We Imagine*, 202.
33. Ibid., 202.
34. Holloway, "Presidents Became Boobs, Bumblers on 'SNL.'"

35. Quoted in Reuters, "Chevy Chase Recalls Ford as 'a Terrific Guy.'"
36. Hendra, *Going Too Far*, 443.
37. Jones, "With All Due Respect," 41.
38. Ibid., 41; the word *gravely* here is as printed in the original source; Rich Little also impersonated both Nixon and Carter (and later Reagan) and was known for his uncannily accurate vocal and physical imitations in his stand-up routines and on various late-night talk and variety shows (Jones, "With All Due Respect").
39. Rollins and O'Connor, *Hollywood's White House*, 338.
40. Matviko, "Television Satire and the Presidency."
41. Quoted in Holloway, "Presidents Became Boobs." While many sources examining *SNL's* Reagan impersonations cite the president's popularity as a reason for the show's weak and sparse impressions, Whalley points out that, despite Reagan's re-election, public opinion polls did not show Reagan to be a popular president.
42. Matviko, "Television Satire and the Presidency," 342.
43. Jones, "With All Due Respect," 42.
44. Ibid.
45. Day and Thompson, "Live from New York, It's the Fake News," 173.
46. Hinckley, "'Saturday Night Live' Is Buzzworthy Again, Thanks to Tina Fey as Sarah Palin."
47. Whalley, *"Saturday Night Live," Hollywood Comedy, and American Culture.*
48. Abel and Barthel, "Appropriation of Mainstream News."
49. See for example, Seelye, "Fey-Palin Character Debuts on S.N.L."; Spillius, "Tina Fey Lands the First Punch at Sarah Palin in *Saturday Night Live* Sketch"; Jones, "Politics and the Brand," 81.
50. Gray, Jones, and Thompson, "Using One of Its Lifelines."
51. Jones, "With All Due Respect," 48.
52. Quoted in Flowers and Young, "Parodying Palin," 54.
53. Sheidlower, "What Kind of Accent Does Sarah Palin Have?"
54. Palin was born in Idaho, but her family moved to Alaska shortly after her birth. They settled in the Anchorage area several years later. Palin, *Going Rogue*.
55. Alaska is the largest and most rural state in the US, making census-taking difficult and likely unreliable. What is known is that Alaska Natives are much more concentrated in rural areas of the state than in Anchorage, the state's primary hub. US Census Bureau, "Decennial Census of Population and Housing."
56. Finkler, "Documentary on Alaska's Great Depression Farm Colonists Worth Watching."
57. Daley and James, "Warming the Arctic Air"; Alaska Advisory Committee to the US Commission on Civil Rights, "Racism's Frontier."
58. Daley and James, "Warming the Arctic Air."
59. Siegel, "Palin's Accent Examined."
60. Siegel; Sheidlower, "What Kind of Accent Does Sarah Palin Have?"
61. Fey, *Bossypants*, 204.
62. Chandler, September 14, 2008, comment on Seelye, "Fey-Palin Character Debuts on S.N.L."
63. Spillius, "Tina Fey Lands the First Punch at Sarah Palin in *Saturday Night Live* Sketch."
64. Ryan, "Did Tina Fey Out-Palin Palin on 'Saturday Night Live,'" 1.
65. McConnell-Ginet, "Intonation in a Man's World."
66. Griffin, "I AM an Angry Black Woman"; Beltrán, *Latina/o Stars in U.S. Eyes.*
67. As I have argued elsewhere, this is exactly the type of pitch pattern that was falsely attributed to Hillary Clinton during the original Benghazi hearings. Edgar, "Toward a Genosonic Lens."

68. Comment on "Obama Impersonated on *Saturday Night Live*," February 24, 2008, *All Things Obama*, February 23, 2008, http://allthingsobama.blogspot.com/2008/02/fauxbama-opening-skit-on-saturday-night.html.
69. According to Baken's authoritative handbook on speech measurement, the average spoken frequency range for women is 165 Hz to 255 Hz; 165 Hz roughly translates to a pitch of E3, represented by the space below the alto clef staff (which I have used throughout this book), and 255 Hz roughly translates to a pitch of C4, represented by the middle line of the staff. The the top of Palin's range aligns with the top average pitch for adult women, but Palin's lower pitch ranges are much lower than is accounted for in the average pitch range for women.
70. I used Baken's work to notate the average pitches by sex. This research does not consider race, but more recent research has suggested that there is no significant difference in pitch between white women and Black women (Xue and Huo, "Normative Standards for Vocal Tract Dimensions by Race as Measured by Acoustic Pharyngometry"). Similarly, Xue and Huo's study found no significant difference between white men and Black men, though the Chinese men in their study showed slightly lower average pitches, attributable to their slightly longer vocal tract lengths. Walton and Orlikoff's ("Speaker Race Identification from Acoustic Cues in the Vocal Signal") study similarly found no significant pitch difference between Black men and white men. As Xue and Huo and others have pointed out, the most important predictors of average vocal pitch are height and weight, rather than racial identification or, as McConnell-Ginet ("Intonation in a Man's World") adds, sex.
71. Palin, *Going Rogue.*
72. Milazzo, "What I Learned at the Sarah Palin Rally before They Threw Me Out."
73. See note 70 and 71.
74. See previous note.
75. Hill Collins, *Black Sexual Politics*, 315.
76. Milazzo, "What I Learned at the Sarah Palin Rally before They Threw Me Out."
77. Seelye, "Fey-Palin Character Debuts on S.N.L."
78. TJW, comment on Ryan, "Did Tina Fey Out-Palin Palin on 'Saturday Night Live,'" *The Watcher*, September 14, 2008, https://web.archive.org/web/20170415215456/http://featuresblogs.chicagotribune.com/entertainment_tv/2008/09/saturday-night.html.
79. As Katie Couric pointed out in Palin's second interview, the politician's comment about Russia still made little sense as a foreign policy credential. My point here is to illustrate that Fey's lines were perceived as being drawn directly from Palin's interviews, despite the fact that they were comic satire.
80. Fey, *Bossypants*, 203.
81. For example, Jessica G., "Tina Fey as Sarah Palin."
82. STV, "Clueless French Newspaper Misidentifies 'Troubled' Tina Fey as Sarah Palin"; "Fox News Shows Tina Fey in On-Screen Graphic for Sarah Palin."
83. Sassette, September 15, 2008, comment on Jessica G., "Amy & Tina Do Hillary & Sarah to Hilarious, Depressing Effect."
84. Brian, September 14, 2008, comment on WSJ Staff, "Tina Fey Returns to '*Saturday Night Live*' to Play Palin."
85. Seelye, "Fey-Palin Character Debuts on S.N.L."
86. Jones, "Politics and the Brand."
87. Ryan, "Did Tina Fey Out-Palin Palin on 'Saturday Night Live.'"
88. Gunn, "On Speech and Public Release," 183.
89. Fey, *Bossypants.*
90. Dwyer, "Getting in Palin's Hair, or Close to It."
91. Diane S., September 14, 2008, comment on WSJ Staff, "Tina Fey Returns to '*Saturday Night Live*' to Play Palin."

92. K2, September 15, 2008, comment on Jessica G., "Amy & Tina Do Hillary & Sarah to Hilarious, Depressing Effect."
93. SydneyGal, September 29, 2008, comment on Jessica G., "Tina Fey as Sarah Palin: 'Katie, I'd Like to Use One of My Life Lines.'"
94. Gilli, September 14, 2008, comment on WSJ Staff, "Tina Fey Returns to 'Saturday Night Live' to Play Palin."
95. SNL Fan of Yore, October 5, 2008, comment on Sweet, "Tina Fey as Sarah Palin Nails It Again on 'Saturday Night Live' Debate Skit."
96. Seelye, "Fey-Palin Character Debuts on S.N.L."
97. Love, "Biden Knows Stuff, Palin Plays Tina Fey."
98. Poniewozik, "Palin vs. 'Palin,'" 29.
99. E. Hussein, September 28, 2008, comment on SilentPatriot, "*SNL* Spoofs Palin/Couric Interview."
100. J. Michael, September 15, 2008, comment on WSJ Staff, "Tina Fey Returns to 'Saturday Night Live' to Play Palin."
101. AgentX, September 28, 2008, comment on SilentPatriot, "*SNL* Spoofs Palin/Couric Interview."
102. Barthes, *Image, Music, Text*, 181.
103. Chester, September 14, 2008, comment on WSJ Staff, "Tina Fey Returns to 'Saturday Night Live' to Play Palin."
104. Noonan, "Palin and Populism."
105. Lisa, September 14, 2008, comment on Sweet, "Tina Fey as Sarah Palin Nails It Again on 'Saturday Night Live' Debate Skit."
106. igda1906, October 5, 2008, comment on Sweet, "Tina Fey as Sarah Palin Nails It Again on 'Saturday Night Live' Debate Skit."
107. Ihde, *Listening and Voice*.
108. Quoted in Frederick, "Sarah Palin Lauds Tina Fey, Perhaps because She Didn't Hear a Word of 'SNL' Skit."
109. annejumps, September 15, 2008, comment on Jessica G., "Amy & Tina Do Hillary & Sarah to Hilarious, Depressing Effect."
110. igda1906, October 5, 2008, comment on Sweet, "Tina Fey as Sarah Palin Nails It Again on 'Saturday Night Live' Debate Skit."
111. Heilemann and Halperin, *Game Change*.
112. Marcus, "Fred Armisen Performs in 'Honeyface.'"
113. Beltrán, "*SNL*'s 'Fauxbama' Debate."
114. Wallenstein, "In Search of a Better Obama Impersonator"; Bennett, "The Tedious Accuracy of Jay Pharoah's Obama impersonation."
115. I do not mean to imply that either sex or authority naturally manifests in the voice. Instead, following McConnell-Ginet ("Intonation in a Man's World"), my argument takes up the assumption that voice is socially constructed in terms of both gender and authority. Additionally, I take the few studies of race and vocal frequency/pitch, which have consistently shown that no significant difference exists between white men's and Black men's average spoken pitch range, as further support for the idea that perceived racial differences in pitch are largely imagined. Much more research is necessary in this area.
116. Anderson and Klofstad, "Preference for Leaders with Masculine Voices Holds in the Case of Feminine Leadership Roles."
117. Anderson and Klofstad, like many scholars of voice, do not indicate the racial identification of the speakers in their study.
118. For example, Simmons-Duffin, "Video: Talking While Female"; Kat, "How to Lower Your Voice"; Louët, "Your Voice."
119. Bergen, "Abraham Lincoln as a Lawyer," 32.
120. Bernstein, "The Speech"; Jenkins, "Obama's One-Man Sing-Along."

121. Browning, "Does Obama's Baritone Give Him an Edge?"
122. Sullivan, "Obama, Romney, and What Their Voices Tell Us."
123. Jenkins, "Obama's One-Man Sing-Along."
124. Obama, *Dreams from My Father*, 67, 220.
125. Clark, "His Late Father Looms Over Obama's Trip to Kenya."
126. Alim and Smitherman, *Articulate while Black*, 26.
127. Obama, *Dreams from My Father*.
128. Alim and Smitherman, *Articulate while Black*.
129. For example, Frank, "The Prophetic Voice and the Face of the Other in Barack Obama's 'A More Perfect Union' Address"; Terrill, "Unity and Duality in Barack Obama's 'A More Perfect Union'"; Utley and Heyse, "Barack Obama's (Im)perfect Union."
130. Pew Research Center for the People and the Press, "Obama and Wright Controversy Dominate News Cycle."
131. Variety Staff, "Commanding Respect Even Sight Unseen," A12.
132. Baken, *Clinical Measurement of Speech and Voice*.
133. See notes 70 and 71; Sadie, *The New Grove Dictionary of Opera*.
134. Beltrán, "*SNL*'s 'Fauxbama' Debate."
135. Milazzo, "What I Learned at the Sarah Palin Rally before They Threw Me Out."
136. Baken, *Clinical Measurement of Speech and Voice*.
137. Xue and Huo, "Normative Standards for Vocal Tract Dimensions by Race as Measured by Acoustic Pharyngometry"; Walton and Orlikoff, "Speaker Race Identification from Acoustic Cues in the Vocal Signal."
138. For example, Somekindofsatan, "Forum: Why Do Black People Have Deep Voices? (No Racist)"; Mysteriousvisitor, "Forum: Why Do Blacks Have Deep Singing Voices?"
139. Hill Collins, *Black Sexual Politics*.
140. Quoted in Gavin, "D.C. Weighs in on SNL's New Obama."
141. NJRightwinger12, September 12, 2012, comment on Toto, "Fred Armisen Out as 'SNL's' Obama Impersonator."
142. Median Democrat, comment on "About That "Obama Playing It Cool" Skit on SNL Last Night?"
143. Quoted in Gavin, "D.C. Weighs in on SNL's New Obama."
144. Comment, November 11, 2012, on "Forum: *SNL* 11/10/12," *Datalounge.com*, https://www.datalounge.com/thread/12119271-snl-11-10-12.
145. Akimbo, September 12, 2012, comment on Obenson, "Jay Pharoah Is Replacing Fred Armisen as President Obama on 'Saturday Night Live.'"
146. Beltrán, "*SNL*'s 'Fauxbama' Debate."
147. Hill Collins, *Black Sexual Politics*.
148. Hill Collins, 315.
149. Billy Bob Jones, April 13, 2012, comment on "Don't You Think President Barack Obama Sounds Like The Rock," *Yahoo! Answers*, https://answers.yahoo.com/question/index?qid=20120413164837AAFT6H3.
150. James S., online poll, January 8, 2008, "Does Barack Obama Sound Like The Rock," *YouChoose.net*, http://www.youchoose.net/campaign/does_barack_obama_sound_like_the_rock.
151. Six years after the original "The Rock Obama" sketch, *SNL* briefly introduced Leslie Jones as She-Rock Obama. In the end portion of a "The Rock Obama" sketch in March 2015, an aide enters the Oval Office to tell Michelle (played by Sasheer Zamata) that "a mentally ill vagrant" has been living in her garden. She transitions, Incredible Hulk style, into She-Rock Obama (played by Leslie Jones). She-Rock Obama's line lasts approximately four seconds in total, and the impression went largely ignored by audience commentary. Furthermore, unlike Fey's and Obama's impersonators, neither Zamata nor Jones seems to perform Michelle in ways that connect to the First Lady's actual vocal

presentation; they are instead fairly generic, albeit, in Jones's case, stereotypical in their reference to the "angry black woman." Since my argument in this chapter is about the layering of bodies that occurs in actual vocal impersonations, I have chosen to focus on the more prominent impressions within *SNL*, specifically those that indicate attempts to actually perform the style of the political speakers in question.
152. joan, 2014, comment on Maltais, "Republican Supporter Dwayne Johnson Demands to Be Removed from Chris Christie Campaign Video He Was Featured In Without Permission."
153. Rebornknight, February 8, 2012, comment on Semigran, "The Rock to Run for President Someday?"
154. Beltrán, "*SNL*'s 'Fauxbama' Debate," 203.
155. Ibid.
156. Falcone, "Obama Gets 'Celebrity Treatment' in New McCain Ad."
157. "Definition of Character."
158. Comment on "Obama Impersonated on *Saturday Night Live*."
159. Comment on "Obama Impersonated on *Saturday Night Live*."
160. Mrs. Shermender, October 10, 2008, comment on Trent, "'*SNL*' Presents the Second Presidential Debate."
161. Browning, "Does Obama's Baritone Give Him an Edge?"

NOTES TO CHAPTER 4

1. Alpinorico2, 1 year ago [accessed November 9, 2014], comment on Guerrillaz, "Richard Pryor - Black Women and White Women," YouTube, March 30, 2010, 4:06, https://www.youtube.com/watch?v=HFD2Y-EgoMc.
2. differentandalike, 10 months ago [archived December 6, 2012], comment on Guerrillaz, "Richard Pryor - Black Women and White Women," YouTube, March 30, 2010, 4:06, https://web.archive.org/web/20121206214454/http://www.youtube.com/watch?v=HFD2Y-EgoMc&gl=US&hl=en.
3. David Beverly, 2 years ago [accessed November 9, 2014], comment on Guerrillaz, "Richard Pryor - Black Women and White Women," YouTube, March 30, 2010, 4:06, https://www.youtube.com/watch?v=HFD2Y-EgoMc.
4. I use Latino, rather than Latinx, here because all of the videos returned in the search for this chapter were performances by cisgender men (see note 43). I discuss this gender disparity later in the chapter but want to note up front that my choice of terms is intentional.
5. Brodie, "Stand-Up Comedy as a Genre of Intimacy," 174.
6. Ibid.
7. Haggins, *Laughing Mad*, 2.
8. Smith-Shomade, *Shaded Lives*.
9. Haggins, *Laughing Mad*, 132.
10. Ibid., 12.
11. Avila-Saavedra, "Ethnic Otherness versus Cultural Assimilation," 290.
12. Dyson, *Open Mike*, 257.
13. Acham, *Revolution Televised*.
14. Hunt, "Off the Record."
15. Ibid.
16. Acham.
17. Haggins, *Laughing Mad*, 10.
18. Ibid.

19. Ibid., 20.
20. Ibid., 50.
21. Henry and Henry, *Furious Cool,* 127.
22. Zoglin, *Comedy at the Edge.*
23. Haggins, *Laughing Mad.*
24. Bogle, *Toms, Coons, Mulattoes, Mammies, and Bucks.*
25. See Gates, "Bringing the Black."
26. Haggins, *Laughing Mad,* 73.
27. Dyson, *Open Mike.*
28. Ibid., 259; Haggins, *Laughing Mad,* 179.
29. Khatchatourian, "Chris Rock Thinks YouTube Has Ruined Stand-Up Comedy."
30. See, for example, Cavendish, "Learn How to Be a Stand-Up Comedian?"; Davis, "How'd You Get There, Standup Comic Kate Wolff?"
31. See, for example, Hanson, Haridakis, and Sharma, "Differing Uses of YouTube during the 2008 U.S. Presidential Primary Election"; see also Guo and Lee, "The Critique of YouTube-Based Vernacular Discourse."
32. Hanson, Haridakis, and Sharma, "Differing Uses of YouTube," 2.
33. Ono and Sloop, "The Critique of Vernacular Discourse," 24; Guo and Lee, "The Critique of YouTube-Based Vernacular Discourse."
34. Baym and Shah, "Circulating Struggle."
35. Hanson, Haridakis, and Sharma, "Differing Uses of YouTube," 2.
36. Hess, "Resistance Up In Smoke," 430.
37. Guo and Lee, "The Critique of YouTube-Based Vernacular Discourse," 400.
38. Dylko, Beam, Landreville, and Geidner, "Filtering 2008 US Presidential Election News," 833.
39. Fattal, "Hostile Remixes on YouTube," 331.
40. Chun, "Ironic Blackness as Masculine Cool," 609.
41. Hall, "Encoding and Decoding in the Television Discourse."
42. Ibid.; Hess, "Resistance Up In Smoke."
43. Since, in this chapter, I was particularly interested in how whiteness impressions circulate through YouTube, I used the site's search function to guide my selection of artifacts. A November 6, 2014, search for "White people impressions" returned 135,000 results, which I sorted by relevance. As I discussed in the above section, YouTube's search function is not a perfect indicator of what is available on the site. Still, given the somewhat problematic gatekeeping processes facilitated by the "thumbs up" and "thumbs down" buttons, using the "sort by relevance" feature offered one way of replicating a typical user's search for impressions of whiteness. I chose to analyze the first thirty videos returned by the search, representing the work of fourteen stand-up comics of color, including eleven Black comedians and three Latino comedians, all of whom are men, and all of whom are discussed, if briefly, in my previous section tracing the history of racial stand-up comedy.
44. Brodie, "Stand-Up Comedy as a Genre of Intimacy."
45. Goodale, *Sonic Persuasion.*
46. Dolar, *A Voice and Nothing More,* 20.
47. Dyson, *Open Mike.*
48. Dolar, *A Voice and Nothing More,* 20.
49. Bucholtz and Lopez, "Performing Blackness, Forming Whiteness."
50. Ibid.
51. Ibid.
52. Ibid.
53. Dolar, *A Voice and Nothing More,* 20.
54. Fleetwood, *Troubling Vision,* 152.

55. Dyson, *Open Mike*, 259.
56. Bucholtz, "The Whiteness of Nerds."
57. Ibid.; Fleetwood, *Troubling Vision*.
58. Fleetwood, *Troubling Vision*, 152.
59. Bouie, "Are Black Names 'Weird,' or Are You Just Racist?"; Matthews, "He Dropped One Letter in His Name While Applying for Jobs, and the Responses Rolled In."
60. Green, *African American English*.
61. Ibid.
62. Carr, "One *Margarita* Please!"
63. Neal, *Looking for Leroy*.
64. Erni, "Queer Figurations in the Media."
65. Gunn, "On Speech and Public Release," 183.
66. Bucholtz, "The Whiteness of Nerds."
67. Hill Collins, *Black Sexual Politics*.
68. Scheff, "Hypermasculinity and Violence as a Social System."
69. Barthes, *Image, Music, Text*.
70. Ibid.
71. Flynt, *Dixie's Forgotten People*; I say the specification of poor white people is "perhaps unfair[ ]" because white people of all economic classes have perpetrated violence against people of color. Focusing on the violence by poor white people only serves to obfuscate the physical and structural violence enacted against people and communities of color, as well as poor whites, by middle-class and wealthy white people, including and especially politicians and conservative voters.
72. In the clips I analyzed, Pryor, Chappelle, Griffin, and Lopez did not raise their pitches in whitevoice. Pryor, Chappelle, and Griffin generally speak in higher voices, making a raised-pitch whitevoice more difficult to achieve. In the Lopez clips, his whitevoice did not change pitch from his standard performance voice.
73. King, *African Americans and the Culture of Pain*.
74. Haggins, *Laughing Mad*, 142.
75. Smyth, Jacobs, and Rogers, "Male Voices and Perceived Sexual Orientation."
76. Kim, "The Racial Triangulation of Asian Americans."
77. See note 43.
78. Alonzo Lockhart, 5 years ago [accessed February 15, 2019], comment on Ghetto Rigged, "Kevin Hart - 'I could never be a rapper,'" YouTube, November 5, 2009, 1:29, https://www.youtube.com/watch?v=C_axfpqRX1w&lc=Ugz2w64zdOBZPgDhvz54AaABAg; Billie Brunson, 6 years ago [accessed February 15, 2019], comment on Ghetto Rigged, "Kevin Hart - 'I could never be a rapper,'" YouTube, November 5, 2009, 1:29, https://www.youtube.com/watch?v=C_axfpqRX1w&lc=UgzUCyCshwzjooxaen54AaABAg.
79. Ravi Parekh, 5 years ago [accessed February 15, 2019], comment on Gabriel Iglesias, "'E-glesias with a I' - Gabriel Iglesias (from my I'm Not Fat. . . I'm Fluffy comedy special)," YouTube, May 12, 2011, 4:17, https://www.youtube.com/watch?v=CxgIbznAV84&lc=UghdZYkPv2VZGngCoAEC; Clinton Cota, 2 months ago [accessed November 9, 2014], comment on Sven Ha, "Dave Chappelle and his white friend Chip," YouTube, November 17, 2008, 5:19, https://web.archive.org/web/20141210182311/https://www.youtube.com/watch?v=JJ3dk6KAvQM.
80. Skerdy, November 8, 2014 [accessed November 9, 2014], comment on Gabriel Iglesias, "'High School Reunion' -Gabriel Iglesias (exclusive bonus footage from 'I'm Not Fat. . . I'm Fluffy')," YouTube, July 28, 2010, 5:23, https://www.youtube.com/watch?v=5QQzusr4IHo.
81. Ladu AU, 6 months ago [accessed November 10, 2014], comment on Codeblack Comedy, "Aries Spears White people do whatever they want Shaq's Five Minute Funnies

Comedy Shaq," YouTube, September 30, 2013, 3:50, https://www.youtube.com/watch?v=7nYngZLjWi0.

82. anniemomi17, 6 years ago [accessed February 15, 2019], comment on Ark adiusz, "Carlos Mencia - white people," YouTube, November 26, 2010, 0:56, https://www.youtube.com/watch?v=speWI30v0S8&lc=UgwnIf2c3wUDRckz3eh4AaABAg.

83. Firstblk, 1 year ago [accessed November 9, 2014], comment on tomdahitman, "Dave Chappelle - Black & White peoples food," YouTube, September 22, 2008, 3:28, https://www.youtube.com/watch?v=SB8A0zV1TD0.

84. DrAbstracked, 6 years ago [accessed February 15, 2019], comment on b31cuzz, "Jamie Foxx stand-up *White ppl* Hilarious!," YouTube, December 22, 2010, 4:51, https://www.youtube.com/watch?v=z-5YNRAg834&lc=Ugxf4aBv7-3UMZWVnk94AaABAg.

85. Bucholtz and Lopez, "Performing Blackness, Forming Whiteness"; this user, DrAbstracked, uploads his own videos to YouTube fairly frequently. In them, he speaks in a clear AAE dialect, though, as he confirms in this comment, he is white.

86. CHEF ASHER, 1 month ago [accessed November 9, 2014], comment on StandupTV13, "DAVE CHAPPELE: why black people hang out with white dudes lmaoo," YouTube, January 7, 2012, 9:24, https://www.youtube.com/watch?v=hIRjB6CPxLE.

87. Green, *African American English*.

88. Castle Coatl, 6 years ago [accessed February 15, 2019], comment on ElSoldao, "White mothers & Latin mothers.wmv," YouTube, November 25, 2008, 2:22, https://www.youtube.com/watch?v=OVjLuL3vijY&lc=UgwaGOKOkdUJvHu6Qh54AaABAg; r0413900, 6 years ago [accessed February 15, 2019], comment on ElSoldao, "White mothers & Latin mothers.wmv," YouTube, November 25, 2008, 2:22, https://www.youtube.com/watch?v=OVjLuL3vijY&lc=UgzzRzmR0leWLSfhxXp4AaABAg.

89. Jason Fontaine, 3 weeks ago [accessed November 8, 2014], comment on DontHateOnJord, "Eddie Murphy's RAW - White People Can't Dance [HD]," YouTube, August 16, 2010, 1:20, https://www.youtube.com/watch?v=KsyYuFv5ltc; Heather Toll, 2 months ago [accessed November 9, 2014], comment on Sven Ha, "Dave Chappelle and his white friend Chip," YouTube, November 17, 2008, 5:19, https://web.archive.org/web/20141210182311/https://www.youtube.com/watch?v=JJ3dk6KAvQM.

90. Annette Jenkins, 3 months ago [accessed November 9, 2014], comment on I watch you post...Simple, "White Families vs. Black Families," YouTube, March 25, 2012, 4:46, https://web.archive.org/web/20141105055140/https://www.youtube.com/watch?v=h_Uj1FRmLao.

91. DALE7XCHAMP, 7 months ago [accessed November 8, 2014], comment on camilo andres, "Eddie Murphy White people and Hauntings," YouTube, July 8, 2013, 1:39, https://www.youtube.com/watch?v=azCCWPcjkJo.

92. For references to mothers, see, for, example the previously cited Castle Cotl and r0413900; for references to fathers, see, for example, Ladu AU; references to fathers included DrAbstracked.

93. Greg Michaels, 8 months ago [accessed November 9, 2014], comment on BigDo, "Eddie Murphy On Michael Jackson," YouTube, July 2, 2009, 4:08, https://web.archive.org/web/20160404212731/https://www.youtube.com/watch?v=gVps8jOl91Q; Matt Ruth, November 8, 2014 [accessed November 9, 2014], comment on Sven Ha, "Dave Chappell and his white friend Chip," YouTube, November 17, 2008, 5:19, https://web.archive.org/web/20141210182311/https://www.youtube.com/watch?v=JJ3dk6KAvQM; Karen Ramos, 6 months ago [accessed November 9, 2014], comment on Gabriel Iglesias, "'High School Reunion' -Gabriel Iglesias (exclusive bonus footage from 'I'm Not Fat. . . I'm Fluffy')," YouTube, July 28, 2010, 5:23, https://www.youtube.com/watch?v=5QQzusr4IH0.

94. Haggins, *Laughing Mad*.

95. TruthfullyRude, 1 year ago [accessed November 8, 2014], comment on machiavel2772, "Dave Chappelle - White People," YouTube, October 3, 2008, 2:14, https://www.youtube

.com/watch?v=6uvg-ug9CvE; Zanny Boy, 6 months ago [accessed November 8, 2014], comment on machiavel2772, "Dave Chappelle - White People," YouTube, October 3, 2008, 2:14, https://www.youtube.com/watch?v=6uvg-ug9CvE.
96. Habanero212, 5 months ago [accessed November 9, 2014], comment on DontHateOnJord, "Eddie Murphy's RAW - Italian's After They Have Seen Rocky [HD]," YouTube, August 16, 2010, 4:12, https://www.youtube.com/watch?v=YMqMKxJJYvY.
97. marliatou Diallov, 3 months ago [Accessed November 9, 2014], comment on b31cuzz, Jamie Foxx stand-up *White ppl* Hilarious!," YouTube, December 22, 2010, 4:51, https://www.youtube.com/watch?v=z-5YNRAg834; Peanut Butter and Jelly, 1 year ago [accessed November 9, 2014], comment on Guerrillaz, "Richard Pryor - Black Women and White Women," YouTube, March 30, 2010, 4:06, https://web.archive.org/web/20121206214454/http://www.youtube.com/watch?v=HFD2Y-EgoMc&gl=US&hl=en.
98. Haggins, *Laughing Mad*, 12.
99. Certainly these hypermasculine ideals also harm women in a variety of ways.
100. Brodie, "Stand-Up Comedy as a Genre of Intimacy," 174.
101. Dolar, *A Voice and Nothing More*, 20.

NOTES TO CONCLUSION

1. Cavarero, *For More Than One Voice*, 177.
2. Barthes, *Image, Music, Text*.
3. Ibid., 181–82; See Introduction, note 21.
4. Douglas, *Listening In*.
5. Ibid.
6. Maurice, "Cinema at Its Source."
7. Butler, *Gender Trouble*.
8. Dolar, *A Voice and Nothing More*, 20.
9. Gunn, "On Speech and Public Release," 183.
10. I used online comment gathering for efficiency while still maintaining rigorous and thorough collection and coding processes for audience data. That is to say that I pulled many more online comments than I included in the write-up of the study. This study is not written as a thematic analysis, because I was interested in placing the text in conversation with the audience comments. Therefore, instead of organizing the project into audience themes, I worked with themes that crossed over between the text and the audience commentary.
11. Middleton, Hess, Endres, and Senda-Cook, *Participatory Critical Rhetoric*; McKinnon, Asen, Chávez, and Howard, *Text + Field*.
12. Tagg, "Caught on the Back Foot."
13. Wing, "When the Media Treats White Suspects and Killers Better Than Black Victims."
14. Stampler, "Twitter Users Ask What Photo Media Would Use #IfTheyGunnedMeDown."
15. See, for example, Wing, "When the Media Treats White Suspects and Killers Better Than Black Victims"; Jacobs, "Research Shows That White Mass Shooters Are Treated More Sympathetically by the Media."
16. Quoted in Chernikoff, "Laverne Cox's Explanation of Why #TransIsBeautiful Will Make You Cheer and Cry."
17. John M. Chu, August 19, 2018, *Twitter*, https://twitter.com/jonmchu/status/1031211945716666368.
18. Tay, "Crazy Rich Asians"; emphasis mine.
19. Ono and Pham, *Asian Americans and the Media*.
20. Nath, "I Can't Stop Thinking About the Accents in *Crazy Rich Asians*."

21. Lu, "What 'Crazy Rich Asians' Left Out."
22. Jackson, "Who Really Owns the 'Blaccent'?"
23. Selk, "'I Wanted to Stop Her Crying.'"
24. Hansen, "The Forgotten Minority in Police Shootings."

NOTES TO APPENDIX

1. Audacity can be downloaded as freeware from http://audacity.sourceforge.net/.
2. MuseScore can be downloaded as freeware from http://musescore.org/.
3. Edgar, "Toward a Genosonic Lens."
4. Ibid.

BIBLIOGRAPHY

"Morgan Freeman Wall." *Fanpop,* http://www.fanpop.com/clubs/morgan-freeman/wall

Abel, Angela D., and Matthew Barthel. "Appropriation of Mainstream News." *Critical Studies in Media Communication* 30, no. 1 (2013): 1–16.

Acham, Christine. *Revolution Televised: Prime Time and the Struggle for Black Power.* Minneapolis: University of Minnesota Press, 2004.

Adelt, Ulrich. *Blues Music in the Sixties: A Story in Black and White.* New Brunswick, NJ: Rutgers University Press, 2010.

Adorno, Theodore W. *The Jargon of Authenticity.* Evanston, IL: Northwestern University Press, 1973.

Alaska Advisory Committee to the US Commission on Civil Rights. "Racism's Frontier: The Untold Story of Discrimination and Division in Alaska." 2002. Accessed September 27, 2018. https://www.usccr.gov/pubs/sac/ako402/main.htm

Alim, H. Samy, and Geneva Smitherman. *Articulate while Black: Barack Obama, Language, and Race in the U.S.* New York: Oxford University Press, 2012.

Altman, Rick. "Television/Sound." In *Studies in Entertainment,* edited by Tania Modleski, 39–54. Madison: University of Wisconsin Press, 1986.

Anderson, Rindy C., and Casey A. Klofstad. "Preference for Leaders with Masculine Voices Holds in the Case of Feminine Leadership Roles." *PLoS ONE* 7, no. 12 (2012): 1–4. https://doi.org/10.1371/journal.pone.0051216.

Ark adiusz. "Carlos Mencia - white people," YouTube, November 26, 2010, 0:56, https://www.youtube.com/watch?v=speWI3ovoS8&lc=UgwnIf2c3wUDRckz3eh4AaABAg.

Asim, Jabari. *What Obama Means: For Our Culture, Our Politics, Our Future.* New York: William Morrow, 2009.

Attali, Jacques. *Noise: The Political Economy of Music.* Minneapolis: University of Minnesota Press, 1985.

Avila-Saavedra, Guillermo. "Ethnic Otherness versus Cultural Assimilation: U.S. Latino Comedians and the Politics of Identity." *Mass Communication and Society* 14, no. 3 (2011): 271–91.

b31cuzz. "Jamie Foxx stand-up *White ppl* Hilarious!," YouTube, December 22, 2010, 4:51, https://www.youtube.com/watch?v=z-5YNRAg834&lc=Ugxf4aBv7-3UMZWVnk94AaABAg.

Baken, R. J. *Clinical Measurement of Speech and Voice.* London: Taylor and Francis, 1987.

Banet-Weiser, Sarah. *Authentic™: The Politics of Ambivalence in a Brand Culture.* New York: New York University Press, 2012.

Barkley, Charles. *Who's Afraid of a Large Black Man?* New York: Penguin Press, 2005.

Barnier, Martin. "The Sound of the First French Television Advertisements." *Music, Sound, and the Moving Image* 2, no. 2 (2008): 149–52.

Barthes, Roland. *Image, Music, Text.* Translated by Stephen Heath. New York: Hill and Wang, 1978.

Barton, Robert, and Rocco dal Vera. *Voice: Onstage and Off.* New York: Routledge, 2011.

Baym, Geoffrey, and Chirag Shah. "Circulating Struggle." *Communication and Society* 14 (2011): 1017–38.

Beltrán, Mary C. *Latina/o Stars in U.S. Eyes: The Making and Meanings of Film and TV Stardom.* Champaign: University of Illinois Press, 2009.

———. "*SNL*'s 'Fauxbama' Debate: Facing Off over Millennial (Mixed-)Racial Impersonation." In Marx, Sienkiewicz, and Becker, 191–211.

Bennett, Laura. "The Tedious Accuracy of Jay Pharoah's Obama Impersonation." *New Republic*, September 15, 2012. Accessed September 24, 2018. http://www.newrepublic.com/article/107338/tedious-accuracy-jay-pharoahs-obama-impersonation.

Benshoff, Harry M. *Monsters in the Closet: Homosexuality and the Horror Film.* Manchester, UL: Manchester University Press, 1997.

Bergen, Abram. "Abraham Lincoln as a Lawyer." In *Proceedings of the Fourteenth Annual Meeting of the Bar Association of the State of Kansas,* edited by Bar Association of the State of Kansas, 31–41. Clay Center, KS: The Times, 1897.

Berland, Jody. "Locating Listening: Technological Space, Popular Music, Canadian Mediations." *Cultural studies* 2, no. 3 (1988): 342–58.

Bernhardt, B. May, and Joseph P. Stemberger. "Translation to Practice: Transcription of the Speech of Multilingual Children." In *Multilingual Aspects of Speech Sound Disorders in Children,* edited by Sharynn McLeod and Brian A. Goldstein, 182–90. Bristol, UK: Multilingual Matters, 2012.

Bernstein, David. "The Speech." *Chicago Magazine,* May 29, 2007. Accessed September. http://www.chicagomag.com/Chicago-Magazine/June-2007/The-Speech/.

"Beyoncé, Adele, Chris Brown up for NAACP Image Awards." *Rolling Stone,* January 20, 2012. Accessed September 25, 2018. https://www.rollingstone.com/music/music-news/beyonce-adele-chris-brown-up-for-naacp-image-awards-97444/.

BigDo. "Eddie Murphy On Michael Jackson," YouTube, July 2, 2009, 4:08, https://web.archive.org/web/20160404212731/https://www.youtube.com/watch?v=gVps8jOl91Q.

Blackman, Lisa. *Immaterial Bodies: Affect, Embodiment, Mediation.* London: Sage, 2012.

Bloom, Gina. *Voice in Motion: Staging Gender, Shaping Sound in Early Modern England.* Philadelphia: University of Pennsylvania Press, 2011.

Bogle, Donald. *Toms, Coons, Mulattoes, Mammies, and Bucks: An Interpretive History of Blacks in American Films.* New York: Bloomsbury, 2001.

Bouie, Jamelle. "Are Black Names 'Weird,' or Are You Just Racist?" *Daily Beast,* September 13, 2013. Accessed September 24, 2018. http://www.thedailybeast.com/articles/2013/09/13/are-blacks-names-weird-or-are-you-just-racist.html.

Boyle, Ellexis, Brad Millington, and Patricia Vertinsky. "Representing the Female Pugilist: Narratives of Race, Gender, and Disability in *Million Dollar Baby.*" *Sociology of Sport Journal* 23 (2006): 99–116.

Brackett, David. "The Politics and Practice of 'Crossover' in American Popular Music, 1963 to 1965." *The Musical Quarterly* 78, no. 4 (1994): 774–97.

Branford, William. "English in South Africa." In *The Cambridge History of the English Language, vol. 5, English in Britain and Overseas: Origins and Development,* edited by Robert Burchfield, 430–96. Cambridge: University of Cambridge, 1994.

Breathwaite, John. "Morgan Freeman . . . *Along Came a Spider.*" *New African* 399 (September 2001): 38.

Brinca, Lilia F., Ana Paula F. Batista, Ana Inês Tavares, Ilídio C. Gonçalves, and Maria L. Moreno. "Use of Cepstral Analyses for Differentiating Normal from Dysphonic Voices: A Comparative Study of Connected Speech versus Sustained Vowel in European Portuguese Female Speakers." *Journal of Voice* 28, no. 3 (2014): 282–86. https://doi.org/10.1016/j.jvoice.2013.10.001.

Brodie, Ian. "Stand-Up Comedy as a Genre of Intimacy." *Ethnologies* 30, no. 2 (2008): 158–80. https://doi.org/10.7202/019950ar.

Browning, Frank. "Does Obama's Baritone Give Him an Edge?" *Salon,* February 28, 2008. Accessed September 24, 2018. http://www.salon.com/2008/02/28/obama_clinton_voices/.

Bucholtz, Mary. "Race and the Re-embodied Voice in Hollywood Film." *Language and Communication* 31, no. 3 (2011): 255–65. https://doi.org/10.1016/j.langcom.2011.02.004.

———. "The Whiteness of Nerds: Superstandard English and Racial Markedness." *Journal of Linguistic Anthropology* 11, no. 1 (2001): 84–100.

Bucholtz, Mary, and Qiuana Lopez. "Performing Blackness, Forming Whiteness: Linguistic Minstrelsy in Hollywood Film," *Journal of Sociolinguistics* 15, no. 5 (2011): 680–706. https://doi.org/10.1111/j.1467-9841.2011.00513.x.

Bugliani, Adriano. "The Ideal and the Real." *Iris* 2, no. 1 (2010): 469–73.

Butler, Judith. *Bodies That Matter.* New York: Routledge, 1993.

———. *Gender Trouble: Feminism and the Subversion of Identity.* New York: Routledge, 1990.

Butler, Mark. "Taking It Seriously: Intertextuality and Authenticity in Two Covers by the Pet Shop Boys." *Popular Music* 22, no. 1 (2003): 1–19.

Butte, Caitlin J., Yu Zhang, Huangquiang Song, and Jack J. Jiang. "Perturbation and Nonlinear Dynamic Analysis of Different Singing Styles." *Journal of Voice* 23, no. 6 (2009): 647–52.

camilo andres. "Eddie Murphy White people and Hauntings," YouTube, July 8, 2013, 1:39, https://www.youtube.com/watch?v=azCCWPcjkJo.

Carr, Jhonni Rochelle Charisse. "One *Margarita* Please! Language Attitudes Regarding Pronunciation in the Language of Origin." *Voices* 2 (2014): 63–73.

Carson, Anne. "The Gender of Sound: Description, Definition and Mistrust of the Female Voice in Western Culture." *Resources for Feminist Research* 23, no. 3 (1994): 24–31.

Casillas, Dolores Inés. *Sounds of Belonging: U.S. Spanish-Language Radio and Public Advocacy.* New York: New York University Press, 2014.

Casillas, Dolores Inés, Juan Sebastian Ferrada, and Sara Veronica Hinojos. "The Accent on *Modern Family*: Listening to Representations of the Latina Vocal Body." *Aztlan: A Journal of Chicano Studies* 43, no. 1 (2018): 61–87.

Caughey, John L. *Imaginary Social Worlds: A Cultural Approach*. Lincoln: University of Nebraska Press, 1984.

Cavarero, Adriana. *For More Than One Voice: Towards a Philosophy of Vocal Expression*. Translated by Paul Kottman. Stanford, CA: Stanford University Press, 2005.

Cavendish, Lucy. "Learn How to Be a Stand-Up Comedian? You're Having a Laugh . . ." *The Telegraph,* October 6, 2014. Accessed September 24, 2018. http://www.telegraph.co.uk/culture/comedy/11143358/Learn-how-to-be-a-stand-up-comedian-Youre-having-a-laugh....html.

Chernikoff, Leah. "Laverne Cox's Explanation of Why #TransIsBeautiful Will Make You Cheer and Cry." *Elle,* September 11, 2015. Accessed September 27, 2018. https://www.elle.com/culture/celebrities/news/a30388/laverne-cox-trans-is-beautiful/.

Chion, Michel. *Audio-Vision: Sound on Screen*. New York: Columbia University Press, 1994.

Chivers, Sally. *The Silvering Screen: Old Age and Disability in Cinema*. Toronto: University of Toronto Press, 2011.

Chun, Elaine W. "Ironic Blackness as Masculine Cool: Asian American Language and Authenticity on YouTube." *Applied Linguistics* 34, no. 5 (2013): 592–612. https://doi.org/10.1093/applin/amt023.

Clark, Lesley. "His Late Father Looms Over Obama's Trip to Kenya." *Seattle Times,* July 18, 2015. Accessed September 24, 2018. https://www.seattletimes.com/nation-world/his-late-father-looms-over-obamas-trip-to-kenya/.

Codeblack Comedy. "Aries Spears|White people do whatever they want Shaq's Five Minute Funnies Comedy Shaq," YouTube, September 30, 2013, 3:50, https://www.youtube.com/watch?v=7nYngZLjWio

Couch, Aaron. "Harrison Ford, Morgan Freeman Top Survey of Fictional Presidents." *The Hollywood Reporter,* November 6, 2012. Accessed September 24, 2018. https://www.hollywoodreporter.com/news/harrison-ford-morgan-freeman-top-387178.

Cucca, Valentina. "Biopics as Postmodern Mythmaking." *Akademisk Kwarter* 2, no. 6 (2011): 166–80.

Daley, Mike. "'Why Do Whites Sing Black?': The Blues, Whiteness, and Early Histories of Rock." *Popular Music and Society* 26, no. 2 (2003): 161–67. https://doi.org/10.1080/0300776032000095495.

Daley, Patrick, and Beverly James. "Warming the Arctic Air: Cultural Politics and Alaska Native Radio." *Javnost* 5, no. 2 (1998) 49–60.

Dalzell, Frederick. "Review: Dreamworking *Amistad*: Representing Slavery, Revolt, and Freedom in America, 1839 and 1997." *The New England Quarterly* 71, no. 1 (1998): 127–33. https://doi.org/10.2307/366728.

Davé, Shilpa S. *Indian Accents: Brown Voice and Racial Performance in American Television and Film*. Urbana: University of Illinois Press, 2013.

Davies, Helen. "All Rock and Roll Is Homosocial: The Representation of Women in the British Rock Music Press." *Popular Music* 20, no. 3 (2001): 301–91.

Davis, Angela Y. *Blues Legacies and Black Feminism: Gertrude Ma Rainey, Bessie Smith, and Billie Holiday*. New York: Pantheon Books, 1998.

Davis, Noah. "How'd You Get There, Standup Comic Kate Wolff?" *The Awl,* July 6, 2012. Accessed September 24, 2018. https://www.theawl.com/2012/07/howd-you-get-there-standup-comic-kate-wolff.

Day, Amber, and Ethan Thompson. "Live from New York, It's the Fake News! *Saturday Night Live* and the (Non)Politics of Parody." *Popular Communication* 10, no. 1–2 (2012): 170–82. https://doi.org/10.1080/15405702.2012.638582.

DeChaine, D. Robert. "Bordering the Civic Imaginary: Alienization, Fence Logic, and the Minuteman Civil Defense Corps." *Quarterly Journal of Speech* 95, no. 1 (2009): 43–65.

"Definition of Character." *Satired,* October 11, 2008. Accessed September 25, 2018. https://policomic.wordpress.com/2008/10/11/definition-of-character/.

Dlanga, Khaya. "*Invictus.*" *Thought Leader,* December 10, 2009. Accessed September 24, 2018. http://www.thoughtleader.co.za/khayadlanga/2009/12/10/invictus-movie-review-freeman-is-mandela/.

Doane, Mary Ann. "Ideology and the Practice of Sound Editing and Mixing." In *Film Sound: Theory and Practice,* edited by Elisabeth Weis and John Belton, 54–62. New York: Columbia University Press, 1985.

———. "The Voice in the Cinema: The Articulation of Body and Space." *Yale French Studies* 60 (1980): 33–50.

Dolar, Mladen. *A Voice and Nothing More.* Cambridge, MA: MIT Press, 2006.

DontHateOnJord. "Eddie Murphy's RAW - Italian's After They Have Seen Rocky [HD]," YouTube, August 16, 2010, 4:12, https://www.youtube.com/watch?v=YMqMKxJJYvY

DontHateOnJord. "Eddie Murphy's RAW - White People Can't Dance [HD]," YouTube, August 16, 2010, 1:20, https://www.youtube.com/watch?v=KsyYuFv5ltc

Douglas, Susan J. *Listening In: Radio and the American Imagination.* Minneapolis: University of Minnesota Press, 2004.

Dwyer, Jim. "Getting in Palin's Hair, or Close to It." *New York Times,* September 16, 2008. Accessed September 24, 2018. http://www.nytimes.com/2008/09/17/nyregion/17about.html.

Dyer, Richard. *Heavenly Bodies: Film Stars and Society.* Oxford: Macmillan Education, 1986.

———. *White: Essays on Race and Culture.* London: Routledge, 1997.

Dylko, Ivan B., Michael A. Beam, Kristen D. Landreville, and Nicholas Geidner. "Filtering 2008 US Presidential Election News on YouTube by Elites and Nonelites: An Examination of the Democratizing Potential of the Internet." *New Media and Society* 14, no. 5 (2012): 832–49. https://doi.org/10.1177/1461444811428899.

Dyson, Michael Eric. *Open Mike: Reflections on Philosophy, Race, Sex, Culture and Religion.* New York: Basic Civitas Books, 2003.

Eberwein, Robert. "Clint Eastwood and Morgan Freeman: Million-Dollar Seniors." In *Shining in Shadows: Movie Stars of the 2000s,* edited by Murray Pomerance, 32–49. Township, NJ: Rutgers University Press, 2012.

Eckstein, Justin. "Sound Arguments." *Argumentation and Advocacy* 53, no. 3 (2017): 163–80. https://doi.org/10.1080/00028533.2017.1337328.

Edgar, Amanda Nell. "Toward a Genosonic Lens: Linking the Anatomy of a 'Screech' to Language and Body." *Velvet Light Trap* 74 (2014): 54–66.

ElSoldao. "White mothers & Latin mothers.wmv," YouTube, November 25, 2008, 2:22, https://www.youtube.com/watch?v=OVjLuL3vijY&lc=UgwaGOKOkdUJvHu6Qh54AaABAg.

Emperor Bell, July 31, 2014, "ITT: We read everything in Morgan Freeman's voice," Forum, *Bungie.net,* https://www.bungie.net/sv/Forums/Post/67162949?sort=0&page=0.

Erni, John Nguyet. "Queer Figurations in the Media: Critical Reflections on the Michael Jackson Sex Scandal." *Critical Studies in Media Communication* 15 (1998): 158–80.

Falcone, Michael. "Obama Gets 'Celebrity Treatment' in New McCain Ad." *New York Times,* July 30, 2008. Accessed September 25, 2018. http://thecaucus.blogs.nytimes.com/2008/07/30/obama-gets-celebrity-treatment-in-new-mccain-ad.

Farhi, Paul. "Does Public Radio Sound Too 'White'? NPR Itself Tries to Find the Answer." *Washington Post,* January 30, 2015. Accessed September 25, 2018. http://www.washingtonpost.com/lifestyle/style/does-public-radio-sound-too-white-npr-itself-tries-to-find-the-answer/2015/01/30/f08f58cc-a899-11e4-a06b-9df2002b86a0_story.html.

Fast, Susan. "Calling Ellen Willis: Quarreling with the 'Radicals,' Loving Consumer Culture, and Hearing Women's Voices." *Women and Music* 12 (2008): 44–53. https://doi.org/10.1353/wam.0.0000.

Fattal, Alex. "Hostile Remixes on YouTube: A New Constraint on Pro-FARC Counterpublics in Colombia." *American Ethnologist* 41, no. 2 (2014): 320–35. https://doi.org/10.1111/amet.12078.

Fearn, Hannah. "Landlords Shunning Foreigners Because of Their Accents, After New Rules Preventing Illegal Migrants from Renting." *The Independent,* February 15, 2015. Accessed September 25, 2018. Retrieved from http://www.independent.co.uk/news/uk/home-news/landlords-shunning-foreigners-because-of-their-accents-after-new-rules-preventing-illegal-migrants-from-renting-10047594.html.

Fey, Tina. *Bossypants.* New York: Little, Brown and Company, 2011.

Finkler, Earle. "Documentary on Alaska's Great Depression Farm Colonists Worth Watching." *Anchorage Daily News,* June 7, 2013. Accessed September 30, 2018. https://www.adn.com/commentary/article/documentary-alaskas-great-depression-farm-colonists-worth-watching/2013/06/08/.

Fleetwood, Nicole. *Troubling Vision: Performance, Visuality, and Blackness.* Chicago: University of Chicago Press, 2011.

Flowers, Arhlene A., and Cory L. Young. (2010). "Parodying Palin: How Tina Fey's Visual and Verbal Impersonations Revived a Comedy Show and Impacted the 2008 Election." *Journal of Visual Literacy* 29, no. 1 (2010): 47–67. https://doi.org/10.1080/23796529.2010.11674673.

Flynt, Wayne. *Dixie's Forgotten People: The South's Poor Whites.* Bloomington: Indiana University Press, 1979.

Fordham, Signithia, and John U. Ogbu, J. "Black Students' School Success: Coping with the Burden of 'Acting White.'" *Urban Review* 18, no. 3 (1986): 176–206.

"Fox News Shows Tina Fey in On-Screen Graphic for Sarah Palin." *The Right Scoop,* June 5, 2011. Accessed September 25, 2018. Retrieved from http://therightscoop.com/fox-news-shows-tina-fey-in-on-screen-graphic-for-sarah-palin/.

Frank, David A. "The Prophetic Voice and the Face of the Other in Barack Obama's 'A More Perfect Union' Address, March 18, 2008." *Rhetoric and Public Affairs* 12, no. 2 (2009): 167–94. https://doi.org/10.1353/rap.0.0101.

Frank, Ze. "True Facts about Morgan Freeman," YouTube Video, 2:06, posted by zefrank1, January 10, 2013, https://www.youtube.com/watch?v=Ch5MEJk5ZCQ.

Frederick, Don. "Sarah Palin Lauds Tina Fey, Perhaps Because She Didn't Hear a Word of 'SNL' Skit." *LA Times Blog,* September 17, 2008. Accessed September 24, 2018. http://latimesblogs.latimes.com/washington/2008/09/sarah-palin-lau.html.

Freeman, Morgan. "Interview with Morgan Freeman; Bergdahl Controversy; Dr. Ben Carson Compares Obamacare to Slavery; Mississippi Primary Results Hold Nation's Attention."

Interview by Don Lemon. *CNN Tonight,* June 3, 2014, Transcript. http://transcripts.cnn.com/TRANSCRIPTS/1406/03/cnnt.01.html.

———. "Interview with Morgan Freeman." Interview by Piers Morgan. *Piers Morgan Tonight,* CNN, September 23, 2011. Transcript. http://www.cnn.com/TRANSCRIPTS/1109/23/pmt.01.html

Gallafent, Edward. "Violence, Actions and Words in *Million Dollar Baby.*" *CineAction* 68, (2006): 45–52.

Gates, Henry Louis Jr. *America: Behind the Color Line.* New York: Warner Books, 2004.

———. *In Search of Our Roots: How 19 Extraordinary African Americans Reclaimed Their Past.* New York: Crown Publishing, 2009.

Gates, Philippa. "Always a Partner in Crime: Black Masculinity in the Hollywood Detective Film." *Journal of Popular Film and Television* 32, no. 1 (2004): 21–29.

Gates, Racquel. "Bringing the Black: Eddie Murphy and African American Humor on *Saturday Night Live.*" In Becker, Marx, and Sienkiewicz, 151–72. Bloomington: Indiana University Press, 2013.

Gavin, Patrick. "D.C. Weighs in on SNL's New Obama." *Politico,* September 17, 2012. Accessed September 20, 2015. https://www.politico.com/story/2012/09/dc-weighs-in-on-snls-new-obama-081290.

Gertz, Emily. "How I Spent My Summer Vacation . . . at the Movies." *Grist,* September 15, 2005. Retrieved from https://grist.org/article/gertz/.

geomandre, "Adele—Someone Like You," YouTube, April 28, 2011, 5:10, https://web.archive.org/web/20121127165504/http://www.youtube.com/watch?v=jCya1yiFFP4.

Ghetto Rigged. "Kevin Hart – 'I could never be a rapper,'" YouTube, November 5, 2009, 1:29, https://www.youtube.com/watch?v=C_axfpqRX1w&lc=Ugz2w64zdOBZPgDhvz54AaABAg.

Gioia, Ted. *The History of Jazz.* New York: Oxford University Press, 1997.

Glenn, Cerise L., and Landra J. Cunningham. "The Power of Black Magic: The Magical Negro and White Salvation in Film." *Journal of Black Studies* 40, no. 2 (2009): 135–52.

Goldsby, Jacqueline. "The High and Low Tech of It: The Meaning of Lynching and the Death of Emmett Till." *Yale Journal of Criticism* 9, no. 2 (1996): 245–82. https://doi.org/10.1353/yale.1996.0016.

Goodale, Greg. *Sonic Persuasion: Reading Sound in the Recorded Age.* Urbana: University of Illinois Press, 2011.

———. "The Sonorous Envelope and Political Deliberation." *Quarterly Journal of Speech* 99, no. 2 (2013): 218–24. https://doi.org/10.1080/00335630.2013.775702.

Gorbman, Claudia. "Aesthetics and Rhetoric." *American Music* 22, no. 1 (2004): 14–26.

Gray, Herman. *Cultural Moves: African Americans and the Politics of Representation.* Berkeley: University of California Press, 2005.

Gray, Jonathan. "Throwing Out the Welcome Mat: Public Figures as Guests and Victims in TV Satire." In *Satire TV: Politics and Comedy in The Post-Network Era,* edited by Ethan Thompson, Jeffrey P. Jones, and Jonathan Gray, 147–66. New York: New York University Press, 2009.

Gray, Jonathan, Jeffrey Jones, and Ethan Thompson. "Using One of Its Lifelines: Does Politics Save *Saturday Night Live* from Oblivion?" *Flow TV,* March 20, 2009. Accessed September 25, 2018. https://www.flowjournal.org/2009/03/%E2%80%9Cusing-one-of-its-lifelines-does

-politics-save-saturday-night-live-from-oblivion-jonathan-gray-fordham-university-jeffrey
-p-jones-old-dominion-university-and-ethan-thompson-texas-a/.

Green, Lisa A. *African American English: A Linguistic Introduction.* Cambridge: Cambridge University Press, 2002.

Griffin, Rachel Alicia. "I AM an Angry Black Woman: Black Feminist Autoethnography, Voice, and Resistance." *Women's Studies in Communication* 35, no. 2 (2012): 138–57. https://doi.org/10.1080/07491409.2012.724524.

Gunn, Joshua. "Mourning Speech: Haunting and the Spectral Voices of Nine-Eleven." *Text and Performance Quarterly* 24, no. 2 (2004): 91–114. https://doi.org/10.1080/1046293042000288344.

———. "On Speech and Public Release." *Rhetoric and Public Affairs* 13, no. 2 (2010): 175–215.

Guerrillaz. "Richard Pryor - Black Women and White Women," YouTube, March 30, 2010, 4:06, https://www.youtube.com/watch?v=HFD2Y-EgoMc.

Guo, Lei, and Lorin Lee. "The Critique of YouTube-Based Vernacular Discourse: A Case Study of YouTube's Asian Community." *Critical Studies in Media Communication* 30, no. 5 (2013): 391–406. https://doi.org/10.1080/15295036.2012.755048.

Haggins, Bambi. *Laughing Mad: The Black Comic Persona in Post-Soul America.* New Brunswick, NJ: Rutgers University Press, 2007.

Hall, Stuart. "Encoding and Decoding in the Television Discourse." In *Culture, Media, Language,* edited by Stuart Hall, Dorothy Hobson, Andrew Lowe, and Paul Willis, 107–16. London: Hutchison, 1980.

———. "Introduction." In *Paper Voices: The Popular Press and Social Change, 1935–1965,* edited by A. C. H. Smith, 11–24 Totowa, NJ: Rowman and Littlefield, 1975.

Hansen, Elise. "The Forgotten Minority in Police Shootings." *CNN,* November 13, 2017. Accessed September 28, 2018. https://www.cnn.com/2017/11/10/us/native-lives-matter/index.html.

Hanson, Gary L., Paul M. Haridakis, and Rekha Sharma. "Differing Uses of YouTube during the 2008 U.S. Presidential Primary Election." *Electronic News* 15 (2011): 1–19.

Hardy, Sarah Madsen, and Kelly Thomas. "Listening to Race: Voice, Mixing, and Technological 'Miscegenation' in Early Sound Film." In *Classic Hollywood, Classic Whiteness,* edited by Daniel Bernardi, 415–41. Minneapolis: University of Minnesota Press, 2001.

Harold, Christine, and Kevin Michael DeLuca. "Behold the Corpse: Violent Images and the Case of Emmett Till." *Rhetoric and Public Affairs* 8, no. 2 (2005): 263–86.

Hartman, S. V., and Farah Jasmine Griffin. "Are You as Colored as That Negro? The Politics of Being Seen in Julie Dash's Illusions." *African American Review* 25, no. 2 (1991): 361–73. https://doi.org/10.2307/3041693.

Heilemann, John, and Mark Halperin. *Game Change: Obama and the Clintons, McCain and Palin, and the Race of a Lifetime.* New York: Harper Collins, 2010.

Hendra, Tony. *Going Too Far.* New York: Doubleday, 1987.

Henry, David, and Joe Henry. *Furious Cool: Richard Pryor and the World That Made Him.* Chapel Hill, NC: Algonquin Books, 2013.

Herndan, James S. "The Police Psychologist on the Silver Screen: Reviewing the Roles on the Reels." *Journal of Police and Criminal Psychology* 15, no. 2 (2000): 30–40.

Hess, Aaron. "Resistance Up In Smoke: Analyzing the Limitations of Deliberation on YouTube." *Critical Studies in Media Communication* 26, no. 5 (2009): 411–34. https://doi.org/10.1080/15295030903325347.

Hill Collins, Patricia. *Black Sexual Politics: African Americans, Gender, and the New Racism.* New York: Routledge, 2004.

Hill Collins, Patricia, and Sirma Bilge. *Intersectionality.* Cambridge: Polity Press, 2016.

Hill, Doug, and Jeff Weingrad. *Saturday Night: A Backstage History of "Saturday Night Live."* New York: Beech Tree Books, 1986.

Hilmes, Michele. "Desired and Feared: Women's Voices in Radio History." In *Television, History, and American Culture: Feminist Critical Essays,* edited by Mary Beth Haralovich and Lauren Rabinovitz, 17–35. Durham, NC: Duke University Press, 1999.

———. "The Evolution of Saturday Night." In Marx, Sienkiewicz, and Becker, 25–39.

———. "Foregrounding Sound: New (and Old) Directions in Sound Studies." *Cinema Journal* 48, no. 1 (2008): 115–17.

———. "Is There a Field Called Sound Culture Studies? And Does It Matter?" *American Quarterly* 57, no. 1 (2005): 249–59.

———. *Radio Voices: American Broadcasting, 1922–1952.* Minneapolis: University of Minnesota Press, 1997.

Hinckley, David. "'Saturday Night Live' Is Buzzworthy Again, Thanks to Tina Fey as Sarah Palin." *New York Daily News,* October 6, 2008. Accessed September 25, 2018. http://www.nydailynews.com/entertainment/tv-movies/saturday-night-live-buzzworthy-thanks-tina-fey-sarah-palin-article-1.303512.

Holden, Stephen. "Film Review; God's Power as an Ego Trip for an Id." *New York Times,* May 23, 2003. Accessed September 25, 2018. https://www.nytimes.com/2003/05/23/movies/film-review-god-s-power-as-an-ego-trip-for-an-id.html.

Holloway, Diane. "Presidents Became Boobs, Bumblers on 'SNL.'" *Washington Times,* February 24, 2001. Accessed September 25, 2018. https://goo.gl/jPjVhB.

hooks, bell. *Art on My Mind: Visual Politics.* New York: New Press, 1995.

———. *Talking Back: Thinking Feminist, Thinking Black.* Cambridge, MA: South End Press, 1989.

"How Do We Stop Racism?" Meme. Accessed September 24, 2018. https://stupidbadmemes.files.wordpress.com/2013/08/stop-talking-about-racism.jpg?w=630.

Hughey, Matthew W. "Cinethetic Racism: White Redemption and Black Stereotypes in 'Magical Negro' Films." *Social Problems* 56, no. 3 (2009): 543–77.

Hunt, Kara. "Off the Record: A Critical Perspective on Def Comedy Jam." *The Journal of Popular Culture* 48, no. 5 (2015): 836–58.

Hutcheon, Linda. *A Theory of Parody: The Teachings of Twentieth-Century Art Forms.* New York: Routledge, 1985.

I watch you post…Simple. "White Families vs. Black Families," YouTube, March 25, 2012, 4:46, https://web.archive.org/web/20141105055140/https://www.youtube.com/watch?v=h_Uj1FRmLao.

Iglesias, Gabriel. "'E-glesias with a I' - Gabriel Iglesias (from my I'm Not Fat. . . I'm Fluffy comedy special)," YouTube, May 12, 2011, 4:17, https://www.youtube.com/watch?v=CxgIbznAV84&lc=UghdZYkPv2VZGngCoAEC.

———. "'High School Reunion' -Gabriel Iglesias (exclusive bonus footage from 'I'm Not Fat. . . I'm Fluffy')," YouTube, July 28, 2010, 5:23, https://www.youtube.com/watch?v=5QQzusr4IH0.

Ihde, Don. *Listening and Voice: Phenomenologies of Sound.* Albany, NY: State University of New York Press, 2007.

Illusions. DVD. Directed by Julie Dash. 1982.

Irby, Trey. "Grammy Performances Range from Authentic to Absurd." *The Crimson White,* February 15, 2012. Accessed September 25, 2018. http://cw.ua.edu/10165/culture/grammy-performances-range-from-authentic-to-absurd/.

Jackson, John L. *Real Black: Adventures in Racial Sincerity.* Chicago: University of Chicago Press, 2005.

Jackson, Lauren M. "Who Really Owns the 'Blaccent'?" *Vulture,* August 24, 2018. Accessed September 28, 2018. http://www.vulture.com/2018/08/awkwafina-blaccent-cultural-appropriation.html.

Jacobs, Tom. "Research Shows That White Mass Shooters Are Treated More Sympathetically by the Media." *Pacific Standard,* July 23, 2018. Accessed September 27, 2018. https://psmag.com/social-justice/white-mass-shooters-are-treated-more-sympathetically-by-the-media.

Jaslow, Ryan. "Meet Adele's Vocal Cord Surgeon, Dr. Steven Zeitels." *CBS News,* February 13, 2012. Accessed September 25, 2018. https://www.cbsnews.com/news/meet-adeles-vocal-cord-surgeon-dr-steven-zeitels/.

Jenkins, Bernard. "Obama's One-Man Sing-Along." *Jornal.Us,* February 20, 2011. Accessed September 25, 2018. http://news.jornal.us/article-5479.Obamas-One-Man-Sing-Along.html.

Jenkins, Henry. "Rowan and Martin's Laugh-In." *The Museum of Broadcast Communications,* n.d. Accessed September 25, 2018. http://www.museum.tv/eotv/rowanandmar.htm.

Jessica G. "Amy & Tina Do Hillary & Sarah to Hilarious, Depressing Effect." *Jezebel,* September 15, 2008. http://jezebel.com/5049863/amy--tina-do-hillary--sarah-to-hilarious-depressing-effect.

———. "Tina Fey as Sarah Palin: 'Katie, I'd Like to Use One of My Life Lines.'" *Jezebel,* September 28, 2008. Accessed January 28, 2019. http://jezebel.com/5056023/tina-fey-as-sarah-palin-katie-id-like-to-use-one-of-my-life-lines/all.

Johnson, Steve. "From Cultural Iconoclast to Cultural Icon." *Chicago Tribune,* October 27, 2002. Accessed September 25, 2018. http://articles.chicagotribune.com/2002-10-27/entertainment/0210260015_1_lorne-michaels-cultural-live-from-new-york.

Jones, Jeffrey P. *Entertaining Politics: Satiric Television and Political Engagement.* Lanham, MD: Rowman & Littlefield, 2010.

———. "Politics and the Brand: *Saturday Night Live*'s Campaign Season Humor." In Marx, Sienkiewicz, and Becker, 77–92.

———. "With All Due Respect: Satirizing Presidents from *Saturday Night Live* to *Lil' Bush.*" In *Satire TV: Politics and Comedy in the Post-Network Era,* edited by Ethan Thompson, Jeffrey P. Jones, and Jonathan Gray, 37–63. New York: New York University Press, 2009.

Jones, Robert P., Daniel Cox, and Juhem Navarro-Rivera. *The 2013 American Values Survey: In Search of Libertarians in America.* Washington, DC: Public Religion Research Institute, 2013. http://publicreligion.org/site/wp-content/uploads/2013/10/2013.AVS_WEB.pdf.

Judy, R. A. T. "On the Question of Nigga Authenticity." *boundary 2* 21, no. 3 (1994): 211–30. https://doi.org/10.2307/303605.

Kainer, Eden Elizabeth. "Vocal Racial Crossover in the Song Performance of Three Iconic American Vocalists: Sophie Tucker (1884–1966), Elsie Janis (1889–1956) and Ella Fitzgerald (1917–1996)." PhD diss., University of Wisconsin-Madison, 2008.

Kalinak, Kathryn. *Settling the Score: Music and the Classical Hollywood Film.* Madison: University of Wisconsin Press, 1992.

Kat. "How to Lower Your Voice." *Corporette,* May 14, 2013. Accessed September 25, 2018. http://corporette.com/2013/05/14/how-to-lower-your-voice/.

Kavka, Misha. *Reality Television, Affect and Intimacy: Reality Matters.* New York: Palgrave Macmillan, 2008.

Khatchatourian, Maane. "Chris Rock Thinks YouTube Has Ruined Stand-Up Comedy." *Entertainment Weekly,* August 9, 2012. Accessed September 25, 2018. http://popwatch.ew.com/2012/08/09/chris-rock-daily-show-youtube/.

Kibler, M. Alison. *Rank Ladies: Gender and Cultural Hierarchy in Vaudeville.* Chapel Hill: University of North Carolina Press, 1999.

Kim, Claire Jean. "The Racial Triangulation of Asian Americans." *Politics & Society* 27 (1999): 105–38.

King, Deborah Walker. *African Americans and the Culture of Pain.* Charlottesville: University of Virginia Press, 2008.

Kinsley, Michael. "Barack Obama and the Voice of God." *Time,* January 15, 2009. Accessed September 28, 2015. http://content.time.com/time/magazine/article/0,9171,1871919,00.html.

Kurtz, Howard. "The *SNL* Effect." *Washington Post,* March 14, 2008. Accessed September 25, 2018. http://www.washingtonpost.com/wp-dyn/content/blog/2008/03/14/BL2008031401607.html.

Kurtzleben, Danielle. "Forget Diversity: *Saturday Night Live* Has a Viewership Problem." *U.S. News and World Report,* January 17, 2014. Accessed September 24, 2018. http://www.usnews.com/news/blogs/data-mine/2014/01/17/forget-diversity-saturday-night-live-has-a-viewership-problem.

Ladino, Jennifer K. "For the Love of Nature: Documenting Life, Death, and Animality in *Grizzly Man* and *March of the Penguins.*" *Interdisciplinary Studies in Literature and Environment* 16, no. 1 (2009): 53–90. https://doi.org/10.1093/isle/isp002.

LaSalle, Mick. "Review: '*Invictus*' Narrows Its Viewpoint." *SF Gate,* December 11, 2009. Accessed September 24, 2018. https://www.sfgate.com/movies/article/Review-Invictus-narrows-its-viewpoint-3278719.php.

Lawrence, Amy. *Echo and Narcissus: Women's Voices in Classical Hollywood Cinema.* Berkeley: University of California Press, 1991.

———. "Staring the Camera Down: Direct Address and Women's Voices." In *Embodied Voices: Representing Female Vocality in Western Culture,* edited by Leslie C. Dunn and Nancy A. Jones, 166–78. Cambridge: Cambridge University Press, 1997.

Liberato, Ana S. Q., and John D. Foster. "Representations and Remembrance: Tracing Civil Rights Meanings in the Narratives of Civil Rights Activists and Hollywood Filmmakers." *Journal of African American Studies* 15, no. 3 (2012): 367–84. https://doi.org/10.1007/s12111-010-9145-y.

Litwack, Leon F. *Trouble in Mind: Black Southerners in the Age of Jim Crow.* New York: Alfred A. Knopf, 1998.

Lott, Eric. *Love and Theft: Blackface Minstrelsy and the American Working Class.* Oxford: Oxford University Press, 2013.

Louët, Sabine. "Your Voice: Your Passport to Authority." *Science,* January 27, 2012. Accessed September 24, 2018. http://sciencecareers.sciencemag.org/career_magazine/previous_issues/articles/2012_01_27/caredit.a1200010.

Love, James. "Biden Knows Stuff, Palin Plays Tina Fey." *Huffington Post,* November 3, 2008. Accessed September 24, 2018. http://www.huffingtonpost.com/james-love/biden-knows-stuff-palin-p_b_131522.html.

Loviglio, Jason. "Sound Effects: Gender, Voice and the Cultural Work of NPR." *Radio Journal: International Studies in Broadcast and Audio* 5, no. 2–3 (2007): 67–81. https://doi.org/10.1386/rajo.5.2-3.67_1.

Lu, Fei. "What 'Crazy Rich Asians' Left Out." *Paper,* September 6, 2018. Accessed September 28, 2018. http://www.papermag.com/crazy-rich-asians-missed-2602612590.html.

Lucaites, John Louis. "Afterword: Border Optics." In *Border Rhetorics: Citizenship and Identity on the US-Mexico Frontier,* edited by D. Robert DeChaine, 227–30. Tuscaloosa: University of Alabama Press, 2012.

Macek, Steve. "Places of Horror: Fincher's '*Seven*' and Fear of the City in Recent Hollywood Film." *College Literature* 26, no. 1 (1999): 80–97.

machiavel2772. "Dave Chappelle - White People," YouTube, October 3, 2008, 2:14, https://www.youtube.com/watch?v=6uvg-ug9CvE.

Maltais, Kirk. "Republican Supporter Dwayne Johnson Demands to Be Removed from Chris Christie Campaign Video He Was Featured In without Permission . . . But Still Insists They Are 'Buddies.'" *Daily Mail,* July 19, 2014, http://www.dailymail.co.uk/news/article-2698462/Dwayne-Johnson-demands-removed-Chris-Christie-campaign-video-says-Democrats-Obama-Clinton-buddies.html.

Marcus, Bennett. "Fred Armisen Performs in 'Honeyface.'" *New York Magazine,* March 13, 2008. Accessed September 24, 2018. http://nymag.com/intelligencer/2008/03/fred_armisen_does_not_wear_bla.html.

Marks, Laura U. *Touch: Sensuous Theory and Multisensory Media.* Minneapolis: University of Minnesota Press, 2002.

Marx, Nick, Matt Sienkiewicz, and Ron Becker. "Introduction: Situating *Saturday Night Live* in American Television Culture." In Marx, Sienkiewicz, and Becker, 1–23.

Marx, Nick, Matt Sienkiewicz, and Ron Becker, eds. *"Saturday Night Live" and American TV.* Bloomington: Indiana University Press, 2013.

Matthews, Cate. "He Dropped One Letter in His Name While Applying for Jobs, and the Responses Rolled In." *Huffington Post,* September 2, 2014. Accessed September 24, 2018. http://www.huffingtonpost.com/2014/09/02/jose-joe-job-discrimination_n_5753880.html.

Matviko, John. "Television Satire and the Presidency: The Case of *Saturday Night Live.*" In *Hollywood's White House: The American Presidency in Film and History,* edited by Peter C. Rollins and John E. O'Connor, 333–48. Lexington: University Press of Kentucky, 2003.

Maurice, Alice. "'Cinema at Its Source': Synchronizing Race and Sound in the Early Talkies," *Camera Obscura* 49, no. 7 (May 2002): 1–71.

McConnell-Ginet, Sally. "Intonation in a Man's World." *Signs* 3, no. 3 (1987): 541–59.

McGraw, Eliza Russi Lowen. "*Driving Miss Daisy:* Southern Jewishness on the Big Screen." *Southern Cultures* 7, no. 2 (2001): 41–59. https://doi.org/10.1353/scu.2001.0023.

McKinnon, Sara L., Robert Asen, Karma R. Chávez, and Robert Glenn Howard. *Text + Field: Innovations in Rhetorical Method.* University Park: Pennsylvania State University Press, 2017.

Median Democrat. December 8, 2008. Comment on FrenchieCat, "About That 'Obama Playing It Cool' Skit on SNL Last Night?" *Democratic Underground,* updated December 7, 2008.

http://www.democraticunderground.com/discuss/duboard.php?az=view_all&address=132x7960834.

Meskimen, Jim. "Morgan Freeman Narrates Your Life: Impressionist Jim Meskimen," YouTube Video, 4:18, posted by Jim Meskimen, March 14, 2014, https://www.youtube.com/watch?v=E6Kjv6me5As.

Middleton, Michael, Aaron Hess, Daniele Endres, and Samantha Senda-Cook, eds. *Participatory Critical Rhetoric: Theoretical and Methodological Foundations for Studying Rhetoric In Situ.* Lanham, MD: Lexington Books, 2015.

Milazzo, Linda. "What I Learned at the Sarah Palin Rally before They Threw Me Out." *Alternet*, October 6, 2008. Accessed September 24, 2018. http://www.alternet.org/story/101903/what_i_learned_at_the_sarah_palin_rally_before_they_threw_me_out.

Milroy, Lesley, and Matthew Gordon. *Sociolinguistics: Method and Interpretation.* Hoboken, NJ: Wiley, 2008.

Modleski, Tania. "Clint Eastwood and Male Weepies." *American Literary History* 22, no. 1 (2009): 136–58. https://doi.org/10.1093/alh/ajp051.

———. "Femininity as Mas(s)querade: A Feminist Approach to Mass Culture." In *High Theory / Low Culture*, edited by Colin MacCabe, 37–52. Manchester: Manchester University Press, 1986.

Mohanty, Satya P. "Drawing the Color Line: Kipling and the Culture of Colonial Rule." In *The Bounds of Race: Perspectives on Hegemony and Resistance*, edited by Dominick LaCapra, 311–43. Ithaca, NY: Cornell University Press, 1991.

"Morgan Freeman." *Urban Dictionary*, 2010. http://www.urbandictionary.com/define.php?term=Morgan+Freeman.

Munroe, Randall. "Fremanic Paracusia." *Xkcd.com*. Accessed September 24, 2018. https://xkcd.com/462/.

Mysteriousvisitor. June 23, 2010. Online Forum. "Why Do Blacks Have Deep Singing Voices?" *Forum Biodiversity*. http://www.forumbiodiversity.com/showthread.php/6086-Why-do-blacks-have-deep-singing-voices.

Nancy, Jean-Luc. *Listening.* Bronx, NY: Fordham University Press, 2007.

Nath, Ishani. "I Can't Stop Thinking About the Accents in *Crazy Rich Asians*." *Flare*, August 15, 2018. Accessed September 28, 2018. https://www.flare.com/tv-movies/crazy-rich-asians-accents/.

Neal, Mark Anthony. *Looking for Leroy: Illegible Black Masculinities.* New York: New York University Press, 2014.

Newcombe, J. August 1, 2012. "Morgan Freeman: Titty Sprinkles." *Urban Sniper*. http://urbansniper.com.

Noonan, Peggy. "Palin and Populism: The Downside of Appealing to Joe Six-Pack." *Wall Street Journal*, October 3, 2008. Accessed September 20, 2015. http://www.wsj.com/news/articles/SB122300786229301597.

O'Sullivan, Sean. "Representations of Prison in Nineties Hollywood Cinema: From *Con Air* to *The Shawshank Redemption*." *The Howard Journal of Communication* 40, no. 4 (2001): 317–34. https://doi.org/10.1111/1468-2311.00212.

Obama, Barack. *Dreams from My Father: A Story of Race and Inheritance.* New York: Times Books, 1995.

Obenson, Tambay A. "Jay Pharoah Is Replacing Fred Armisen as President Obama on 'Saturday Night Live.'" *IndieWire,* September 12, 2012, https://www.indiewire.com/2012/09/jay-pharoah-is-replacing-fred-armisen-as-president-obama-on-saturday-night-live-141955/.

Oliver, Kelly. *Witnessing: Beyond Recognition.* Minneapolis: University of Minnesota Press, 2001.

Ong, Walter J. *Orality and Literacy.* New York: Routledge, 2002.

Ono, Kent A. "Borders That Travel: Matters of the Figural Border." In *Border Rhetorics: Citizenship and Identity on the US–Mexico Frontier,* edited by D. Robert DeChaine, 19–32. Tuscaloosa: University of Alabama Press, 2012.

Ono, Kent A., and Vincent N. Pham. *Asian Americans and the Media.* Cambridge: Polity Press, 2009.

Ono, Kent A., and John M. Sloop. "The Critique of Vernacular Discourse." *Communication Monographs* 62 (1995): 19–46. https://doi.org/10.1080/03637759509376346.

Orgeret, Kristin Skare. "Mediated Culture and the Well-informed Global Citizen: Images of Africa in the Global North." *Nordicom Review* 31, no. 2 (2010): 47–61.

Palin, Sarah. *Going Rogue: An American Life.* New York: HarperCollins, 2009.

Patz, Kally. "Raise Your Voice: Why Women with High-Pitched Voices Face Trouble in the Workplace." *Columbia Spectator,* November 23, 2014. Accessed September 24, 2018. http://columbiaspectator.com/eye/2014/11/23/raise-your-voice.

Peters, Jenny. "Morgan Magic: The Golden Globes 2012: The Cecil B. DeMille Award." *Variety,* January 13, 2012. Accessed September 24, 2018. https://variety.com/2012/film/awards/morgan-magic-1118048333/.

Pew Research Center for the People and the Press. "Obama and Wright Controversy Dominate News Cycle." March 27, 2008. Accessed September 24, 2018. http://www.people-press.org/2008/03/27/obama-and-wright-controversy-dominate-news-cycle/.

Poniewozik, James. "Palin vs. 'Palin': When SNL Parody Becomes Campaign Reality." *Time,* October 9, 2008. Accessed September 25, 2018. http://content.time.com/time/magazine/article/0,9171,1848735,00.html.

Port, Ian S. "Adele's Grammy Performance: A Reminder of the Scary Power of an Honest, Gorgeous Song." *San Francisco Weekly,* February 13, 2012. Accessed September 24, 2018. http://www.sfweekly.com/music/adeles-grammys-performance-a-reminder-of-the-scary-power-of-an-honest-gorgeous-song/.

Randall, Don Michael. *The Harvard Dictionary of Music.* Cambridge, MA: Belknap Press, 2003.

Reuters. "Chevy Chase Recalls Ford as 'a Terrific Guy.'" *Today,* December 27, 2006. Accessed September 25, 2018. https://www.today.com/popculture/chevy-chase-recalls-ford-terrific-guy-wbna16370028.

Richards, Sam. "The-Dream: R&B Super-Producer on Rihanna, Beyoncé and Tulisa." *The Guardian,* March 16, 2012. Accessed September 24, 2018. https://www.theguardian.com/music/2012/mar/17/terius-nash-the-dream.

Ridgway, Sam, Donald Carder, Michelle Jeffries, and Mark Todd. "Spontaneous Human Speech Mimicry by a Cetacean." *Current Biology* 22, no. 20 (2012): R860–61.

Rollins, Peter C., and John E. O'Connor. *Hollywood's White House: The American Presidency in Film and History.* Lexington: University of Kentucky Press, 2003.

Ryan, Maureen. "Did Tina Fey Out-Palin Palin on 'Saturday Night Live.'" *Chicago Tribune,* September 14, 2008. Accessed September 24, 2018. https://web.archive.org/web/20170415215456/http://featuresblogs.chicagotribune.com/entertainment_tv/2008/09/saturday-night.html.

Sadie, Stanley. *The New Grove Dictionary of Opera*. Oxford: Oxford University Press, 2004.

Schafer, R. Murray. *The Soundscape: Our Sonic Environment and the Tuning of the World*. Rochester, VT: Destiny Books, 1993.

Scheff, Thomas J. "Hypermasculinity and Violence as a Social System." *Universitas* 2 (2006): 1–10.

Seelye, Katharine Q. "Fey-Palin Character Debuts on S.N.L." *New York Times: The Caucus*, September 14, 2008. Accessed September 25, 2018. http://thecaucus.blogs.nytimes.com/2008/09/14/fey-palin-character-debuts-on-snl/.

Selk, Avi. "'I Wanted to Stop Her Crying': The Image of a Migrant Child That Broke a Photographer's Heart." *Washington Post*, June 18, 2018. Accessed September 28, 2018. https://www.washingtonpost.com/news/post-nation/wp/2018/06/18/i-wanted-to-stop-her-crying-the-image-of-a-migrant-child-that-broke-a-photographers-heart/?utm_term=.a3d4646a2e3b/.

Semigran. "The Rock to Run for President Someday? 'Don't Forget, I Am G.I. Joe,' He Reminds America." *Entertainment Weekly*, February 8, 2012, http://www.ew.com/article/2012/02/08/the-rock-to-run-for-president-someday-dont-forget-i-am-g-i-joe-he-reminds-america.

Shado85. "What If Morgan Freeman Really Is God?" *Cheezburger*, 2008. Retrieved from https://cheezburger.com/5600533504.

Shales, Tom. "Zingers on Saturday Night." *Washington Post*, November 8, 1975. A19.

Shands, Hubert Anthony. *Some Peculiarities of Speech in Mississippi*. Boston: Norwood Press, 1890.

Sheidlower, Jesse. "What Kind of Accent Does Sarah Palin Have?" *Slate*, October 1, 2008. Accessed September 25, 2018. http://www.slate.com/articles/life/the_good_word/2008/10/what_kind_of_accent_does_sarah_palin_have.html.

Siegel, Robert. "Palin's Accent Examined." *NPR*, October 2, 2008. Accessed September 24, 2018. http://www.npr.org/templates/story/story.php?storyId=95306504.

SilentPatriot. "*SNL* Spoofs Palin/Couric Interview." *Crooks and Liars*, September 28, 2008, http://crooksandliars.com/2008/09/28/snl-spoofs-palincouric-interview.

Silverman, Kaja. *The Acoustic Mirror: The Female Voice in Psychoanalysis and Cinema*. Bloomington: Indiana University Press, 1998.

Simmons-Duffin, Selena. "Video: Talking While Female." *NPR*, October 24, 2012. Accessed September 24, 2018. http://www.npr.org/blogs/health/2014/10/24/357584372/video-what-women-get-flak-for-when-they-talk.

Sklar, Robert, and Tania Modleski. "A Split Decision." *CineAste* 30, no. 2 (2005): 6–11.

Smith-Shomade, Beretta. *Shaded Lives: African-American Women and Television*. New Brunswick, NJ: Rutgers University Press, 2002.

Smith, Jacob. *Vocal Tracks: Performance and Sound Media*. Berkeley: University of California Press, 2008.

Smith, Jeff. *The Presidents We Imagine: Two Centuries of White House Fictions on the Page, on the Stage, Onscreen, and Online*. Madison: University of Wisconsin Press, 2009.

Smyth, Ron Smyth, Greg Jacobs, and Henry Rogers. "Male Voices and Perceived Sexual Orientation: An Experimental and Theoretical Approach." *Language in Society* 32, no. 3 (2003): 329–50. https://doi.org/10.1017/S0047404503323024.

Somekindofsatan. February 23, 2011. Online Forum, "Why Do Black People Have Deep Voices? (No Racist)." *BodyBuilding.com*. http://forum.bodybuilding.com/showthread.php?t=132101503.

Son, April, "Morgan Freeman Being Inspirational Will Get You Through Another Week," *Slate.com,* September 15, 2014, https://slate.com/culture/2014/09/morgan-freeman-inspirational-sayings-collected-wisdom-of-the-actor-with-the-great-voice-video.html.

SpacePerson. "Forum: Race and Sound of Voice." *Biology Online,* December 9, 2009. https://www.biology-online.org/biology-forum/viewtopic.php?t=17638.

Spielberg, Theo. "'Magnetic Fields' Stephin Merritt: Adele Is Loved Because She's White & Sounds Black." *Spinner,* March 23, 2012. Accessed August 12, 2012. https://web.archive.org/web/20121109235625/http://www.spinner.com/2012/03/23/stephin-merrit-adele-racism/.

Spillius, Alex. "Tina Fey Lands the First Punch at Sarah Palin in *Saturday Night Live* Sketch." *The Telegraph,* September 14, 2008. Accessed September 24, 2018. http://www.telegraph.co.uk/news/2958696/Tina-Fey-lands-the-first-punch-at-Sarah-Palin-in-Saturday-Night-Live-sketch.html.

Squires, Catherine, Eric King Watts, Mary Douglas Vavrus, Kent A. Ono, Kathleen Feyh, Bernadette Marie Calafell, and Daniel C. Brouwer. "What Is This 'Post-' in Postracial, Postfeminist . . . (Fill in the Blank?)" *Journal of Communication Inquiry* 34, no. 3 (2010): 210–53. https://doi.org/10.1177/0196859910371375.

Stampler, Laura. "Twitter Users Ask What Photo Media Would Use #IfTheyGunnedMeDown." *Time,* August 11, 2014. Accessed September 30, 2018. http://time.com/3100975/iftheygunnedmedown-ferguson-missouri-michael-brown/.

StandupTV13. "DAVE CHAPPELE: why black people hang out with white dudes lmaoo," YouTube, January 7, 2012, 9:24, https://www.youtube.com/watch?v=hIRjB6CPxLE.

Stephen, Lauren C. "'At Last the Family Is Together': Reproductive Futurism in *March of the Penguins.*" *Social Identities* 16, no. 1 (2010): 103–18. https://doi.org/10.1080/13504630903465944.

Sterne, Jonathan. *The Audible Past: Cultural Origins of Sound Reproduction.* Durham, NC: Duke University Press, 2003.

Stilwell, Robin J. "Sound and Empathy: Subjectivity and the Cinematic Soundscape." In *Film Music: Critical Approaches,* edited by Kevin J. Donnelly, 167–87. Edinburgh: Edinburgh University Press, 2001.

Stoddard, Jeremy D., and Alan S. Marcus. "The Burden of Historical Representation: Race, Freedom, and 'Educational' Hollywood Film." *Film & History* 36, no. 1 (2006): 26–35. https://doi.org/10.1353/flm.2006.0018.

Stoever, Jennifer Lynn. *The Sonic Color Line: Race and the Cultural Politics of Listening.* New York: New York University Press, 2016.

Stras, Laurie. "White Face, Black Voice: Race, Gender, and Region in Music of the Boswell Sisters." *Journal of the Society for American Music* 1, no. 2 (May 2007): 207–55.

STV. "Clueless French Newspaper Misidentifies 'Troubled' Tina Fey as Sarah Palin." *Gawker,* October 3, 2008. Accessed September 24, 2018. http://gawker.com/5058797/clueless-french-newspaper-misidentifies-troubled-tina-fey-as-sarah-palin.

Suisman, David. *Selling Sounds: The Commercial Revolution in American Music.* Cambridge, MA: Harvard University Press, 2009.

Sullivan, Barbara Apple. "Obama, Romney, and What Their Voices Tell Us." *Forbes,* October 11, 2012. Accessed September 25, 2018. http://www.forbes.com/sites/forbesleadershipforum/2012/10/11/obama-romney-and-what-their-voices-tell-us/.

Sven Ha. "Dave Chappelle and his white friend Chip," YouTube, November 17, 2008, 5:19, https://web.archive.org/web/20141210182311/https://www.youtube.com/watch?v=JJ3dk6KAvQM.

Sweet, Lynn. "Tina Fey as Sarah Palin Nails It Again on 'Saturday Night Live' Debate Skit." *The Scoop from Washington,* October 4, 2008. Accessed January 28, 2018. https://web.archive.org/web/20151118152054/http://blogs.suntimes.com/sweet/2008/10/tina_fey_as_sarah_palin_nails.html.

Tagg, Philip. "Caught on the Back Foot: Epistemic Inertia and Visible Music." *IASPM@Journal* 2, no. 1–2 (2011): 3–18. https://doi.org/10.5429/2079-3871(2011)v2i1-2.2en.

Tate, Greg. *Everything but the Burden: What White People Are Taking from Black Culture.* New York: Broadway Books, 2003.

Tay, Karen. "Crazy Rich Asians: Power in Seeing Faces Like Mine on Screen." *Stuff,* August 30, 2018. Accessed September 27, 2018. https://www.stuff.co.nz/entertainment/film/106686686/crazy-rich-asians-power-in-seeing-faces-like-mine-on-screen.

Taylor, Jessica. "'Speaking Shadows': A History of the Voice in the Transition from Silent to Sound Film in the United States." *Journal of Linguistic Anthropology* 19, no. 1 (2009): 1–20.

Terrill, Robert E. "Unity and Duality in Barack Obama's 'A More Perfect Union.'" *Quarterly Journal of Speech* 95, no. 4 (2009): 363–86. https://doi.org/10.1080/00335630903296192.

Test, George A. *Satire: Spirit and Art.* Tampa: University of South Florida Press, 1991.

Texhnician. "Adele Performing Someone Like You | BRIT Awards 2011." YouTube, February 15, 2011, 5:50, https://www.youtube.com/watch?v=qemWRToNYJY.

Thomas, Erik R. "Phonological and Phonetic Characteristics of African American Vernacular English." *Language and Linguistics Compass* 1, no. 5 (2007): 450–75. https://doi.org/10.1111/j.1749-818X.2007.00029.x.

THR Staff. "Morgan Freeman Narrates New Gay Marriage Ad (Video)." *The Hollywood Reporter,* November 26, 2012. Accessed September 24, 2018. https://www.hollywoodreporter.com/news/morgan-freeman-narrates-gay-marriage-393943.

Timm, Jordan. "But Morgan Freeman Is So Perfect." *Maclean's* 122, no. 33 (August 25, 2008): 57.

Tomdahitman. "Dave Chappelle - Black & White peoples food," YouTube, September 22, 2008, 3:28, https://www.youtube.com/watch?v=SB8A0zV1TD0.

Toto. "Fred Armisen Out as 'SNL's' Obama Impersonator." *Breitbart,* September 12, 2012, https://www.breitbart.com/big-hollywood/2012/09/12/armisen-out-as-snl-obama/.

Tracy, Kathleen. *Morgan Freeman: A Biography.* Fort Lee, NJ: Barricade Books, 2006.

Trent. "'*SNL*' Presents the Second Presidential Debate." *Pink Is the New Blog,* October 10, 2008, https://web.archive.org/web/20121113194500/http://www.pinkisthenewblog.com/2008-10-10/snl-presents-the-second-presidential-debate.

US Census Bureau. "Decennial Census of Population and Housing." Accessed September 24, 2018. https://www.census.gov/programs-surveys/decennial-census/decade.2010.html.

Utley, Ebony, and Amy L. Heyse. "Barack Obama's (Im)perfect Union: An Analysis of the Strategic Successes and Failures in His Speech on Race." *The Western Journal of Black Studies* 33, no. 3 (2009): 153–63.

Variety Staff. "Commanding Respect Even Sight Unseen." *Variety,* June 9, 2011, p. A12.

Wallenstein, Andrew. "In Search of a Better Obama Impersonator." *NPR,* November 4, 2008. Accessed September 24, 2018. http://www.npr.org/templates/story/story.php?storyId=96574088.

Walton, Julie H., and Robert F. Orlikoff. "Speaker Race Identification from Acoustic Cues in the Vocal Signal." *Journal of Speech & Hearing Research* 37, no. 4 (1994): 738–46.

Watts, Eric King. *Hearing the Hurt*. Tuscaloosa: University of Alabama Press, 2012.

———. "'Voice' and 'Voicelessness' in Rhetorical Studies." *Quarterly Journal of Speech* 87, no. 2 (2001): 179–96. https://doi.org/10.1080/00335630109384328.

Weiss, Dan. "The Magnetic Fields' Stephin Merritt on Why Adele Fans Are Racist, and Other Topics." *L.A. Weekly*, March 22, 2012. Accessed September 25, 2018. https://www.laweekly.com/music/the-magnetic-fields-stephin-merritt-on-why-adele-fans-are-racist-and-other-topics-2410460.

Wexler, Rebecca. "Onward, Christian Penguins: Wildlife Film and the Image of Scientific Authority." *Studies in History and Philosophy of Biological and Biomedical Science* 39, no. 3 (2008): 273–79. https://doi.org/10.1016/j.shpsc.2008.06.001.

Whalley, Jim. *"Saturday Night Live," Hollywood Comedy, and American Culture: From Chevy Chase to Tina Fey*. New York: Palgrave Macmillan, 2010.

Williams, Megan. "In the Ring with Mildred Pierce: *Million Dollar Baby* and Eastwood's Revision of the Forties Melodrama." *Arizona Quarterly* 67, no. 1 (2011): 161–86. https://doi.org/10.1353/arq.2011.0002.

Wilstein, Matt. "Rep. Louie Gohmert Quotes Sarah Palin and Tina Fey on House Floor." *Mediaite*, March 18, 2014. Accessed September 24, 2018. https://www.mediaite.com/tv/rep-louie-gohmert-quotes-sarah-palin-and-tina-fey-on-house-floor/.

Wing, Nick. "When the Media Treats White Suspects and Killers Better Than Black Victims." *Huffington Post*, August 14, 2014. Accessed September 27, 2018. https://www.huffingtonpost.com/2014/08/14/media-black-victims_n_5673291.html.

Wolfram, Walt. "African American Englishes." In *The Handbook of World Englishes*, edited by Braj Kachru, Yamuna Kachru, and Cecil L. Nelson, 328–45. Malden, MA: Blackwell Publishing, 2009.

WSJ Staff. "Tina Fey Returns to '*Saturday Night Live*' to Play Palin." *Wall Street Journal*, September 14, 2008, http://blogs.wsj.com/washwire/2008/09/14/tina-fey-returns-to-saturday-night-live-to-play-palin/tab/comments/.

Wyatt-Brown, Bertram. "*Amistad*." *The Journal of American History* 85, no. 3 (1998): 1174–76.

Xue, Steve A., and Jianping G. Huo. "Normative Standards for Vocal Tract Dimensions by Race as Measured by Acoustic Pharyngometry." *Journal of Voice* 20, no. 3 (2006): 391–400. https://doi.org/10.1016/j.jvoice.2005.05.001.

Zoglin, Richard. *Comedy at the Edge: How Stand-up in the 1970s Changed America*. New York: Bloomsbury, 2008.

Zumthor, Paul. *Oral Poetry: An Introduction*. Translated by Kathryn Murphy-Judy. Minneapolis: University of Minnesota Press, 1990.

INDEX

Adele, 21, 24–27, 29, 31, 33–49, 52, 150, 152–53; audience response, 40–42, 46–47; lyrics, 39–43; vocal racial passing, 33–39

African American English, 60–61, 119, 129–31, 133, 138, 143, 146, 154, 160; diction, 60, 133; stand-up comedy, 129; stereotyped in media, 130–31; written, 143–44

Afrikaans dialect, 72–73

Alaska, 83, 92–93, 97, 99, 102, 115, 178n1, 179n54; Alaska natives, 92–93, 99, 102, 115, 179n55; white Alaskan dialect, 92–93, 99; whiteness and colonization, 99, 102, 115. *See also* Sarah Palin

Apollo Theater, The, 117, 120

appropriation, 21, 30–35, 39, 42–45; as gentrification, 42–43

Apu (character from *The Simpsons*), 9

Armisen, Fred, 22, 85, 102–3, 106–13, 152; audience response to Barack Obama impression, 113; Barack Obama impression, 106–7

Asian and Asian American representation, 2, 11, 13–14, 130, 158–60; yellowvoice, 11, 158–59, 171n15

Audacity, 18, 153–67, 171n76; 176–77n84, 188n1

authenticity, 26–27, 30–31, 33–35, 39–40, 42, 45, 47–48, 51, 95; discursive, 31, 33–34; masculine, 27, 45; racial, 26, 30–34, 39–40, 42; rock and roll, 33–34

Awkwafina, 160

Aykroyd, Dan, 89–90

Baker, Josephine, 38

Barthes, Roland, 4, 7–8, 26, 33, 35, 39–40, 61–63, 74, 137, 148–49

biological determinism, 6, 29, 43, 48, 113, 141, 148–49; racialized voice, 36, 48, 59; voice/body match, 148–49. *See also* technological determinism

Blaccent, 160. *See also* Blackvoice

Black feminism, 27, 29, 43

Black Lives Matter, 157. *See also* social movements

Black music, 27, 29, 33–34

Blackvoice, 21, 26–30, 32–42, 44–45, 47–49, 59–60, 65, 149, 160; defined, 26. *See also* linguistic minstrelsy

blues, 20–21, 24–33, 35–43, 45–49, 150, 153

bordering rhetoric, 25, 27, 29, 31, 34–35, 39–40, 44, 46–48, 160; defined, 25; in music industry, 46–47

breathiness, 21, 37, 39–40, 44, 58, 61–63, 65–66, 73–74, 78, 110, 176n72

brown voice, 2, 9, 26, 171n15. *See also* Apu (character from *The Simpsons*); dialects (Indian)

Brown, Michael, 157

Bush, George H. W., 90

Butler, Judith, 6, 10, 28, 33, 68, 92, 127, 150; citationality, 3, 10, 26, 92, 104

Carter, Jimmy, 89, 179n38

Carvey, Dana, 90

Chappelle, Dave, 22, 116, 118, 120, 122–23, 126, 129–30, 132, 134–40, 142–45, 185n72; Chip

207

character, 129–30, 134–35, 138, 147; grape drink joke, 144; white shopping joke, 138; white suburbs joke, 140

Chase, Chevy, 88–91

Chitlin' Circuit, 120. *See also* The Apollo Theater

citationality (Judith Butler), 3, 10, 26, 92, 104

Civil Rights Movement, The, 30, 120–21. *See also* social movements

Clinton, Bill, 90

Clinton, Hillary, 18, 95, 104, 161–67

code-switching, 13. *See also* whitevoice

colonization, 25, 33–34, 37 43–45, 73, 102, 115. *See also* Alaska

conventions, 11, 13–14; of musical genres, 26; of soundtrack music, 70; of synchronization, 9, 149; of television news, 157–58; of television satire, 83–84

coolness, 126, 128, 131–37, 141; and Black vernacular, 131–37

coon shouting, 32–33, 38

Couric, Katie, 92, 94–97, 101, 180n69

Cox, Laverne, 157–58

Crazy Rich Asians (film), 158–60

critical cultural vocalics, 3–4, 7–10, 15–17, 19–23, 26–27, 39, 47, 59, 148–50, 161; defined, 3, 17; future research in, 159; theoretical tenets, 135, 150–53

crossover in media, 30, 121–22; and social media, 122–23

culturally privileged voices, 5, 10–15, 20, 25, 28, 37, 41, 43, 45, 47–48, 50, 52, 62, 71, 78, 92, 98, 103–4, 112, 115, 135, 150–52; defined, 3, 5

Dash, Julie, 28–29, 43

dialects, 2, 4, 12, 28, 59, 60–61, 72–73, 92–93, 98–99, 102–3, 115, 129–31, 133–34, 154, 157, 160, 186; and community building, 133–34; received pronunciations, 159; Southern US white and racism, 138; white, 129. *See also* African American English; Afrikaans dialect; Alaska; Asian and Asian American; Indian dialect

direct address, 66, 75–76

discipline, 2–3, 5–6, 10–17, 25, 34, 84–87, 125–26, 130, 143, 150, 154–55; through laughter, 13, 14, 84, 149

discursive authenticity, 31, 33–34. *See also* authenticity

exhalation, 40, 61–62, 73–74

Fey, Tina, 22, 83–85, 91–115, 98–99, 138–39, 150–53, 159, 178n1, 182–83n151; Couric-Palin interview, 101; "I can see Russia from my house" (*Saturday Night Live*), 83, 95–97, 178n1, 180n79; "A Non-Partisan Message" (*Saturday Night Live*), 95–96; popularity of Palin impression, 91, 98

Ford, Gerald, 88–91

Foxx, Jamie, 122, 132, 138, 140, 143, 145; on Rodney King, 138; white audience member joke, 140; "white people can't dance" joke, 146

Foxx, Redd, 120

Freeman, Morgan, 21–22, 50–53, 66, 67, 71–80, 82–85, 103, 105–06, 110, 151–54, 157, 159, 177n91; audience response, 76–80; and Barack Obama, 105; as God, 57–58; in *Amistad*, 67–68; in *Bruce Almighty*, 57, 60; in *The Bucket List*, 58; in *Deep Impact*, 56, 65, 69; in *Driving Miss Daisy*, 54–55; in *Evan Almighty*, 57, 60, 65, 74; in *Invictus*, 57, 60, 72–73; in *Kiss the Girls*, 55; in *March of the Penguins*, 56, 57–58; in *Million Dollar Baby*, 53, 55–56, 57, 63–65; in *Olympus has Fallen*, 56, 68–69; in *Seven*, 53; in *The Shawshank Redemption*, 53, 62, 76; in *Unforgiven*, 53; as president, 68–71, 73; postracialism, 51, 52–55, 58, 79. *See also* voice-over

Fresh Prince of Bel-Air, The, 136

gay voice, 14, 135, 141, 159

genres, musical, 21, 24–25, 29, 30, 42–47

Goldberg, Whoopi, 118, 140–41

grain of the voice, the. *See* Roland Barthes

Gregory, Dick, 121–22

Griffin, Eddie, 132, 135

growl, 33, 37

Hammond, Darrell, 90

Hart, Kevin, 123, 126, 134–36, 142

Hartman, Phil, 90

Harvey, Steve, 127, 129, 132–33, 137

Hillbilly music, 27–28, 171–72n20
homophobia, 4, 141
Horne, Lena, 29

identification: with media characters, 68–69; and vocal intimacy, 77. See also parasocial relationships
Iglesias, Gabriel, 116, 123, 128–29, 133, 142, 145; high school reunion joke, 142
Illusions (Dash), 29, 43
immigration, 25, 122; anti-immigrant sentiment, 2, 9, 13, 104, 133, 149
impersonation, 32, 83–115, 138–39, 178n31
Indian dialect, 2, 9. See also brown voice; Apu (character from *The Simpsons*)
intersectionality, 2–4, 13–20, 23–24, 33, 39–40, 59, 63, 83, 91, 110, 119, 141, 148–50, 153, 155–56, 159; defined, 16, 170n70
intertextuality, 19, 27, 31, 35, 39–41, 47, 83–84, 92
Irwin, May, 32

Jim Crow South, 60, 78; and Black masculinity, 110; and Morgan Freeman, 21, 52, 59, 71, 78, 80, 152; music industry, 25–27
Johnson, Dwayne, 85, 111; Barack Obama impression, 110–11

Laugh-In, Rowan and Martin's, 87–88
laughter, 124. See also discipline; stand-up comedy
Lincoln, Abraham, 103
linguistic minstrelsy, 2. See also minstrelsy
listening, 7, 8; as rhetorical element, 67–69. See also method; speaking and listening (cycle); vocal intimacy
Lopez, George, 22, 116, 118, 122–23, 130, 132–33, 143; parental discipline joke, 143–44; Spanish names joke, 132–33
lynching, 22–23, 59, 61, 110; and racial slurs, 138. See also Jim Crow; racism

Magical Negro, The, 55, 77–78; defined, 54
materiality, 4–8, 25, 31, 43, 46, 59, 66, 118, 123, 144, 149–50. See also voice (as interior body)
Media, 2, 6–7, 11, 13–14, 91–93, 121; campaign ads, 56, 75, 80, 83, 105–6, 108, 112; circulation, 85–86, 118; culturally privileged voices, 5, 135; Tina Fey's Sarah Palin impression, 101; film industry practices, 52, 62, 123, 158; music industry practices, 10–11, 12, 21, 24–25, 27–35, 41–43, 46–48, 171–72n20; Obama's speeches, 105; online commentary, 123–24; political deliberation, 89. See also genres, musical; music industry; silent film; sound film; synchronization; television
Mencia, Carlos, 122; anti-immigrant white person joke, 138; waving at cars joke, 142–43; white laughter joke, 127–28; white people and wild animals joke, 129
method, 17, 153–54
Michaels, Lorne: goals of *Saturday Night Live*, 88; as *Laugh-In* writer, 87–88; on Reagan impression, 89
minstrelsy, 2, 28, 31, 59, 61
Mississippi: dialects, 60, 65, 73; Morgan Freeman's childhood home, 21, 52, 59; racism in education, 59
Murphy, Eddie, 116, 118, 120–22, 145; Italians watching *Rocky* joke, 140; racists at dance club joke, 129, 138; *Raw*, 140; "white people can't dance," 136
music industry, 10–11, 12, 21, 24–25, 27–35, 41–43, 46–48, 171–72n20. See also Adele; blues; Hillbilly music; race music

National Public Radio, 14, 93
naturalization: Blackvoice, 28–29, 41, 149; brown voice, 9; colonization, 43, 102; identities and stereotypes, 118; musical genres, 47; presidential voice, 114–15; synchronization, 29; vocal training and whiteness, 128, 131, 135, 146; vernacular, 144; voice and race, 31, 59; voice and sex, 113; voice/body match, 10–11, 14–15, 31, 113, 118
neoliberalism, 121–22
nerds, 131–32, 134, 136, 146
Nixon, Richard, 89, 179n38

Obama, Barack, 22, 85, 103–06, 112; "A More Perfect Union" speech, 105; Black preacher sound, 104; campaign ads, 56, 79–80, 106; first Black president, 55; Morgan Freeman's support, 75, 79–80; The Rock Obama, 102, 110–11; *Saturday*

Night Live impressions, 102, 106–15, 152; State of the Union address, 107; vocal adaptation, 104. *See also* Fred Armisen; Dwayne Johnson; Jay Pharoah

Obama, Michelle, 182–83n151

OscarsSoWhite, 158

ostinato, 64–66, 71, 154

Palin, Sarah, 22, 83–84, 95–97, 179n54; confusion with Tina Fey, 98, 101–2; Couric-Palin interview, 101; dialect, 91–93; "I can see Russia from my house" (*Saturday Night Live*), 83, 95–97, 178n1, 180n79; white femininity, 93–94, 99, 103, 115. *See also* Alaska; Tina Fey

parasocial relationships, 6; with Adele, 37–38, 40–42, 46–48; with Tina Fey, 100–101; with Morgan Freeman, 75–80; with Dwayne Johnson, 111; and political affiliation, 79–80; with stand-up comedians, 142, 144–46

Peters, Russell, 123, 129; white people as bobblehead joke, 135–36; "white people sound like donkeys" joke, 134–35

Pharoah, Jay, 22, 85, 107–10; audience response to Obama impression, 109; compared with Fred Armisen, 109; Barack Obama impression, 102–3, 107–09, 112, 115, 151–52

pitch, 62; and age, 74; and authority, 95, 103–15, 179n67; and musical style, 38, 52; and recording technologies, 12; and sex/gender, 2, 14, 74, 85, 93–94, 96, 139–41, 179n67, 180n69, 181n115; transcribing, 18, 153, 156, 159–67; and vocal identity, 4, 36–37, 64–65; and vocal intimacy, 73–74; and white femininity, 93–99, 102, 119

Poehler, Amy, 95–96, 101

pop (musical genre), 25, 30, 45; Adele, 42–43; feminization, 27, 45–48, 54–55

postracialism, 42, 54–55. *See also* Morgan Freeman

presidency, US, 22, 58; *See also* George H. W. Bush; Bill Clinton; Abraham Lincoln; Barack Obama; Ronald Reagan, *Saturday Night Live* (television series)

Presley, Elvis, 33

Price, Vincent, 14

privilege, 2–6, 12–20, 25–30, 34–38, 45–52, 146–48. *See also* culturally privileged voices; white privilege

proximity: defined, 66–67; and vocal intimacy, 71

Pryor, Richard, 22, 116–18, 121–23, 136–37, 139, 144–45; generic white person, 130; "white people eat quiet" joke, 126–27, 132; white people sex joke, 128–29

queerness, vocal, 14, 102, 159; and gender, 141; mismatch vocal/visual gender, 141; as white, 134–35. *See also* gay voice

race records, 27

racial authenticity, 26, 30–34, 39–40, 42. *See also* authenticity

racism, 105, 120–21, 137–38. *See also* Michael Brown; brown voice; colonization; immigration (anti-immigrant sentiment); Jim Crow South; linguistic minstrelsy; lynching; minstrelsy; Mississippi (racism in education); OscarsSoWhite; postracialism; segregation; stereotypes; white privilege

radio, 3, 12–13, 16, 27–28, 30, 86, 128, 149, 151, 156. *See also* National Public Radio

Reagan, Ronald, 89, 121–22, 179n38

repetition, 15, 150, 152; and authenticity, 106; and naturalization, 4, 10; and pitch patterns, 21, 64–65; and racial difference, 3, 36–37; and vocal identity, 81; and vocal intimacy, 81

rhetorical elements of voices. *See* breathiness; dialects; direct address; exhalation; growl; listening; pitch; proximity; repetition; shimmer; silence; synchronization; underscore; voice-over; whisper

Ribeiro, Alfonso, 136

rock and roll, 33

Rock, Chris, 118, 120, 122; rejection of YouTube, 123; white people and the n-word joke, 138

Rock Obama, The (*Saturday Night Live* character). *See* Dwayne Johnson

Sanford and Son (television series), 120

Saturday Night Live (television series), 87–91; ratings, 90–91; The SNL Effect, 84–85. *See also* Fred Armisen; Tina Fey;

Dwayne Johnson; Lorne Michaels; She-Rock Obama; Jay Pharaoh; Amy Poehler

segregation, 54–55, 59, 92, 118, 120. *See also* racism

She-Rock Obama (*Saturday Night Live* character), 182–83n151

shimmer (vocal effect), 37

silence, 21, 62, 66, 136; as subordination, 67–69, 71, 81

silent film, 11, 28. *See also* sound film

simultaneity: defined, 68; and identification, 71; and musical listening, 38; and shared histories, 142–44, 146; and vocal intimacy, 69

slang, 131–32, 143, 145–46

Smith, Bessie, 32–33

Smothers Brothers Comedy Hour, The (television series), 87–88

social media, 25–26, 41, 46–47, 122–23, 157–58. *See also* YouTube

social movements: Black Lives Matter, 157; The Civil Rights Movement, 121; online activism, 123–24, 157–58; speaking about protests, 120

sociophonetics, 15, 18, 153–54

Sonic Color Line, The, 31

sound film transition, 11, 28–29

soundscapes, 7, 11, 13

South African dialect. *See* Afrikaans dialect

speaking and listening (as cyclical), 2, 4, 7–10, 19–22, 43, 48–49, 52, 63, 90–92, 114, 148–49; audience expectations, 11, 31, 81; on YouTube, 123

Spears, Aries, 123, 132, 144; African Americans and Black Africans joke, 142; mother/child relationship joke, 127, 139–40

stand-up comedy, 116–17, 132, 145–46; anti-femme, 118, 140–41; as political resistance, 119–23

star images, 39; and Adele, 40–41; authenticity, 42

stereotypes: Asian and Asian American, 2, 11, 158–59; Black masculinity, 78, 85, 128, 107–8, 110, 113, 132, 135, 136; Black femininity, 96, 182–83n151; as casting practice, 11, 28, 58; Latinx, 119, 132; masculinity, 94, 134; white femininity, 12, 96, 99, 114–15, 118, 140, 167. *See also* Blackvoice; brown voice; coolness; gay voice; linguistic minstrelsy; minstrelsy; nerds; Uncle Tom

subordination, 51–54, 58, 60–69, 71, 75–82, 151. *See also* Morgan Freeman; racism; silence; Uncle Tom

synchronization, 2, 9–10, 149; manipulation of vocal sound, 28–29; naturalization of Blackvoice, 28. *See also* naturalization

talkies. *See* sound film

technological determinism, 6–7. *See also* biological determinism

television, 1, 3, 5, 12, 15–16, 20, 24, 38, 55, 61–62, 66, 82; politics, 105, 121–23; satire, 86–88, 93, 114, 151; variety shows, 86, 88. *See also Saturday Night Live* (television series)

transcribing pitch, 18, 153, 156, 159–67

Tucker, Sophie, 32

Uncle Tom, 60, 61, 64, 76; and silence, 69

underscore, 63, 68–71

Vaudeville, 32–33, 87. *See also* minstrelsy

vernacular rhetoric, 123–24, 126, 131, 135–36, 143–44

vocal acquisition, 1–2, 12, 43. *See also* speaking and listening (cycle); vocal training

vocal identity, 7, 48; defined, 4, 149

vocal intimacy, 7–8, 61–62, 66, 99–100, 127, 142–43, 145; and community, 144–45; defined, 4, 148–49

vocal racial passing, 21, 27, 31–33, 35, 43, 150; defined, 26

vocal training, 12, 33, 126, 177n92; and Blackvoice, 28; as discipline, 12; as oppositional to coolness, 131; as privilege, 59, 135; and voice/body match, 48; and whiteness, 127, 59, 135

vocal transcription, 18, 153–54, 156, 161–67. *See also* method; sociophonetics

vocalic bodies, 8–9

voice, 2, 5–6, 10, 15, 63, 103, 110; as community, 1–2; as emotional conduit, 5; as instrument, 8; as interior body, 1, 5, 7–9, 33, 48, 62, 74, 90, 101, 106, 110, 137, 149

voice-over, 19, 63, 69, 70, 75–76; and authenticity, 76; Morgan Freeman, 21, 53, 57–58,

63, 69, 80–82; and vocal intimacy, 75–76, 151
voice/body match, 9–10, 13–14, 31, 46–47, 131; gender, 45; naturalization, 4, 6, 35; race, 28, 35, 51, 149. *See also* synchronization

Walker, Jay, 128
Waters, Ethel, 38
whisper, 19, 52, 61–63, 65–66, 71, 74, 110
white privilege, 118–19, 126–31, 135. *See also* privilege
whiteness, 24, 26–29, 35, 59, 107; as animalistic, 134; and femininity, 42–49, 93; resistance, 117–19, 126–43, 146, 150–51, 154. *See also* Alaska; appropriation; colonialism; white privilege; whitevoice

whitevoice, 22–23, 28, 119, 132, 134–35, 138; defined, 117–18
Wilson, Flip, 121–22
women's representation, 150–51; in media, 11–12, 14; in music, 27–30, 34, 45–48; in politics, 103; in stand-up comedy, 118–19, 140–42

xkcd.com (web comic), 78

YouTube, 20, 22, 38, 123–26; comedy, 50, 116–19; comment sections, 41, 46–47, 142–45; community, 124–26; gatekeeping, 125–26; social movements, 124, 146, 151; and vernacular rhetoric, 123–24

www.ingramcontent.com/pod-product-compliance
Lightning Source LLC
Chambersburg PA
CBHW030137240426
43672CB00005B/160